CLEVELAND

Prodigy of the Western Reserve

by George E. Condon

Cleveland: Prodigy of the Western Reserve

a pictorial and entertaining commentary on the growth and development of Cleveland, Ohio

By George E. Condon

Dedicated to the author's grandson, Peter George Brereton

South side of Superior Avenue, looking east from Seneca Street (now Third Street), circa 1873

Editors:
Larry P. Silvey
Douglas S. Drown

Associate Editor:
Peggi Ridgway

Art Director:
Rusty Johnson

Assistant Art Director:
James Michael Martin

Cleveland: Prodigy of the Western Reserve is sponsored by The Greater Cleveland Growth Association.

Published in 1979 by Continental Heritage Press, Inc.

Library of Congress Catalog Card Number 79-53562.

ISBN 0-932986-060-4

Cleveland: Prodigy of the Western Reserve is part of The American Portrait Series of premium books published by The Continental Heritage Press; others include:
Houston: a history of a giant
The Saint Louis Portrait
The San Antonio Story
Des Moines: Capital City
Detroit: American Urban Renaissance
The Tulsa Spirit
In 1980, The American Portrait Series will add to its list the cities of Los Angeles, San Diego, San Jose, Fort Worth, Charlotte and Columbus.

Contents

G. S. NEWCOMB & CO.
PHOTOGRAPH GALLERY
WILLIAM KIDD
& CO.
FINE JEWELRY
CHILDRENS CARRIAGES
WILLOW & WOODEN
WARE.
KLEINSCHMIDT & AMBR
TOYS & FA
ODS.

North side of Superior Avenue, looking east from Seneca Street (now Third Street) to the Public Square, circa 1873

The Flats, circa 1873

The Flats, circa 1873

Prologue

There was nothing explosive or flamboyant about the natural site of Cleveland; nothing as spectacular as a Niagara River tumbling over a high escarpment in a free fall whose roar could be heard for miles around.

Cleveland was a quiet place in the wilderness. Its Cuyahoga River hardly murmured as it came off its meandering way out of the overgrown, high-walled flats and spilled into Lake Erie.

Not that the Cuyahoga was an ordinary, no-nonsense river. It was exasperatingly complex in the way it traveled. It followed an elliptical, exhausting course, one that persistently twisted and turned, looping about in a contrary way, bending into impossible ox-bows that slowed the waters so drastically they hardly had enough strength left to empty into the southernmost of the Great Lakes.

As if that were not enough, those last few feet at the end of the river's journey were made even more difficult by the sand bars that accumulated in the mouth of the waterway. Sometimes they grew to such size as to close off the river's access to the lake entirely. When that happened, all the river could do was swirl around in frustration until it could breach a part of the sand barrier and find release.

The early visitors noted all this and the wise ones saw beyond the crooked river (which is what the Indian name, Cuyahoga, means) to gain a vision of greater things.

The Indians had a special feeling about the Cuyahoga Valley. It was a place where tribal conflicts were put to one side so that all could use this gateway to the interior of the Ohio country, a paradise for hunters.

The early white visitors also felt the magic that irradiated here; the instinct that is so often stirred by the right combination of important elements, such as those that blessed this place.

Excellence, it has been noted philosophically, is a long time in reaching maturity. The Western Reserve is a good example.

The natural forces at work here reached back at least 300 million years, to the time when a great saline sea covered this part of North America and settled its salty deposits deep in the earth.

More recently on the time scale (a mere 20,000 years ago or so) the Great Ice Age had set in motion a widespread glacier as much as 1,000 feet thick that moved deeply into Ohio from the north, traveling as far south as the Ohio River and reaching close to the site of future Cincinnati.

When the glacier finally withdrew, it performed a farewell service of infinite value by grinding the rocky outcropping and pulverizing the boulders in its northward path to create deposits of new, fertile soil to enrich the fields. At the same time, it was leveling the topography to make it ideal for agriculture. Finally, as a last flourish, it scooped out an enormous basin to contain its own melting waters.

Lake Erie was the end result of the massive evolutionary geologic process. In its genealogy, it is the legitimate descendant of a series of inland seas created by the receding ice field.

Geologists have determined that the mightiest of the ancient glacier-created lakes was a vast body of water called Lake Maumee, which stood 760 feet above sea level and covered infinitely more territory than Lake Erie. By way of comparison, Cleveland's Public Square stands 668.69 feet above sea level.

The successors to Lake Maumee as it dwindled in size through thousands of years were Lake Whittlesey, Lake Arkona, Lake Warren, Lake Wayne, Lake Lundy, and, finally, Lake Erie.

The present lake, while small in comparison with its predecessors, is still counted as one of the largest fresh water lakes in the world and stands as a national asset beyond price. Its beaches have varied in their height above sea level from a former 573 feet to the present 540 feet.

Each of the prehistoric lakes made a distinct contribution to the existing topography of Cleveland; to the plan and reality of the city itself, if you please. Their receding waters left behind a series of ancient shorelines — level, sandy ridges that are nothing more than abandoned beaches, stepped down in terrace effect like the benches of a mighty amphitheater.

Those level, easy-to-traverse ridges running through the thickets and twisted forests of the lakeshore were put to good use as highways by Indian travelers looking for the paths of least resistance. The oldest Indian trails from Cleveland to Buffalo and from Cleveland to Detroit followed the prehistoric beachlines.

The same ridges made travel indescribably easier for the first white settlers in the region because, being flat and level, they were ideal for use as roads and major highways. They still serve to this day; many of the principal avenues of today's Cleveland, such as Euclid Avenue, Detroit Avenue, Center Ridge Road and Terrace Road, rest on prehistoric beaches.

The illusion given by the terraced ridges of an amphitheater built to giant scale was more than appropriate in Cleveland's case because there was a great drama waiting to be played in this unusual setting. History was in the wings, waiting for the cue. The stage was set. From that moment on it was up to the cast of players.

MAP
of the
WESTERN RESERVE
Including the
FIRE LANDS
IN
Ohio
September 1826
Cedar Point
PERKINS
HURON
VERMILLION
Brownhelm
BLACKRIVER
Elyria
SHEFFIELD
DOVER
ROCKPORT
MIDDLEBURGH
LORAIN COUNTY
OXFORD
ELDRIDGE
FLORENCE
RUSSIA
EATON
COLUMBIA
STRONGS VILLE
MONROE
NORWALK
TOWNSEND
WAKEMAN
GRAFTON
LIVERPOOL
BRUNSWICK
HURON COUNTY
VREDENBURG
BRONSON
CLARKSFIELD
WELLINGTON
PENFIELD
MEDINA
GREENFIELD
FAIRFIELD
NEW-LONDON
MONTVILLE
NEW-HAVEN
RIPLEY
SULLIVAN
HARRISVILLE
WESTFIELD
GUILFORD
Surplus Lands

Birth of a city

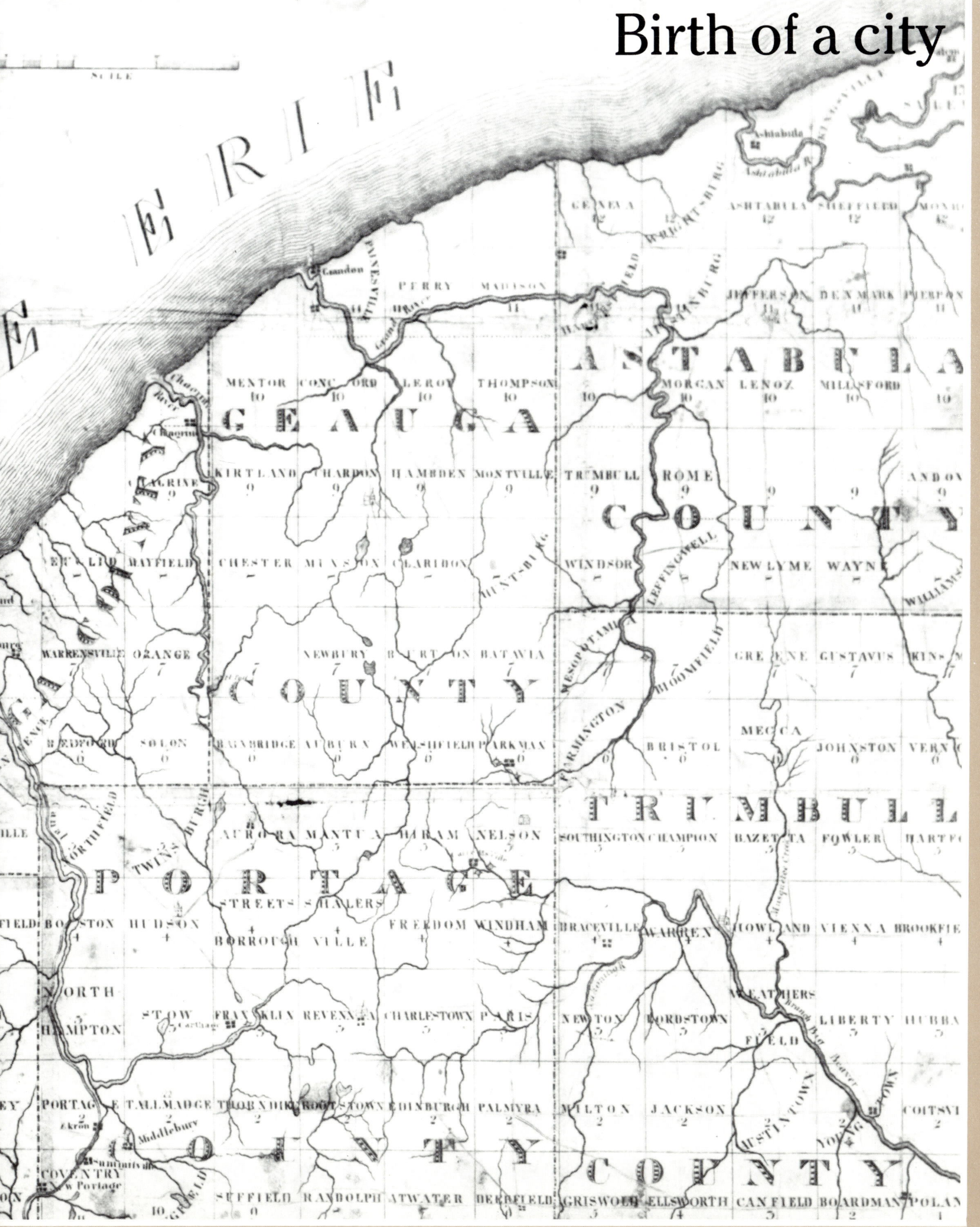

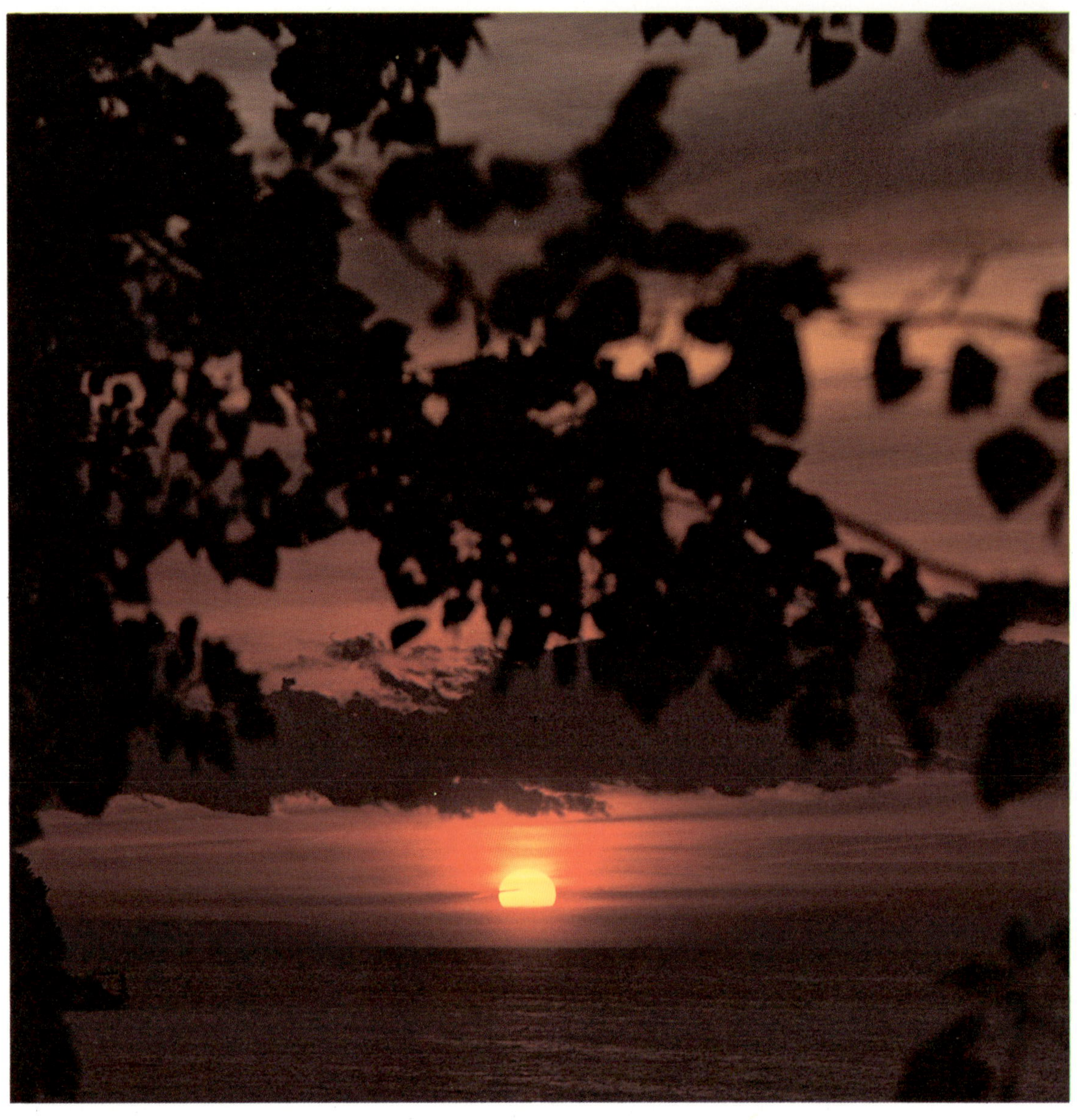

'Tis here, when nature reigned supreme,
That General Cleaveland trod the wild;
And saw an infant in his dream,
And with his name baptized the child.

— Harvey Rice

1. The beginning

The isolation that the Ohio Country had enjoyed through the centuries, the existence apart from the civilized world, showed signs of being breeched in the 17th century. The outside world was probing. But it would not be the first time that the old had given way to the new in this magnificent wilderness.

Once, in pre-Columbian time, a race of Mound Builders had claimed this area as their home, and they had left behind them impressive memorials in the mysterious mounds that incredibly were able to weather the centuries.

Where the Cuyahoga River emptied into Lake Erie, for example, to the west of its mouth, there was a towering mound, said to be about 70 feet high, crowned with large trees. It was eroded away, partly by the river and partly by man, when a new mouth was cut through to the lake. Early settlers also reported a mound where Ontario Street and Prospect Avenue met, and another one on the site of Newburgh.

The Mound Builders disappeared from the scene at some indeterminate time and were succeeded by the modern Indians. It was their rule over the forested empire that was challenged as the 17th century wore on.

The problem of the white man's trespass was not the only jurisdictional question in the Ohio Country at that time. There was a larger dispute, a civil war, that climaxed a long-standing feud among the Indians themselves. The principal disputants were two powerful tribes: the Eries, commonly known as the Cat People, and the Senecas, members of the Iroquois Confederation.

Some historians say that the Eries and the Senecas were blood relatives, which would help to explain the terrible intensity of the fighting that ensued between the two tribes. Family battles are often the worst kind.

The Eries lived along the southern shores of the lake that bore their name. The Senecas had their principal settlement in New York State.

The enmity between the two tribes finally came to a head in bloody battle, waged sometime around 1750. The victory went to the Senecas, who not only defeated the Eries, but virtually annihilated them. The victory gave the Senecas control over the Ohio Country as far west as the Cuyahoga River, whose valley was respected as a sort of neutral zone, used peacefully by many tribes as a passageway to the south.

The significance of the Cuyahoga route was that it was a portage trail, allowing the use of waterways, all the way from Lake Erie to the Ohio River. The Cuyahoga led to the Tuscarawas, then to the Muskingum, and on to the Ohio.

There undoubtedly were white hunters and trappers who found their way to the mouth of the Cuyahoga in the course of their travels without leaving behind any record of their visits. It is more than likely that many of the religious missionaries, the real trailblazers of the wilderness, passed through the Cleveland area in the course of their evangelistic pursuits. One of them probably was Father La Roche Daillon, a French Recollect missionary who made his way along the southern shore of Lake Erie as early as 1626.

An afternoon in the year 1679 could have presented a novel sight off the Cleveland shoreline: the white sails of a white man's vessel out on the blue waters of the lake. It would have been the Griffin, a 60-ton sailing ship that the great French explorer, La Salle, caused to be built above the falls of the Niagara River.

The Griffin's maiden voyage, a westward journey to Green Bay, Wis., would not have escaped the notice of the Indians camped on the high bluffs near the mouth of the Cuyahoga.

La Salle's return trip, by land, may have taken him along the southern shore of the lake and through the future site of Cleveland, but his route is not known.

One of the earliest visitors to the mouth of the Cuyahoga was Sir William Johnson, the architect of the alliance between the British and the Indians of the Six Nations.

Sir William's diary, recording details of a trip to Detroit in 1761, contained the following notation: "Embarked this morning at six of ye clock, and intend to beach near Cuyahoga this day."

A few years earlier, in 1755, an 18-year-old Pennsylvanian, James Smith, held prisoner by the Indians for four years, remembered being taken on a hunting trip to the Cuyahoga River valley and out into the lake itself.

"It is a very gentle river," he wrote, "with but few ripples or swift running places."

Those were qualities that were appreciated in a valley serving as a gateway to important hunting country.

Major Robert Rogers

The next known visitor was the famous Maj. Robert Rogers, commander of a New Hampshire company of Provincial Rangers, who had been ordered west from Fort Niagara to take possession of a French post. According to historical account, Rogers arrival at the mouth of the Cuyahoga brought about an historic meeting with another famous personality, Chief Pontiac.

"On the 7th of November, 1760," wrote Historian Francis Parkman in *Conspiracy of Pontiac*, "they reached the mouth of the Cuyahoga River, the present site of Cleveland. No body of British troops had ever advanced so far. The day was dull and rainy, and, resolving to rest until the weather should improve, Rogers ordered his men to prepare their camp in the neighboring forest.

"The place has seen strange changes since that day. Soon after the arrival of the Rangers, a party of Indian chiefs and warriors entered the camp. They proclaimed themselves an embassy from Pontiac, ruler of all that country, and directed in his name that the English should advance no further until they had had an interview with the great chief, who was close at hand.

"He (Pontiac) greeted Rogers with the haughty demand, what his business was in that country, and how he dared enter

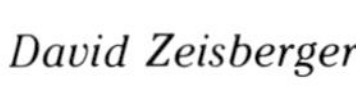

David Zeisberger

John Heckwelder

it without his permission."

Apparently the great chief was open to argument and presents. The Rogers party was allowed to resume its journey.

Only three years later, Cleveland's shoreline was the setting for another historic occurrence — this one clouded with tragedy. An expedition of some 600 British regulars under the command of a Major Wilkins, on its way to relieve the garrison of Detroit, then under French attack, encountered a bad storm as it was traveling in a fleet of bateaux off the mouth of Rocky River. Many of the small, flat-bottomed boats capsized. Others took on water dangerously.

"Thus threatened," relates a description of the crisis, "they sought safe harbor within the mouth of Rocky River. East of the narrow channel was a high cliff where a hidden sandbar, covered by shoal water, extended at right angles. Over this swept waves with tremendous force, breaking 60 to 80 feet high against the cliff...Some boats drove upon the bar and, sinking in the quicksands, were dashed to bits. Some beached high and dry on a marsh to the east. Others made safe harbor within the river's mouth.

"Seventy men, three officers, and a French pilot drowned. Twenty boats, 50 barrels of provisions, some field pieces and all ammunition were lost."

The survivors clambered up to the bluff of the west bank, where they built a campfire within a circle of rocks.

The site of that post-wreck campground was rediscovered in 1863 after a bayonet had been found nearby. Four years later, two knives were found near the circle of rocks, and in the decades that followed, residents of the Rocky River area reported finding bayonets, coins, and other memorabilia, still being washed ashore onto the beaches.

One of the side effects of the French and Indian War, quite naturally, was the attention it drew to the wilderness lands west of the Allegheny Mountains. The conflict between the great European powers for possession of the vast inland territory made a better knowledge of the frontier's geography a military imperative.

The old, crude, sometimes fanciful maps of the interior, based on the observations, rumors, and imaginations of hunters, trappers and missionaries, had to be put aside in favor of more accurate, scientific cartography.

Among the earlier maps of the Great Lakes region, for example, was one that entirely omitted Lake Erie; a major oversight, certainly.

As better maps became available, military eyes alighted with considerable interest on the place where the Cuyahoga River was shown to be emptying into Lake Erie. They saw the same possibilities for portage travel between the Ohio River and the great lake to the north, via the Muskingum-Cuyahoga route.

Benjamin Franklin in 1765 saw the junction of the Cuyahoga and Lake Erie as the obvious place for a military post.

George Washington suggested "the practicability of a route from Lake Erie, by way of the Cuyahoga, Tuscarawas and Muskingum into the Ohio, as an outlet to the future inland commerce of the lakes."

He pointed out that it would necessitate only "a portage near Akron of less than seven miles, whereby shipments were to be transferred from the lakes to the river Ohio, thence to ascend its upper tributaries into the mountains, from whence, by another portage, would be reached the navigable rivers falling into the Atlantic."

"Where the Cuyahoga River flows into Lake Erie," prophesied Washington, "shall arise a community of vast commercial importance."

The first organized settlement in the Cleveland area was a colony of Moravian Christians and their Indian converts — the sad survivors of a terrible massacre at Gnadenhutten Village near the Muskingum River in Tuscarawas County.

The group, led by David Zeisberger and John Heckwelder, two German missionaries, in 1786 settled in the Cuyahoga Valley, near the mouth of Tinker's Creek, on the site of an abandoned Ottawa Indian town. They gave the name of Pilgerruh, or "Pilgrim's Rest," to the settlement.

Hunger and a warning from some militiamen that the colony illegally occupied land owned by Connecticut discouraged the Moravians and they pulled up stakes and moved on in the spring of 1787.

During their brief stay, interestingly enough, the residents of Pilgrim's Rest were furnished with some flour by agents of an Indian trade enterprise, Duncan, Wilson & Co. of Pittsburgh, whose agent, a James Hillmann, apparently operated out of a supply cabin at the mouth of the Cuyahoga.

The story also has it that Hillmann and one of his employees, finding the entrance to the Cuyahoga River choked with sand and impassable, removed a section of the sandbar with wooden shovels so that their supply schooner, Mackinaw, was able to enter the river and sail to a docking point approximately where Main Street ends at water's edge.

Some of the pioneers arriving early on the Cleveland scene reported that a fur trading post, supposedly owned by John Jacob Astor, stood at the mouth of the Cuyahoga River, on the west bank. The claim is blurred by conflicting accounts.

This much is clear: the site at the junction of the Cuyahoga River and Lake Erie had become something of a wilderness crossroads by the time Moses Cleaveland and his party arrived on the scene.

It was a timely arrival. One century was ending and a new one was beginning.

The thick, dark forests that still curtained the ancient shores of Lake Erie were about to be parted. The silence and the solitude would be broken. A new drama was about to begin.

2. Opening the Western Reserve

What Moses Cleaveland had in mind on the warm summer day of July 22, 1796, when the bateau carrying him and his advance party found its way into the Cuyahoga River, was to select something more significant than the site of a frontier settlement: he was looking for a new state capital.

The Western Reserve tract of some 3 million acres that the State of Connecticut had sold to the group of 40 investors who were banded together as the Connecticut Land Company certainly was large enough to be a state. Its area was, in fact, four times the size of Rhode Island.

Connecticut had acquired title to the far-off land through some circuitous twists and turns of history.

Moses Cleaveland

King Charles II of England, by the way of generous reward to those enterprising subjects who were willing to endure the American wilderness, in 1662 had given the Connecticut colony a grant of land between the 41st and 42nd parallels, beginning at the border of Pennsylvania and extending westward as far as the "South Sea" — the name then for the Pacific Ocean.

The Connecticut land claim, based on the old grant, was one of several that had to be resolved in 1786 by the new federal government.

The compromise arrived at by the leaders of the young republic and the member state allowed Connecticut to reserve a strip of land in the western wilderness, staying within the 41st and 42nd parallels, along the southern shore of Lake Erie, from Pennsylvania to Sandusky Bay.

This was called Connecticut's Western Reserve. It was estimated to represent some 4 million acres. Of this, 500,000 acres were set aside by the Connecticut legislature to be awarded to citizens of the state whose property had been burned by British troops in the War of Independence. That allotment, at the western end of the reserve, was given the name of the Fire Lands.

The remaining area, actually containing about 3 million acres, was authorized by the state to be sold in 1795. The purchasing group was the Connecticut Land Company, a hastily formed syndicate of well-to-do citizens who hoped to make a worthwhile profit from the resale of the western lands.

Their initial investment in the land purchase was $1,200,000, less than 40 cents an acre.

What that sum of money had bought the investors was a small empire. Considering the modest size of eastern states such as Connecticut, Vermont, New Hampshire, Maine, Massachusetts, and Rhode Island, it was little wonder that the real estate developers thought of their land in terms of a new state.

The man who was selected by the company to open up this new territory to colonization was Moses Cleaveland, himself a principal investor in the speculation. He was a stern, swarthy, stocky, no-nonsense type — just the kind the other investors could trust to look out for their best interests and make sensible decisions out in the field.

Cleaveland was named the company's agent and general field superintendent, in charge of a party of surveyors who would constitute the first mission into the Western Reserve. Theirs was a basic preliminary. The land could not be sold until it had been surveyed and partitioned.

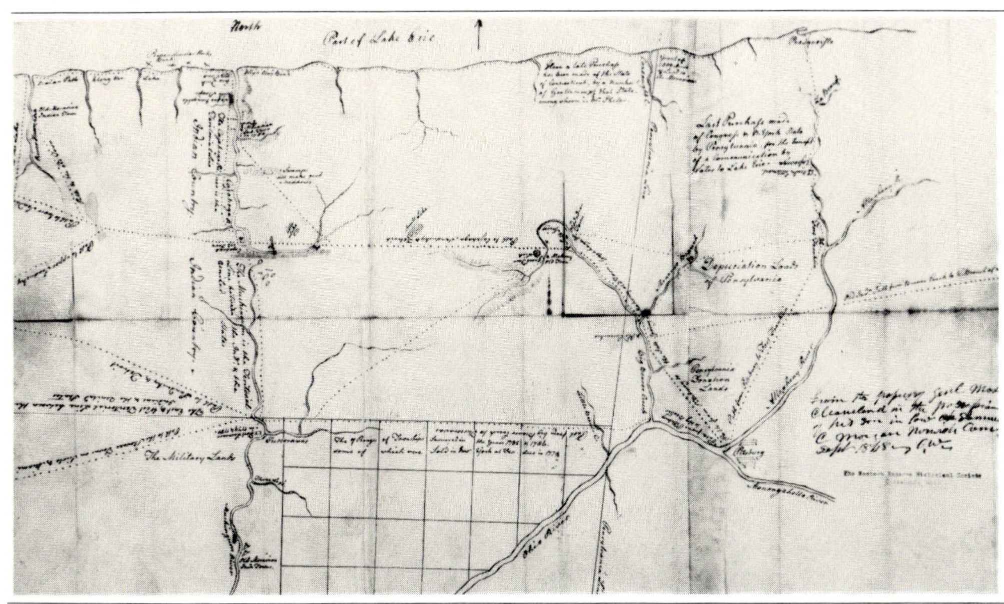

First map of the Cleveland area by John Heckwelder, 1795

Cleaveland, a general in the Connecticut state militia, was a prominent citizen; he was a graduate of Yale in a time when higher education was reserved for the patrician few. It is still a source of inspiration to some Clevelanders to know that an old Eli was the father of their city.

While the first expedition sent by the company into its western lands was primarily bent on surveying, Cleaveland was a practicing lawyer, not a surveyor. But he was, by all accounts, a born leader.

The company expected Cleaveland, as its representative, to confer with the Seneca Indians in upstate New York and get them to yield whatever claims they still had to territory within the Western Reserve.

Such a concession was essential to the successful disposal of the land to eastern purchasers. Indian hostility could discourage pioneer settlement and delay any return on the investment for many years.

It also fell upon Gen. Cleaveland to select the site of a principal settlement in the vast tract of land, which already had been given the name of New Connecticut.

The favored site, based on the study of crude maps and the recommendations of wise leaders such as Benjamin Franklin and George Washington, was the place where the Cuyahoga River flowed into Lake Erie, 80 miles west of the Pennsylvania line.

The spelling of the river's name, by the way, was as uncertain as its meaning. Some old maps spelled it Caujahoga. The Moravian missionaries wrote it, Gajahaga. The Mohawks called it Cayagaga. The Seneca version was Cuyohaga. The Delawares favored Diohaga. At least one missionary, John Heckwelder, wrote it, Cujahaga. And there were some who preferred to call it Cauahogue.

Under the confused circumstances, it wasn't unreasonable for people finally to settle on Cuyahoga. That spelling has been accepted, but the pronunciation remains a matter of minor controversy. Most people prefer: Ky-a-hoga.

It was up to Gen. Cleaveland and his chief assistants, Augustus Porter, head surveyor, and Seth Pease, astronomer and surveyor, to examine the Cuyahoga site with critical objectivity and make the final decision. The expedition from Connecticut numbered 50 persons. They came together for the westward journey in Schenectady, N.Y., in early June, 1796.

The first objective was the site of Buffalo, on Lake Erie's shores, where a meeting had been arranged with representatives of the Senecas and the Mohawks on the issue of Western Reserve land ownership.

Some of the Cleaveland party traveled the full distance by land because they had horses and cattle to lead. The main group followed the water route: the Mohawk River, Wood Creek, the Oswego River and, finally, Lake Ontario.

The meeting in Buffalo with the Indians followed the slow protocol of the day. It took three days of talking, orating, dancing and drinking before the two sides arrived at a peaceful settlement of the issues at hand.

The Indian representatives, Chief Red Jacket of the Seneca Nation and Joseph Brant (Thayendanega) of the Mohawks, liked Moses Cleaveland's looks and his forthright manner of speaking. The Connecticut Yankee, fortunately, was swarthy enough after weeks of travel under the summer sun, to pass for an Indian himself.

Under terms of the agreement reached, the Indians withdrew their claim to the Western Reserve and promised to let white settlers move into the territory without harm. In return for this pledge, Gen. Cleaveland paid $1,500 to the Indians and gave them two beef cattle and several barrels of whiskey.

With the Indian claim thus extinguished, the Connecticut expedition pushed on westward, arriving at the mouth of Conneaut Creek in Ohio, fortuitously, on July 4, 1796. The coincidence gave them double reason to celebrate, and they took full advantage of the situation.

After the revelry had ended, the men set about the job of establishing the land company's first base of operations in the Western Reserve by building a large log structure which they named "Castle Stow" after a member of the expedition, Joshua Stow, who was in charge of the commissary. The city of Stow, Ohio, today marks his memory.

Once the base was established, the surveyors dug into their job, a truly formidable assignment that called for them to lay out New Connecticut into townships five miles square, and then to subdivide each township into 100-acre lots.

Gen. Cleaveland and his small advance party, meanwhile, took to their bateau and began the final lap of their western odyssey by water: the trip to the westernmost edge of the territory made available through the Indian treaty, where the Cuyahoga River flowed into Lake Erie.

The boat carrying Cleaveland and his chief assistants hugged the Erie shoreline, blundered up the Chagrin River, hastily returned to the lake, and finally slipped into the Cuyahoga River on the morning of July 22, 1796.

When the men set foot ashore on the east bank of the river,

Cleaveland meets with the Mohawks and Senecas at Buffalo, from a painting by Fred Dana Marsh

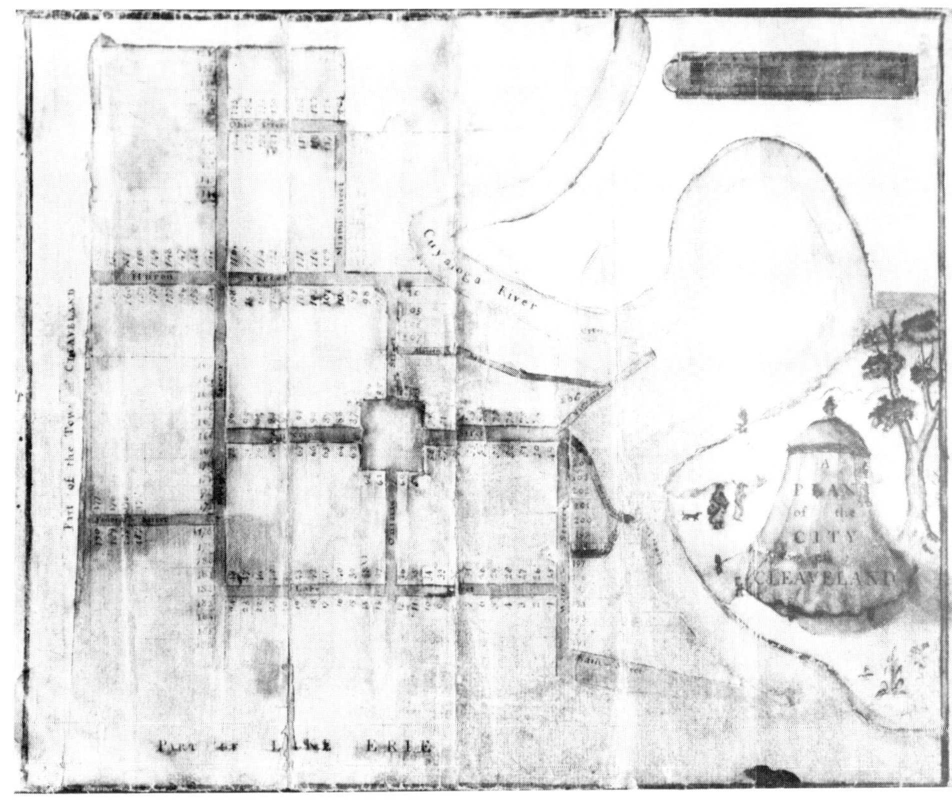

Second town map of Cleveland, drawn by Seth Pease, 1796

Seth Pease, surveyor

approximately at the foot of Superior Hill, it was a rather unceremonious conclusion to a long, historic journey. There were no speeches or heroic gestures. These pioneers were, in the best New England tradition, businesslike and unemotional.

What they saw in the flats of the river valley was an unprepossessing sight. A marshy growth of wild vegetations concealed most of the riverside and the slow-moving waters of the Cuyahoga, darkened with silt, were overlaid by the shadows of the hillsides and the tall trees.

A more cheerful vista awaited the party when they climbed to the top of the 80-foot high hillside on the eastern edge of the valley and discovered "a broad and beautiful plain of woodland stretching far away to the east, west and south."

What the newcomers from Connecticut were admiring on this plateau was the final tapering-off of the Appalachian Mountains, for it is here that the great eastern range, after slumping downward from the Pennsylvania border, finally subsides entirely and levels off into the gentle river plain on the valley's edge.

Gen. Cleaveland, after extensive examination of the terrain, a cruise up the river and one along the lakefront, returned to Camp Stow to ponder what he had seen and to make his final decision on the choice of the settlement site.

While at the Conneaut base, he recorded his impressions and his uncertainty in a report to the land company investors back home in Connecticut. His letter, dated Aug. 5th, said:

"The Cuyahoga is navigable for sloops about eight miles as the river runs, and for boats to the portage, if the immense quantity of trees drove down and lodged are cleared out. The land excellent, the water clear and lively current, and streams and springs falling into all three rivers.

"We went in a Schenectady boat, the 'Cuyahoga,' about 25 miles to the old Moravian Indian town*, and I imagine on a meridian line, not more than 12 or 15 miles. Here the bottoms widen, and as I am informed, increase in width, and if possible in quality x x x at this place we found a stream that empties into the river which will make a good mill seat.

"x x x On the east of the Cuyahoga are clay banks from 20 to 40 feet high, on the top the land level, covered with chestnut, oak, walnut, ash, and some sugar maple. There are but few hemlocks, and those only on a swamp, pond or lake, and in the immense quantity of flood wood lodged on the lakes and rivers, I rarely found any of that wood.

"The shore west of the mouth of the Cuyahoga is a steep bank for ten miles, the quality of the soil I know not, but from the growth and kind of timber, these present no unfavorable aspect. I should with great pleasure, readily comply with what I suppose you have heretofore expected that I should leave this country about this time..."

At this point in his report, a note of bitterness crept into the Cleaveland voice:

"Those who are meanly envying the compensation and sitting at their ease and see their prosperity increasing at the loss of health, ease, and comfort of others," he complained, "I wish might experience the hardships for one month; if not then satisfied their grumbling would give me no pain.

"x x x It is impossible at present to determine on the place for the capital. More information of the extent of the ceded lands and ye traverse of the lakes and rivers wanted, this will cause delay and require examination. I believe it will be on the Cuyahoga it must command the greatest communication, either by land or water of any other place on the purchase or on any ceded lands west of the head of the Mohawk.

"I expect soon to leave this for the westward and shall make my residence there until I am ready to return to Connecticut. The men are remarkably healthy, though without sauce or vegetables, and in good spirits. I hope they will continue so."

Upon dispatching that progress report, clearly revealing the strain and pressures of the mission, Cleaveland returned to the Cuyahoga site and peremptorily ordered two of his assistants, Seth Pease and Amos Spafford, to survey a square mile of the place for future settlement.

The decision had been made. The die was cast.

This was to be Cleveland.

3. Mapping the new town

The first street plans for Cleveland were drawn, as ordered, at summer's end by the two surveyors, Seth Pease and Amos Spafford. It was a time when the entire mile-square tract of land atop the eastern bluff of the Cuyahoga, extending down the hillside to the water's edge, was covered still by dense virgin forest. The first tree had yet to be felled.

The two men made their surveys independently of each other, working under the supervision of Chief Surveyor Augustus Porter. Thanks to this unusual arrangement, two separate maps of the future town were produced.

Even though there had been no official decision as to the name of the settlement, each of the surveyors referred to the capital-to-be of New Connecticut as Cleaveland.

This may have been out of admiration for the general or simply to force his hand in the matter. Some consideration had been given, it seems, to the name, Cuyahoga. Cleaveland, at any rate, did not allow his own name to be chosen for the honor until "the earnest suggestion and advice of the surveyors" led him into the decision.

The spelling of the town's name was a subject of confusion from the very beginning. On Spafford's map, the name is spelled "Cleveland." On one of Pease's maps (he drew two), the name is spelled both ways: Cleveland and Cleaveland.

Credit for the shorter spelling that came to be adopted later usually is given to a newspaper, the Cleveland Advertiser, which dropped the "a" one day without offering any explanation. It was said that the newspaper was short an "a" in a certain font of type and revised the spelling for its own convenience.

Whatever the reason, it didn't take too much boldness, really, to alter the spelling because it was controversial from the beginning. There long had existed a basic difference of opinion on the orthographic question even in the Cleaveland (Cleveland) family itself.

Gen. Cleaveland himself sometimes used the shorter spelling. And some years later, President Stephen Grover Cleveland, who was related to Gen. Cleaveland, said that his father had made a determined investigation of the family tree and had come to the conclusion that the correct spelling would have to be Cleveland.

Both names, in any event, sprang out of the same genealogical source — a family of Saxons whose place of origin was the Yorkshire countryside in northeastern England.

The terrain in that area is characterized by fissures and clefts, and the people of the vicinity, not surprisingly, became known as clevelanders or cleftlanders. Out of this group grew the family known as Cleaveland, or Cleveland. Other branches of the family used the surname Cleffland, Clifland, and Cleiveland.

The first of Gen. Cleaveland's ancestors to migrate to America also bore the given name, Moses. He arrived in Boston in 1635. A few years later he was one of the founders of the

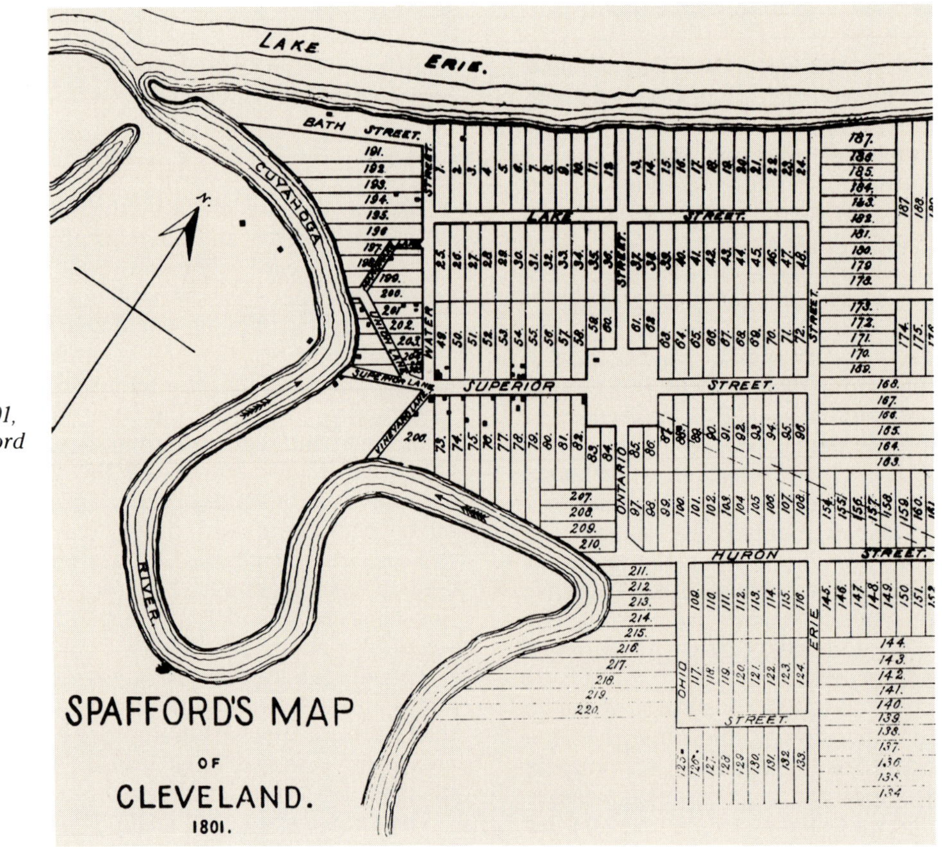

Map of Cleveland, 1801, by Major Amos Spafford

North side of Euclid Avenue, looking west in 1889, with construction of the Arcade

town of Woburn, Massachusetts. There must have been something in the Cleaveland blood that inspired its men to go about siring new settlements.

* * *

Pease and Spafford had to work swiftly on their layout of the first Western Reserve settlement. Summer already was waning as they set to work. But the resulting maps were carefully precise and showed no sign of pressure.

The remarkable thing, really, is that what later came into being actually was in close adherence to the earliest diagrams of the surveyors. There was such strength in those original layouts, however hastily improvised, that their basic outline still is clearly apparent in the street scheme of the modern downtown. Surveyors Pease and Spafford can take credit for having governed the design of the central city for more than 180 years.

Interestingly enough, there was no Euclid Avenue in the original plans. The dominant downtown thoroughfare, by design, was to be Superior Avenue (originally Superior Street). Spafford at first used the name Broad Street, but later substituted Superior. He also abandoned "Court Street" in favor of Ontario Street, and "Deer Street" in favor of Miami Street.

The plan overall was a conventional grid pattern with the traditional New England commons, or public square, as a focal feature. The 10-acre square was set aside for the communal grazing of cattle.

If there was anything remarkable about the plan, it probably was the far-sightedness of the surveyors in alloting extra width to the two main streets: Superior, running east and west; Ontario, running north and south.

Superior Street was planned to be 132 feet wide, a dimension worthy of a Parisian boulevard. Ontario was given a generous 90-feet of width.

Traffic engineers in later years would be grateful to Pease and Spafford for not having stinted on those dimensions. Another aspect of the original plan, on the other hand, stirs a certain amount of rue and critical wonderment.

There is no ready explanation for the fact that only two major north-south streets were provided in the Spafford-Pease plans, and even they were widely separated. One was Ontario Street, the other was Erie Street (E. 9th).

The city has lived uncomfortably with this oversight. It never has been corrected. The problem of north-south movement continues to be a downtown dilemma for those caught in the traffic.

The difficulty of pedestrian movement was eased through the years by the creation of some of the country's most interesting arcades, serving as pedestrian pass-throughs.

The famous Euclid Arcade, just west of E. 6th Street, better known as "The Old Arcade," was created as such a combination shortcut and shopping mall before the turn of the 19th century with the financial backing of John D. Rockefeller. The existence of this building alone should make Clevelanders grateful for the Pease-Spafford stinginess with streets. It consists of two 10-story buildings, one on Euclid Avenue and the other on Superior Avenue, which are joined by a 400-foot esplanade under a glass-domed roof.

Pedestrians who travel today between Prospect Avenue and Euclid Avenue are helped by two arcades: the Colonial Arcade and the Euclid Arcade.

The surveyors in Moses Cleaveland's crew little knew the problems and the wonders that would grow out of their ad-lib schematics in the forest back in 1796. But the cause and effect relationship is clearly visible today.

The shape of downtown Cleveland was determined in that early day. Moses (Cleaveland) had not received his street plan in a miraculous mountaintop manner, nor were they engraved on stone tablets, but they might as well have been because they had such a commanding influence.

Cleaveland, a lawyer by profession, was out of his element when it came to surveying and its problems. In such areas he wisely deferred to the knowledge and experience of the mathematical experts. In his one major conflict with the surveyors, he also demonstrated a commendable flexibility.

In what perhaps was the most unusual incident growing out of the first Connecticut Land Company expedition to the Western Reserve, a number of the surveyors got into a mutinous frame of mind and threatened to quit work if their terms of employment were not bettered.

Cleveland's first strike threat was met diplomatically by the general, who obviously had nowhere to turn in the wilderness for replacement surveyors. He made the men a generous offer. If they would continue their work, they could have an entire township to divide among themselves providing they met certain terms in the offer.

The township tendered to the men was the one directly to the east of Cleveland, and it was given a name appropriate to the mathematical calling of the unhappy help: Euclid.

The offer was accepted and the labor unrest quelled. But the surveyors never did take advantage of the offer.

4. Expedition's end

Cleveland in 1800 — A sketch indicates early landmarks, from left to right, the old river bed, mouth of the Cuyahoga River, Lorenzo Carter's first cabin, log warehouse of the surveyors, surveyors' cabin or Pease's hotel.

By the middle of that first October on the site of Cleveland in 1796, the principals and their followers in the Connecticut Land Company's first expedition into the Western Reserve had grown visibly anxious about the length of their stay in the wilderness country.

Their basic objectives had been met. The Indian question had been settled — up to the line of the Cuyahoga River, at least. A large part of New Connecticut had been surveyed and mapped. A site for the capital city had been found and prepared, in a limited way, for future occupation.

What now was demanding everyone's full attention were the signs of seasonal change that were everywhere to be seen. The Cleveland autumn is not one easily to be ignored. It is a time that is flamboyantly demanding of attention still, but no doubt more vividly then than now. The universal spread of green forest, numbering heavy stands of sugar maples, were turning into a blaze of color. Thick, rolling mists of white hung low in the river valley in the early mornings, and hoar frost covered the meadows up on the Cuyahoga bluff.

The sharp edge of the message from the north was felt most keenly in the bracing cold morning air that hardly had time to soften under the mellow light of the afternoon before the abbreviated day had ended.

Gen. Cleaveland, anxious to return home anyway, heeded the signs, finally, and gave orders to prepare for departure. There is no indication that it was for him an emotional wrench. He had accepted a difficult assignment, worked out some difficult problems in a manner that to him seemed to have produced satisfactory results, and now he could go home without any need to apologize for the results of the expedition.

He wrote, somewhat stolidly, of the experience in later days.

"While I was in New Connecticut I laid out a town on the bank of Lake Erie, which was called by my name, and I believe the child is now born that may live to see that place as large as old Windham."

Old Windham, Conn., at that time had a population of about 1,500.

* * *

The expedition departed the site of Cleveland at 3 in the afternoon of Oct. 17, 1796; a day that had started out gray and rainy, but which had cleared up by mid-afternoon.

"There were 14 men on board the boat," wrote 18-year-old John Milton Holley in his journal, "and never, I presume, were fourteen men more anxious to pursue an object that we were to go forward..."

But Cleveland was not abandoned entirely. The expedition did leave behind small holding parties to maintain possession of the sites staked out until the first contingents of settlers could be recruited to go west and become a permanent part of the pioneer scene in the Ohio country.

Elijah Gun and his wife, Anna, were left in residence at Camp Stow in Conneaut. Three persons agreed to spend the winter in Cleveland. They were Job P. Stiles, his wife, Tabitha, and a man named Joseph Landon.

History was in the making in the Stiles cabin on top of the east bluff (near W. 6th and Superior) that winter — in more ways than one.

A son, Charles Phelps Stiles, was born to the couple on Jan. 23, 1797. He was the first white child born in Cleveland.

It is an incredible fact of history that this child, born on the Cleveland site before the town itself really had begun to live, when the full population numbered a mere 3 persons, lived to see Cleveland grow into a city of some 100,000 population by the time of his death in 1882.

Joseph Landon changed his mind about spending the winter of 1796-97 in Cleveland and moved on, but another white man, Edward Paine, who later founded the city named in his honor, Painesville, took his place.

Paine was a frequent visitor to the Stiles cabin, but he preferred to spend most of his time with the Indian tribes that made their winter camps on the west side of the Cuyahoga. The Chippewas and the Ottawas were among those friendly Indians who lived across the river. There also was an encampment of Seneca Indians at the foot of the bluff between Superior Street and the river.

Besides the Stiles cabin on the top of the bluff, the Cleaveland expedition had left behind two other log buildings. They were close together in the flats, on the east bank of the river, on what today would be Old River Road. One, which served as a dormitory for the surveyors, was humorously called, "Pease's Hotel." The other was a storage cabin. The only other sign of the white man's presence was the log cabin on the other side of the Cuyahoga, close to the river's mouth, that supposedly had served as a fur trading post before the arrival of Moses Cleaveland on the scene.

That was Cleveland, then, as winter closed in and brought about a recess in the difficult and dangerous attempt to open this part of the New World to white settlement in 1796.

And while there was some discontent back in the east over the progress attained, the members of the surveying expedition could look back on a time of high achievement.

Moses Warren, a member of the pioneer party, wrote the following poetic expression of his feeling as he and other members of the Cleaveland expedition rode the waters of Lake Erie, homeward bound, and cast a last backward look at the townsite on the high Cuyahoga bluff:

The Explorer's Farewell

From Erie's shore and Cleveland's street
The woods-worn lads at length retreat
With scanty means of living
Again approach the Orient East,
To celebrate the autumnal feast
That Yankees call Thanksgiving.

The cloud-topped trees and purling rills,
The flowery meads and swelling hills,
Have claim for us no more;
The explorer's path and artist's line
Neglected lie: We all combine
And seek our native shore.

The elk, the deer and beasts of prey
Are left to range the forests gay
Till savage hand destroy;
And soon give place to flowing fields
With all the crops that nature yields
To crown the tiller's joy.

The saline spring on Beaver's flood,
Chenango's flats, Mahoning's wood,
and Cuyahoga's trade;
Geneva's hills, LeChagrin's vales
And Tuscarora's plain prevails
To invite the undismayed.

Then rouse, ye men, whose native soil
Eludes your most laborious toil
With scanty crops and blasts;
Far in the West your work renew,
Nor dread the dire corrosive dew
That Eastern fields lay waste.

But when you journey, leave behind
The bigot's stern, unsocial mind.
On sterile stony hills;
These Western lands are far too good
To cherish such a rankling brood —
The worst of human ills.

The sciences do not forget,
But them transplant and cultivate
By precept and example,
Till Western students shall outdo
The schools of Yale and Harvard, too,
And on the pedants trample.

5. Life on the frontier

Those first company-sponsored residents of the Cleveland site in that first winter of 1796-97 were not alone. Besides the presence of the neighboring Indians, there were the comings and goings of the fur trappers, hunters, military couriers, and a certain breed of wilderness itinerants, including the individual explorers and adventurers.

Among the visitors to the place on the Cuyahoga, it is said, was the famous Indian chief, Seneca, whose presence in the Cleveland area continued as late as 1809. His tribesmen, friendly to the settlers, supplied them with fresh game during the winter months.

With the awakening of the countryside in the spring, there was a freshet of people to Cleveland. Most prominent of these were the members of the Connecticut Land Company's second expedition.

Conspicuously missing from this group was Gen. Moses Cleaveland. There had been some displeasure in the home office of the company over his groundbreaking efforts of the previous year, and he had been displaced as superintendent by Rev. Seth Hart.

Some familiar names and faces were to be found among the members of that second expedition, however. They included Seth Pease, now the principal surveyor; Amos Spafford, his son, Samuel Spafford, Richard M. Stoddard, Moses Warren, Joseph Landon, Theodore Shepherd, and Joseph Tinker.

There were, in all, 51 persons in the Connecticut Land Company's second expedition into the Western Reserve.

The newcomers to the town that spring also included Elijah Gun and his wife, who had chosen to move from the company's Conneaut camp at the end of the rigorous winter to take up residence in Cleveland.

They were joined in the decision to forsake Conneaut in favor of the Cuyahoga settlement by James Kingsbury and his wife. This pioneer couple from New Hampshire, and their three children, had gone through a chilling experience at Conneaut in the winter just ended. One of their children had died in the terrible privation.

James Kingsbury

Lorenzo Carter

Perhaps the most important of all the new arrivals in Cleveland in that springtime of 1797, historically speaking, was Lorenzo Carter, a native of Rutland, Vermont.

Carter, who had traveled to the Western Reserve by way of Canada, quickly became the strong man of the new settlement. He was, in a real sense, Cleveland's first law enforcement officer, its first judge and jailer, its first policeman, its first inn-keeper, and its first civic leader. And on the side he operated the first ferry across the Cuyahoga.

The return of the land company's official party, who traveled the final lap of the trip by water, was marked by a last-minute tragedy. One of the young men in the party, David Eldridge of Connecticut, was drowned while trying to cross the Grand River. His body was carried to Cleveland and he was buried in a hastily selected cemetery site, the city's first, on the east side of Ontario, just north of Prospect Avenue. The Episcopal rites in that first funeral service was read by the leader of the expedition, Rev. Hart.

Everything that happened that year seemed to qualify as an historic "first," of course. But among the significant entries in the record book was the town's first wedding, which took place on July 4, 1797. Miss Choe Inches and a Canadian by the name of Clement were married on that holiday by the same Rev. Hart, who apparently was just as busy being a minister of the Lord as an emissary of the Connecticut Land Company.

The population count in that first full year of Cleveland's existence fluctuated with the coming and going of surveyors and wilderness travelers, but at one time it reached a high of 24 persons.

One of the compelling reasons for the population fluctuation, by the way, was the dawning realization that Cleveland was coming to be viewed as a hazardous place to live.

Apart from the routine dangers of rugged frontier life, Cleveland presented two special threats to everybody's health: Rattlesnakes and malaria-spreading mosquitoes.

The rattlesnakes were everywhere. Most common was the great yellow rattlesnake, a reptile not to be taken lightly. When the first white settlers entered the Western Reserve, they were amused by the way the native Indians leaped in crazy zigzag fashion and yelped as they made their way through the woods and across the creeks. When the presence of the snakes underfoot became known to the whites, they soon were outleaping and outyelping the Indians. Rattlesnakes had a way of giving wings to the heels of the slowest pioneers.

Southeast of Cleveland — Early settlers' favorite refuge from the mosquito-infested Cuyahoga flats was the high, dry ground of nearby Newburgh where the remains of the Old Grist Mill (below) stood near the falls along Mill Creek (above).

On the bright side, however, Joshua Stow, the commissary of the Connecticut Land Company's survey party, was said to have "a positive liking for snake meat," according to Historian James Harrison Kennedy.

That interesting fact must not have advanced Stow's cause with his earlier superior, Gen. Cleaveland, and might even have caused Cleaveland to sniff Stow's stew suspiciously because, wrote Kennedy in his,*A History of the City of Cleveland*,: "General Cleaveland was disgusted with snakes, living or cooked, and with those who cooked them."

But the major health problem in the new settlement was more serious: the high incidence of malaria that was directly attributable to the heavy presence in the Cuyahoga flats area of the female of the anopheles mosquito, the carrier of the malaria germ.

Mosquitoes thrived in the valley, many parts of which were marshy and stagnant, perfect breeding places for the deadly insects. Most likely the worst place of all was close to the mouth of the Cuyahoga, on the west side, where there was a stagnant body of water that once had been a part of the river. A sand bar had accumulated, separating it from the rest of the river, which was diverted and forced to find a new outlet to the lake. The abandoned section of river, land-trapped, existed only as a dead pool and was called, by the earliest settlers, "Sun Fish Pond." Its water was foul and stagnant, repulsive to

Samuel Huntington

Turhand Kirtland

the pioneers, but appreciated by the mosquitoes.

The malarial disease struck swiftly and spared few and represented a most serious threat to the success of the Connecticut colonization attempt in the Cuyahoga region. And while it was not scientifically established as yet that the mosquitoes were the villains of the malaria problem, it wasn't long before the early settlers began to put two-and-two together. The Cuyahoga flats was the place of high malarial incidence and there the mosquitoes were most numerous.

Most of the settlers sensibly sought to put some safe distance between themselves and the flats. They did this by selecting their cabin sites on the high eastern plain above the river and far enough inland as possible. Their favorite refuge was the high, dry ground of Newburgh, some six miles to the southeast. To the humiliation of Clevelanders, it became fairly common for some people to describe Cleveland as the town near Newburgh.

One of the pioneers, Timothy Doan, settled his family to the east of Public Square on the Buffalo Road at a place identified later as E. 105th Street and Euclid Avenue. That intersection to this day is still known as Doan's Corner.

There was good reason for that flight inland. The diaries and writings of many of the settlers are replete with references to the suffering and deaths from malaria.

Seth Pease's journal for the months of August, September and November of 1797 is full of notations about sickness and fever in the little settlement.

Under these trying circumstances, nevertheless, there was a pair of newcomers to Cleveland who not only elected to live in the flats, but who chose a site on the west bank very close to stagnant Sunfish Pond. The two who dared virtually to put their heads inside the mosquitoe's jaws were father and son, David and Gilman Bryant.

The Bryants arrived in the Cuyahoga valley in June, 1797, and shortly thereafter established a whisky distillery next to the dank, dangerous site. That they were able to do so and survive, even prosper, was held by some Clevelanders to be among the most stirring testimonials of all time to the efficacy of whisky as a medical potion and as an effective antidote to the bites of snakes, mosquitoes, mad dogs and other enemies of man.

Lorenzo Carter's first log cabin was on the east side of the river, near the foot of Superior Hill. Close by was the wooden dock for the ferry service that Carter established in one of his first actions. He also built the ferry boat. Whether due to a fire blamed on one of his sons, or to the virulent presence of the mosquitoes, Carter eventually moved the family to a new house at the top of the hill, on Superior Street.

The second Carter house was the biggest and most elaborate, by far, at the time. A log building, it enjoyed impressive dimensions, containing two apartments on the ground floor and a large garret. It was a cabin for all seasons and all occasions. It served as an inn, a variety store, a social center, and even as a courthouse and jail.

Turhand Kirtland, an agent of the Connecticut Land Company, was visibly impressed by the importance of Lorenzo Carter in the Cleveland scheme of things when he visited the settlement in the summer of 1800.

The investors in the land company by that time had gotten themselves into a nervous state about the prospects of their Western Reserve investment. Pioneers were not pounding at the company door trying to buy land out west. The Cleveland population, for example, included only the families of Lorenzo Carter, David Clark, and Maj. Amos Spafford. (The Bryants presumably did not count because they lived on the other side of the river.)

The price of city lots in Cleveland, illustrating the depressed nature of the land business at the time, had been reduced to $25 apiece from the previously fixed price of $50 apiece.

A distinguished newcomer to Cleveland in that critical year was Samuel Huntington, nephew and namesake of Gov. Samuel Huntington of Connecticut. Young Huntington had decided to cast his lot with the Western Reserve. In his diary, he wrote the following impression of the Cleveland settlement as it appeared to him in October, 1800:

"Left David Abbot's mill (Willoughby) and came to Cleveland. Stayed at Carter's at night. Explored the city and town; land high and flat, covered with white oak. On the west side of the river is a long deep stagnant pond of water, which produces fever and ague, among those who settle near the river. There are only three families near the point, and they have the fever.

"Sailed out of the Cuyahoga along the coast, to explore the land west of the river. Channel at the mouth about five feet deep. On the west side is a prairie, where one hundred tons of hay might be cut each year. A little way back is a ridge, from which the land descends to the lake, affording a prospect indescribably beautiful..."

Huntington did not linger long in Cleveland. He went on, in a rapid sequence of successes, to become a militia officer, a state senator, a state supreme court justice, and, in 1807, governor of the state.

Huntington Park, west of Cleveland, memorializes him as a pioneer resident, however briefly.

6. Education's beginning

It stands as something of a testimonial to the scale of values held by Cleveland's pioneer few that even while their settlement was clawing for a foothold in the wilderness, the amenities of civilized life still were accorded an important place in the primitive scheme of things.

The first priorities of the time, naturally, were food, clothing and shelter. But the need for law and education were not far behind in the attention of the community. As early as 1800, for example, education had been given a rude beginning in a log schoolhouse built near the home of Judge James Kingsbury "on the ridge road." This presumably referred to Euclid Avenue; specifically, to the vicinity of Euclid and E. 105th Street, still known as Doan's Corner. It was there that Nathaniel Doan, an early settler, had chosen to settle after escaping the malarial mosquitoes in Moses Cleaveland's settlement. Sara Doan, Nathaniel's daughter, was the teacher in the first school.

Education came to Cleveland proper — that is, the area in the vicinity of the Cuyahoga Valley — in 1802. In that year, Miss

High school built in 1852, from a student's drawing before the razing of the building.

Daguerreotype of a chemistry class, probably in Cleveland's first high school (Central High), circa 1850

Anna Spafford, daughter of Maj. Amos Spafford, began to conduct classes for about a dozen children of the settlement in the large front room of Maj. Carter's inn.

The first schoolhouse in Cleveland was built in 1806 at the foot of Superior Street. Some 21 children from the families of George Kilbourne, Samuel Huntington, James Hamilton, James Kingsbury, David Kellogg, and W. W. Williams attended the school.

The teacher was Asael Adams, a young Connecticut native who had lived previously in Liberty Township near Youngstown. The founder of Liberty Township was Camden Cleaveland, brother of Moses and brother-in-law of Asael Adams.

Adams was paid $10 a month, "to be paid in money or wheat at the market price," and his contract called for him not only to teach, but to "furnish benches and fire-wood sufficient."

A much larger schoolhouse was built in 1817; a frame building built by private subscription on St. Clair Street, near Bank (W. 3rd). The village acquired that schoolhouse by purchase in June of that year, refunding the donations of the private citizens.

Library at Woodland Hills School, circa 1900

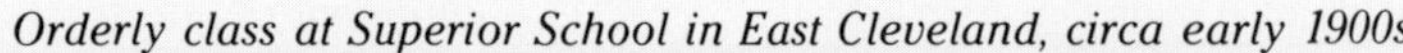

Orderly class at Superior School in East Cleveland, circa early 1900s

Government and order

EXPEDITION

STAGE LINE!

From Seville and Medina, via. Brunswick, Strongsville, Middleburgh, Parma, Brighton and Brooklyn to Cleveland, and return Daily except Sundays.

The Stage will leave Seville at 6:30 A. M., and Medina at 8:15 A. M., arriving in Cleveland in time to do business for several hours same day and in time for the evening Trains and Boats going east, west and south.

The Stage will leave Cleveland (Russells Forest City House,) at 8:15 A. M., arriving in Seville in time for the trains going east on the A. & G. W. R.

This is the best and most direct Route of travel for all persons doing business at Cleveland, or that wish to take the Cars at Seville Station, whose residence is at or near the Towns above named.

The Proprietor being grateful for past favors, solicits a continuance of patronage from the traveling public.

RULES:

Fare must be paid in advance; seats are engaged when paid for to an authorized Agent

Extra baggage over 40 lbs to be paid for when put on or marked for collection on delivery, but if, as it sometimes happens that the amount is not known to the Agent at the place of departure, in this case any Agent is authorized to make and collect the charges.

Drivers are prohibited from taking passengers from or past a Station, until the fair is paid.

If any passengers wish to get on and off between Stations, the Driver is required in all such cases to collect the fare at the usual rates and pay it over at the next Station, and see it entered on the Way-Bill.

Drivers will be accomodating and gentlemanly to passengers, and take especial care of all Packages entrusted to them, and see that they are in all cases properly entered on the Way-Bills and forwarded to the nearest Station where directed.

No package will be delivered elsewhere than to an Agent, unless the charges are paid in advance, and not then except by special agreement.

It is the Drivers duty among other things to keep the Coaches in good running order at all times, and clean inside and outside, and to always have the Way-Bill in safe keeping, and know what is on it and to report to the first Agent seen what has been received after leaving a former Station.

Agents and passengers will do a favor by reporting all delinquences to the undersigned.

Agents will attend promptly to the business relating to their Agencies and prevent any unnecessary delay at their respective Stations.

D. D. DOWD, Prop.

P. S—Drivers will furnish themselves with Cleaning Tools, Whips and Hitch Reins.

7. The evolution of government

Long before Cleveland became an active center of civilization, it was part of a shifting pattern of sovereignty.

In the beginning, thanks to Christopher Columbus, it was part of the continental claim of Spain. Later, it was within the territory to which the French asserted title. After the French and Indian War, it went under the flag of Great Britain. Ultimately, of course, it was part of the territory absorbed by the new United States of America just 20 years before Moses Cleaveland's party arrived.

There has been almost as rich a variety of jurisdiction and control on the lower levels of government affecting the city.

At the time Cleveland was founded, the land on the east side of the Cuyahoga River was officially a part of Washington County, whose seat was Marietta on the Ohio River, about 175 wilderness miles distant.

General Arthur St. Clair

The land on the west side of the Cuyahoga was counted then as part of Wayne County, whose government was administered from Detroit, Mich.

The Cuyahoga River, it is seen, was the great divider in Cleveland in the old days, just as it is in modern times.

When the site of Cleveland still was in the hands of the Indians, the river served as the boundary between the Senecas in the east and the several Indian tribes to the west.

As white civilization encroached on the Indian territory, the Cuyahoga was the line of separation between the eastern lands of the Western Reserve which had been yielded by the Indians in a treaty, and the Connecticut-claimed lands west of the river which still were regarded by the Indians as their property.

When the first county lines were drawn, it was the river that separated Wayne County on the west from Washington County on the east.

Cleveland was less than a year old when, in 1797, Gen. Arthur St. Clair, the governor of the Northwest Territory, created a new county, Jefferson by name, that took in the Connecticut settlement on the east bank of the Cuyahoga. The county seat of Jefferson County was Steubenville.

Gov. St. Clair created Trumbull County in July, 1800, including in its jurisdiction the entire territory of the Western Reserve, including all the former Indian country to the west of the Cuyahoga River. Warren was the county seat. This marked the first time that Cleveland's east and west sides had been united within the same county framework.

Those were unsettled political times, of course. It was a period of political ferment and change at every level of government as westward expansion and the beginning of immigration began to have their effect. No system could remain static under the pressures of the time and the shifting about of population. Newly opened lands and new migratory trends meant, necessarily, new patterns of government.

The most important of those new units of government to the settlers in Cleveland was the state of Ohio, which emerged as a political entity in 1803.

But while the creation of Ohio was a welcome development to the pioneers who may have felt themselves disenfranchised by the move to the west, the news probably was received with mingled emotions back home in Connecticut. It quelled forever whatever hopes may have remained among the investors in the Western Reserve that their large Ohio holdings would one day become an independent state called New Connecticut.

The shift from existence under a territorial government to life under the rule of a full-fledged sovereign state had an immediate effect on the political and personal lives of Clevelanders. It gave them — as it gave all Ohioans — a more direct participation and representation in their government. It gave them also an enhanced sense of dignity, security and progress. It meant that the frontier barrier at last had been downed. The wilderness had achieved statehood. Civilization had assumed command.

Out of statehood grew several important developments.

One was a renewed effort to resolve the question of the Connecticut Land Company's title to the lands west of the Cuyahoga River.

A conference between representatives of the company, the government, and seven Indian tribes was held at the western edge of the Western Reserve, near Sandusky, in July, 1805, to resolve the issue.

The negotiating sessions were brief. The impression is inescapable, from all accounts, that the Indians approached the conference in the slow, fatalistic manner of people who believed the outcome to be fore-ordained.

On July 4, ironically enough, the tribal representatives yielded some more of their independence and another sizeable piece of their home territory: all the land claimed by the Connecticut Land Company to the west of the Cuyahoga River.

After the papers were signed, according to one account, "many of the Indians wept."

The agreement meant that the way now was open for the settlement, survey and sale of the land on Cleveland's west side. It was laid out as the new township called Brooklyn and it became, almost immediately, a rival of Cleveland Township on the east side.

Two years later, in February, 1807, there was still another significant political development when the state legislature established the new Cuyahoga County, making Cleveland the county seat.

It was Cleveland's first governmental distinction; a most important recognition for a struggling village with but a few inhabitants.

* * *

Drawing of the first capitol of Ohio at Chillicothe

Perhaps made giddy by the town's fresh political prestige, the civic leaders in Cleveland in that same year of 1807 aggressively recruited the support of the state legislature for a scheme to improve travel between Cleveland and the all-important Ohio River, the principal highway of travel between east and west.

Only a thin trickle of people was finding its way to Cleveland by way of the difficult wilderness route across New York State. Not many more were challenging the overland route through the Pennsylvania mountains and eastern Ohio.

The easiest way for eastern migrants to get to Cleveland was for them to travel the Ohio River from Pittsburgh to Marietta, and from there to proceed north on the Muskingum and Tuscarawas Rivers to the carrying place in Summit County. A short portage there and the northward journey could be carried to its conclusion via the Cuyahoga River to Lake Erie.

Cleveland leaders persuaded the legislature in 1807 to authorize a state lottery, of all things, to raise the money to improve that river-and-portage route between the Ohio River and Lake Erie. It was basically the same kind of lottery scheme that the state placed in operation in 1974.

It was estimated that $12,000 would be enough to clear the Cuyahoga and Tuscarawas rivers of obstructions, deepen them where needed and improve the portage paths so that they could be used by wagons transferring cargoes, passengers and boats from one waterway to the next.

The state lottery commission included a number of prominent Clevelanders: Lorenzo Carter, Timothy Doan, Samuel Huntington, James Kingsbury, Turhand Kirtland, Amos Spafford and John Walworth.

The scheme improvised by the commission called for the sale of 12,800 tickets at $5 apiece. The revenue to be produced by that sale would amount to $64,000. Out of that grand sum would be extracted the $12,000 needed for the improvement of the river route. The rest of the money would be distributed to lucky ticket buyers in the form of 3,568 prizes ranging in amount from $10 to $5,000.

The Ohioans of 1807 either were more frugal or more moral than the Ohioans of 165 years later. The lottery failed miserably. No more than one-fourth of all the tickets offered were purchased.

The lottery officially was admitted to be a failure. Purchasers of tickets were given a refund. The people had answered the $64,000 question of 1807 with a resounding, "No!", and the travelers of the portage route had to go on paddling their own canoes without any help from the state.

8. The history-makers

Almost everything that happened in the opening years in Cleveland was of landmark quality; material ready-made for the historian's notebook. The slate was new and clean, and historic firsts were commonplace.

For example, the village in 1805 was given its own postoffice, and a man named Elisha Norton was honored with appointment as the first postmaster.

It may have been that he did not regard the honor in an important light. He held the post less than a year. His successor was a newcomer to town, John Walworth, who had moved to Cleveland from a farm near Grand River in April, 1806. His name is recalled in the modern city's Walworth Run.

There were, apparently, more titles and more jobs available in that early time than there were qualified job applicants. Walworth, besides being postmaster and customs collector, was appointed "inspector of revenue for the port of Cuyahoga" by President Thomas Jefferson.

Gov. Tiffin, that same year, named Walworth an associate judge of the Court of Common Pleas of Geauga County. And he found time, somehow to serve also as Cuyahoga County clerk of courts and county recorder. On the side, he sold salt.

The strength and length of some of the threads of history are astonishing. Those that bind the Nathan Perry mosaic into the Cleveland tapestry are an example.

Nathan Perry was a Connecticut native who moved to Ohio in 1796, the year of Moses Cleveland's expedition, and shortly afterward bought 1,000 acres of land, at 50 cents an acre, in Lake County. He also purchased several parcels of land in Cleveland after the Connecticut Land Company had selected the new town-site.

One of Perry's land acquisitions was a 5-acre tract in the woods on top of the hill overlooking the Cuyahoga Valley from the east.

As the town's street pattern asserted itself, Perry's land could be described as the area between Superior and St. Clair avenues, bounded on the west by W. 9th Street and on the east by W. 6th Street. In short, prime downtown real estate.

Perry was appointed a county judge in 1809 and went on to distinction in that post. Meanwhile, his son and namesake, Nathan Perry, Jr., an enterprising young merchant who owned a prosperous Indian trading post on the Black River in Lorain, moved to Cleveland and built a frame store and dwelling on his father's property at the corner of Superior and Water (W. 9th) streets.

One of the younger Perry's children, a daughter, became the wife of Henry B. Payne, later a United States senator from Ohio. The merger of these early, prominent families is memorialized by the presence in the modern city of the Perry-Payne Building, which stands on the site of the original Perry home and store dating back to the beginning of the city.

Senator Payne's family, incidentally, owned a large tract of land farther to the east, beyond Erie (E. 9th) Street and south of Superior. The land was called Payne's Pastures. Through it today runs Payne Avenue.

Among the important newcomers to Cleveland as it first dug in to the appointed site were the likes of Abram Hickox, Levi Johnson, Dr. David Long and Alfred Kelley. They arrived in a

Perry-Payne Building, circa 1890, on Superior Avenue

First county court house, on the Public Square of Cleveland

John Walworth

Nathan Perry

Henry B. Payne

Abram Hickox

Levi Johnson

Dr. David Long

Alfred Kelley

John W. Allen

The famous Buckeye House, a hostelry built by Levi Johnson

close cluster: Hickox in 1808, Johnson in 1809, and Kelley and Long in 1810.

Of most immediate importance, perhaps, was the arrival of Abram Hickox. He was a blacksmith and the services he was able to render were of fundamental importance in a primitive settlement. The scholars, preachers, lawyers and philosophers would have their turns later. What Cleveland needed at the outset was builders.

But there was something else that recommended Abram to the community. He was the father of five daughters, and that alone would have made him warmly welcome in a town badly in need of population.

Hickox, more familiarly known as "Uncle Abram," arrived at the right time. The village desperately needed a replacement for its previous blacksmith, Nathaniel Doan, who had fled across the malaria-ague line into the eastern highlands out on Euclid Avenue to escape Cuyahoga's mosquitoes.

But Hickox was a big help to the town in another way; his presence was a morale-booster because of his cheerful, outgoing personality. The townspeople liked to congregate at his shop on the north side of Superior, which later became the site of his home when he moved his forge to a site south of Superior, and, finally, to Euclid Avenue. Over the doorway to his shop was the cheerful slogan, "Uncle Abram Works Here." Underneath that, burned into the wood, was the imprint of a horseshoe.

Besides his blacksmithing, Uncle Abram served as the town sexton, and, in effect, the town undertaker because all the arrangements for the burial of the dead were his responsibility. Beyond that, he voluntarily kept the town on its patriotic toes.

On each 4th of July, by the dawn's early light, Uncle Abram would begin hammering on his anvil with all his might, setting up a terrible, ringing clangor that could not be ignored by the sleeping townspeople. They had no alternative to arise and celebrate their country's independence because there was no letup by Uncle Abram. He kept up the hammering on the anvil all day long.

Levi Johnson was another man whose services were of vital, immediate importance to the village.

This 24-year-old native of Herkimer County, N.Y., was a highly skillful builder — a talent of incalculable value in a community that was little more than a wilderness clearing, whose streets still were cluttered with tree stumps, and whose rude log buildings were little more than temporary shelters awaiting more permanent replacement.

Johnson was the builder of most of the important structures that were erected in Cleveland in the beginning decades, and he continued to make valuable contributions to the community through a long lifetime that did not end until 1871.

Johnson's first effort was a log cabin for himself on the ridge, later Euclid Avenue, near Public Square. He later built a log county courthouse and jail on the northwest corner of Public Square, and the first frame house in town for Judge Walworth on the site later occupied by the American House. He also built the famous hostelry called the Buckeye House on Woodland Hills Avenue, and numerous houses and barns throughout Cleveland and Newburgh.

It was as a boat-builder that Johnson achieved special fame. His first effort was a schooner called "Ladies Master," which he built in 1813 on his Euclid Avenue property, which was, of course, a considerable distance from the water. When it was finished, it had to be towed down to the river, at the foot of Superior Hill, by ox teams. It was a sight that had the town buzzing for weeks.

In 1817, Johnson built another schooner, the "Neptune," but this time he built the boat at river's edge, near the foot of Eagle Street. Seven years later, he built the craft that won him special fame. It was the "Enterprise," and it had the distinction of being the first steamboat built in Cleveland.

Johnson had a love of the water and sailed Lake Erie for many years. But his contribution to the maritime scene was not limited to his boats or his sailing. In 1830, he built a stone lighthouse at the entrance to Cleveland's harbor and followed that achievement with a similar lighthouse at Cedar Point. Several years later he built a 1,700-foot government pier off the Cleveland lakefront that gave the Cleveland port a badly-needed facility.

* * *

A big gap in the social structure of Cleveland was filled in 1810 with the arrival of Dr. David Long. The townspeople greeted him with special warmth because the nearest practicing physicians at that time were to be found either in Hudson or in Painesville.

Dr. Long, graduate of a New York City medical school, quickly found a sizeable practice in Cleveland, but he did not limit himself to medicine. He was active in the public and social life of the town and became an important person in community affairs. He was elected a county commissioner in 1826 and became deeply involved in certain business enter-

Dr. Jared P. Kirtland, in his later years

prises, including the building of the Ohio Canal.

In any judgment of Cleveland's early leaders, the name of Alfred Kelley undoubtedly would have to be given the highest rating; indeed, in any review of the city's leadership from the very beginning to the present, Kelley probably would have to be among the top three or four leading statesmen.

Remarkably, he was Cleveland's first executive leader. After Cleveland was officially incorporated as a village by the Ohio General Assembly on Dec. 23, 1814, the community had its first general election in June, 1815, and Alfred Kelley was unanimously elected first president of the village.

Kelley had moved to Cleveland from the upstate New York town of Lowville in 1810. He was from a large family that exerted considerable influence on the development and growth of Cleveland.

His father, Judge Daniel Kelley, and his three brothers, Datus, Irad and Reynolds, all played active roles in the little settlement on the Cuyahoga.

There was a special family reason for the interest the Kelleys took in Cleveland, and for their transfer here from New York. Judge Kelley's wife, Jemima, was the sister of Joshua Stow, who was one of the 35 original members of the Connecticut Land Company and who served as commissary of Moses Cleaveland's 1796 founding party.

Alfred, the first member of the family to make Cleveland his home, had practiced law in New York for three years before moving to Cleveland in 1810. He accompanied on that trip his uncle, Joshua Stow, and Dr. Jared P. Kirtland, another outstanding man who would make his mark in history. Kelley, within less than a year, was made Cleveland's public prosecutor — a likely appointment in light of the fact that he was the town's first practicing attorney. He held the post until 1822.

The 1815 election that made Kelley village president brought out only 12 voters — an impressive turnout considering that there were only 12 persons eligible to vote — all males, of course. In addition to electing Kelley, they gave their approval to Horace Perry, recorder; Alonzo Carter, treasurer; John A. Ackley, marshal; George Wallace and John Riddle, assessors; Samuel Williamson, David Long, and Nathan Perry, Jr., trustees.

Alfred Kelley held the post of village president less than a year. He resigned and was succeeded by his father, Daniel Kelley, who presided over the Cleveland village government until 1819.

The last person to fill the office of president of the village was John W. Allen, who served from 1832 to 1835. The following year, 1836, the Ohio General Assembly granted Cleveland its charter as a city. Henceforth, the chief administrative officer would be a mayor.

Ironically, the charter came too late to give Cleveland the distinction it sought so badly, that of becoming the first city in Cuyahoga County, an honor achieved by Brooklyn.

9. The hanging of O'Mic

The year of 1812 was in every way the most exciting time in Cleveland's brief history.

There was, in the springtime, news of a sensational double murder near Sandusky, a trial, a conviction, and, finally, a public execution.

Then, in the late summer, there was the outbreak of war with Great Britain that had been threatening for so long, and the immediate effect was to bring about a shivery apprehension.

The victims in the springtime murders, committed by three Indians, were two white trappers named Buel and Gibbs. The suspects had been arrested almost immediately after the terrible crime, which took place on April 3, but even their seizure had tragic overtones. One of the three, apparently unable to bear the dishonor, committed suicide after he was captured.

A second suspect was released because of his extreme youth. The third, an Indian named O'Mic, was a familiar figure in the Cleveland vicinity. He was turned over to the custody of Maj. Lorenzo Carter in Cleveland because Huron, where the crime was committed, was within the jurisdiction of Cuyahoga County.

There was no foot-dragging by the courts in those pioneer days. The wheels of justice turned quickly. Before the month of April had ended, the murder trial of O'Mic was underway in Cleveland. It was not held in any austere courtroom setting, however, but was conducted outdoors, under the shady branches of a large tree at the corner of Water (W. 9th) and Superior streets.

Two judges, William W. Irvin and Ethan Allen Brown, presided over the hearings. Alfred Kelley was the prosecuting attorney. Peter Hitchcock was the counsel for the defense.

Members of the petit jury were Hiram Russell, Levi Johnson, Philemon Baldwin, David Bunnel, Charles Gunn, Christopher Gunn, Samuel Dille, Elijah Gunn, David Barret, Dyer Shearman, William Austin, and Seth Doan.

The formal indictment charged O'Mic specifically with the murder of Daniel Buel "with a certain Tomahawk, made of iron and Steele."

There was little wrangling in the courtroom. Indeed, if there was any defense it must have been presented in minutes. A verdict of guilty was reached quickly and O'Mic was sentenced to death for the crime. The date of execution was set at June 26th, the following month.

Word of the impending hanging spread quickly through the state and overlapped into Pennsylvania, Indiana and Michigan. By the time June 26th rolled around, the sightseers from hundreds of miles away joined nearby settlers in crowding the Cleveland clearing for the big event.

Levi Johnson, who had helped convict O'Mic in his role as a trial juror, now made a further contribution to the hapless Indian's departure by putting his master-builder skills to work in the construction of a stout gallows. The site was a cleared space in the northwest corner of Public Square, close to the city's first log courthouse and jail that was still a building under Johnson's direction. The combination-purpose building would not be ready for official use until 1813.

O'Mic, while awaiting execution, was confined to the garret of Lorenzo Carter's all-purpose inn, where he was chained to an attic rafter for the month following the trial.

There are conflicting descriptions of O'Mic, but a consensus would indicate that he was not really one of those legendary Indian braves, tall and slim and silent, with nobility of bearing. From most accounts, he was on the short side, overweight and given to garrulity.

Among the subjects on which O'Mic lectured while awaiting execution was the striking difference between the ways that white men and Indians approached death. He spoke scornfully of the paleface fear of death and he boasted that when his hour on the gallows platform arrived, he would give an example to one and all of the stoical, fearless manner in which an Indian brave could meet the end.

The execution itself was not one of the smoothest in the history of such affairs — not even on the frontier, where life and death were commonly casual. The mounted military guard, under Maj. Samuel Jones, was supposed to form a hollow square about the prisoner as he rode — seated on his own coffin in the sheriff's newly painted wagon — from Maj. Carter's inn to Public Square. Maj. Jones, however, had trouble remembering which orders would bring about that nice military effect and the result was confusion, with horses and riders colliding with a great medley of neighing and shouting.

"Perhaps," ventured one eyewitness, Elisha Whittlesey, "the major had lingered too long at Lorenzo Carter's tavern."

In spite of all the confusion in the ranks of the mounted guard, the wagon managed to transport O'Mic to the Public Square, through the huge assemblage, and up to the gallows. There it was met by Sheriff Samuel S. Baldwin and Lorenzo Carter.

O'Mic's face was a mask as the sheriff fitted a noose around his neck while Carter stepped down, clearing the platform for the grim proceeding.

The critical moment for O'Mic to show the white man how to die had arrived, without question, but the Indian was of a different mind at the moment. Dipping his head suddenly, he was able to wrench the cap that had been pulled over his head and, at the same time, grab one of the posts of the platform. To this he clung, one could say, for dear life.

When Sheriff Baldwin approached the prisoner, O'Mic made threatening gestures in his direction. Maj. Carter promptly

climbed to the platform and harshly called on O'Mic to explain his peculiar resistance to the planned proceedings, addressing him in his native Indian dialect.

O'Mic's reply, in so many words, was he needed a drink, and that if Carter would provide him with a half-pint of whisky — one for the road, so to speak — he would become the most cooperative Indian in town.

Carter, a reasonable, understanding sort, agreed. He produced a bottle of Old Monongahela, a frontier standby, and offered it to O'Mic, who tipped it to his lips and swallowed it in a few gulps.

Then, to everybody's surprise, the Indian grabbed the platform post again and issued another ultimatum. He would not die, he said, until he had had another drink. He was still thirsty. Carter came out of the ringside crowd again with another half-pint of Old Monongahela, and O'Mic downed the second drink with considerable gusto. But even as he was pouring it down his throat, Sheriff Baldwin cut the rope, causing O'Mic to be jerked upward by the tightened noose and then to swing back and forth like a pendulum over the gallows platform while the large crowd involuntarily exclaimed in horror.

Some doubt was expressed that the Indian's neck had been broken in that first attempt and the authorities began to raise the body on high again for a second attempt, but at that moment a bad storm that had been brewing at last burst. Most of the spectators fled from Public Square in search of shelter. O'Mic's body was placed in a coffin that had been kept nearby.

"The storm was heavy and all scampered but O'Mic," wrote one Cleveland historian, James Harrison Kennedy.

A mystery grew out of the interrupted hanging, nevertheless. Reports circulated for years that O'Mic had survived the hanging; that several doctors who were present at the execution had taken the body out of its coffin that same night and found that "it was easier to restore life than to prevent it."

Another popular story had it that some of the doctors in town to witness the execution were hard pressed for a cadaver, and that, with the help of Sheriff Baldwin, they had snatched the body and hid it below a spring on the bank of the lake, east of Water Street (W. 9th) until the hanging had been forgotten, a year later, goes the story, they retrieved the body.

O'Mic, in a "properly articulated" condition, was supposed to have been in the possession of Dr. Long for a long time, then to have been transferred to the office of Dr. Town in Hudson for a while. The macabre journey finally is said to have taken poor O'Mic to the town of Penn, near Pittsburgh, where it was reportedly given over to the care of a Dr. Murray, a son-in-law of Dr. Town.

Whatever O'Mic had been in life, all Cleveland agreed that he certainly was a standout in death.

10. The War of 1812

The War of 1812, as it turned out, swirled menacingly around and about the village where the Cuyahoga River flowed into Lake Erie, but it never really came close enough for discomfort. The community's chief involvement was to serve as a supply base and as a mobilization center for the army.

One of the most memorable incidents came at the beginning of the war, in the summertime. Congress had declared war against the British in June and considerable fear had built up in Cleveland over some of the dread possibilities in the situation, including the danger of the village being shelled by British warships and the threat of land invasion by combined British and Indian forces.

Commodore Oliver Hazard Perry

The spectre of massacre became even more real in August when the news of the surrender of Detroit by General Hull burst on the already apprehensive Clevelanders. An attack on the virtually defenseless settlement occupying the strategic Cuyahoga site at once became a distinct probability to the people of the town. A quick follow-up attack by the British to consolidate their control of Lake Erie would have been a logical military action. And, for a while, it seemed as if such a move were underway.

Alfred Kelley, recalling the wartime scare, described it later in a letter:

"Information was received at Cleveland, through a scout from Huron, that a large number of British troops and Indians were seen from the shore, in boats, proceeding down the lake, and that they would probably reach Cleveland in the course of the ensuing night.

"This information spread rapidly through the surrounding settlements. A large proportion of the families Cleveland, Newburgh, and Euclid, immediately on the receipt of this news, took such necessary articles of food, clothing and utensils as they could carry, and started for the more populous and less exposed parts of the interior.

"About thirty men only remained, determined to meet the enemy if they should come, and, if possible, prevent their landing. They determined at least to do all in their power to allay the panic, and prevent the depopulation of the country."

What amounted to near-panic in the village, resulting in the evacuation of the buildings close to the river, had been brought about by a courier from Huron who spread the word that a number of British and their Indian allies were coming ashore at that settlement west of Cleveland.

Upon receipt of this report in Cleveland, a Maj. Samuel Jones, riding wildly about on horseback in the manner of a latter-day Paul Revere, urged people to flee to Doan's Corner, where a military guard would try to protect them from the enemy.

Meanwhile, a doughty band of men came together in the abandoned village and made plans to resist a British-Indian landing as best they could. Sentinels were posted along the downtown waterfront at sunset.

Before many hours had passed, the alarm was sounded. A sailing vessel that appeared to be a British warship had appeared off the Cuyahoga and was moving in towards port. The Clevelanders took their positions and when they were all properly stationed, a challenge was shouted across the water to the oncoming ship.

There was an immediate response. A voice from the ship called out that the men aboard were Americans who were among the survivors of Gen. Hull's ill-fated Detroit garrison.

The reassuring news was carried to the refugee Clevelanders huddled together at Doan's Corner by a Captain Allen Gaylord, who probably qualified for top melodramatic honors of the day when he approached the frightened civilians on horseback, waving his sword in the air and crying out:

"To your tents, oh Israel! General Hull has surrendered to the British general, and our men, instead of Indians, were seen off Huron. They are returning to their homes!"

That momentary scare was enough to spur the villagers into an appeal to the army for some kind of defense force to augment the area's two companies of militia, one from Cleveland and one from Newburgh, numbering some 50 men each.

Gen. Elijah Wadsworth, a Revolutionary War veteran who was in command of military operations in the northeastern part of Ohio, responded by moving the militia of this division from Canfield, O., to Cleveland. Gen. Wadsworth also appealed to the War Department to send regular army troops to help in Cleveland's defense.

In response, a company of regular army troops was dispatched to Cleveland in May, 1813. It was under the command of Captain Stanton Shoes, who, in a memoir penned some 45 years later, recalled the appalling lack of preparedness that greeted him upon his arrival in the frontier town. His description provides a good picture of the Cleveland of that time.

"I found no place of defense, no hospital, and a forest of larger timber (mostly chestnut) between the lake and the lake road," he wrote. "There was a road that turned off between Mr. Perry's and Major Carter's that went to the point, which was the only place that the lake could be seen from the buildings. This little cluster of buildings was all of wood, I think none painted.

"There were a few houses further back from the lake road. The widow Walworth kept the post-office, or Ashbel, her son. Mr. L. Johnson, Judge Kingsbury, Major Carter, N. Perry, Geo. Wallace, and a few others were there.

"At my arrival I found a number of sick and wounded who were of Hull's surrender, sent here from Detroit, and more coming. They were crowded into a log-cabin, and no one to

Commodore Perry transfers his flag to The Niagara during the Battle of Lake Erie, September of 1813.

"Burial of the Officers Slain at the Battle of Lake Erie," a painting by Louis Chevalier, circa 1835

care for them. I sent one or two of my soldiers to take care of them, as they had no friends. I had two or three good carpenters in my company, and set them to work to build a hospital . . .

"I next went to work and built a small fort, about fifty yards from the bank of the lake, in the forest. This fort finished, I set the men to felling the timber along and near the bank of the lake, rolling the logs and brush near the brink of the bank to serve as a breastwork."

Fort Huntington, as it was called, was on the bluff at the foot of Water (W. 9th) Street. It was a star-shaped stockade built of chestnut logs with a capacity of 200 men. One small cannon was its only armament.

It seemed, suddenly, as if Captain Sholes' timing in these hasty defense preparations was incredibly opportune. Some enemy ships were spotted off the Cleveland shore.

"On the 19th of June," wrote Sholes, "a part of the British fleet appeared off our harbor, with the apparent design to land.

"When they got within one and a half miles of our harbor, it became a perfect calm, and they lay there till afternoon, when a most terrible thunderstorm came up, and drove them from our coast. We saw them no more as enemies. Their object was to destroy the public or government boats, then built and building, in the Cuyahoga River, and other government stores at that place."

The British warships later were identified as the "Lady Provost," the "Queen Charlotte," and several smaller vessels.

The highlight of the war for Clevelanders came with the passage westward on Lake Erie of Commodore Oliver Hazard Perry's hastily built fleet, sailing to meet the British naval forces gathered at the western end of the lake, near Put-in-Bay.

Perry's ships anchored briefly off Cleveland Harbor for a while on its way to its historic engagement and the commodore came ashore for a quick visit. Two of the ships in his fleet, the Porcupine and the Portage, had been built in the Cuyahoga River by Cleveland labor.

The Battle of Lake Erie was fought in the waters off Sandusky a few weeks later. About 60 miles of water separate Cleveland from the scene of that famous battle, but a lot of people in the village swore through the remaining years of their lives that they heard the booming of the warship cannons in the distance on that historic day of Sept. 10, 1813.

Perhaps they did. Sound carries over water amazingly well sometimes.

Except for the visit of the great naval hero, Perry, to Cleveland the following October, the rest of the War of 1812 passed without incident in Cleveland.

11. The opening of the west side

The lifting of the curtain that separated the land on the west side of the Cuyahoga River from the eastern part of the Western Reserve was tantalizingly slow after the Indian claims to the territory finally were extinguished by the treaty of July, 1805.

What was involved overall was a tremendous tract of land consisting of 1,300,000 acres reaching from the Cuyahoga westward to the islands of Sandusky Bay.

Of this, the westernmost 500,000 acres had been set aside as the Fire Lands, to be parceled out to the Connecticut citizens who had seen their properties put to the torch by the British in the War of Independence.

The settlement of the Indian claims removed the last barrier to the survey, sale and settlement of the 800,000 acres of land between the Cuyahoga River and the Fire Lands.

Of immediate interest to Clevelanders, of course, was the land directly across the river. It had been acquired in a drawing of Connecticut Land Company investors by Samuel and Richard Lord.

The surveying of the newly-released land began on May 15, 1806, but the sale of the acreage that followed, and its settlement, were disappointingly slow.

It was not until 1818 that the territory on the west bank of the river was organized into a township. It was given the name of Brooklyn; a name, incidentally, that was a second choice. The first proposal had been to call the new township "Egypt," because the corn grew so well in its soil.

A major discouragement to newcomers from the east who were contemplating further westward travel was the forest barrier on the river's west bank. Wagon trains, carriages and horses bearing riders had only one traversable route through Brooklyn, an Indian trail that followed a prehistoric beach ridge near the lakeshore.

The state sought to ease westward travel from Cleveland in 1809 by authorizing the clearing of a road from the river to the mouth of the Huron River. It followed, quite logically, the same ancient ridge trail. This first highway west of Cleveland was called the Cleveland-Huron Road. Later it was called the Milan State Road; and some years afterward it became the Detroit Road — today's Detroit Avenue.

The first settler on the West Side is believed to have been Gideon Granger, whose cabin was on the high bluff that later became part of Riverside Cemetery. It was a spectacular site for a home, commanding as it did a view of the Cuyahoga River and its deep valley.

Granger was a squatter, having arrived on the West Side before the area was surveyed. He lived on the site, though, until 1815, when he sold it to some newly-arrived settlers named Brainard — a name that in time became most prominent in West Side affairs.

The first permanent white settler west of the river usually is conceded to be James Fish of Groton, Conn., who took up life in Brooklyn with his wife, four children, his mother-in-law, and two cousins, Moses and Ebenezer Fish.

They arrived in Newburgh, in mid-winter of 1812. The following spring they built a modest log cabin at a cost of $18 in the heart of the township. The Fishes could claim to be the only inhabitants of the near West Side until the arrival later in the year of the Brainards.

Brooklyn Township, as defined by the Connecticut Land Company for Samuel Phillips Lord at the time of his purchase on April 2, 1807, was that land west of the river bounded by Lake Erie to the north, a line that later became Highland Road (W. 117th Street) to the west, and the township lines of Inde-

Josiah Barber

Cleveland in 1834, looking east from the corner of Bank (West 6th) and St. Clair Streets

pendence and Parma to the south. The eastern boundary was the center of the river. All told, Brooklyn contained somewhat less than 16,000 acres, the standard township of the Western Reserve.

West of Brooklyn was Rockport Township, including within its boundaries the area known today as Lakewood and Rocky River. Its pioneer settlers included John Haberton and Philo Taylor, who settled east of Rocky River. One William McConley is said to have built a place in the Rocky River flats area.

John Haberton in 1807 had built a cabin on the Lakewood (east bank) side of the Rocky River. George Peake and his family arrived on the scene in 1809, followed in 1810 by John Nicholson and his family.

Dr. John Turner, Van Scoter, Datus Kelley, and Chester Dean arrived in 1812. The Alger family, John Kidney, Ben Rabinson and Dyer Nichols came in 1812; Moses Eldred in 1813, and Joseph Larwell in 1815.

The first of these settlers to use the newly-prepared ridge road (Detroit Avenue) was a family of blacks: the George Peake family. The road by 1809 had been cleared as far as Rocky River. The wagon carrying Peake and his family crossed the Cuyahoga by log ferry near the foot of St. Clair and proceeded up the hill between Pearl Street (W. 25th) and Washington Avenue, through dense woods, on to Detroit Avenue at a point about Kentucky Avenue (W. 38th Street), and then westward to Rocky River.

Peake's two sons, George and Joseph, rode in the wagon with the father and mother. Two other sons, James and Henry, joined them later. Together they built a log cabin on what was known as the Barnum tract, about a mile south of the lake, on the banks of the Rocky River.

The 16,000 acres in Brooklyn Township owned by Samuel P. Lord were but a part of his entire holding in the Western Reserve. His initial investment of $14,092 in the Connecticut Land Company entitled him to 35,230 acres in the company's Ohio empire.

Lord dispatched his son, Richard, and his son-in-law, Josiah Barber, as his representatives on the scene in the Western Reserve. They were charged with the sale of lots, the plotting of streets, the development of farm allotments, and all the other details that were part of the profitable liquidation of the township property.

The two men, working as the firm of Lord & Barber, broke up the huge tract into small units that gradually were sold to the incoming pioneers. Upon the death of Josiah Barber, his son, Epaphras Barber, stepped into the firm.

Josiah Barber and Richard Lord journeyed to Cleveland from Hebron, Conn., in 1818, leading an impressive train of horses, wagons, oxcarts, carriages and cows.

Barber, his wife, Sophia, and their four children built a log house on the high western bluff across from Cleveland, just south of Detroit Avenue.

The site enjoyed a splendid view of the river valley, and most of what could be seen below was part of the holdings of Samuel P. Lord and his land company associates. The Lord interests claimed nearly all of the land in the Flats between W. 25th Street and the river, from Franklin Avenue hill to Lake Erie.

When Brooklyn Village was incorporated as The City of Ohio in 1836, bringing about wild celebration, Josiah Barber, then 65 years old, was elected mayor of the new city which he had been instrumental in bringing out of the forest.

The Barber name is memorialized today by Barber Avenue, which runs west from W. 25th Street beyond Walworth Road.

Trestle over Kingsbury Run on the Newburgh Dummy Railroad Line, 1873

Growing pains

12. Shipping, the canal, and growth

There was a lot of excitement on the Cleveland waterfront one day in the late summer of 1818. The first steamship ever to visit the settlement, "Walk-in-the-Water," out of Buffalo, had anchored off the mouth of the Cuyahoga River.

The date was August 25, a day to remember because a steamship was a wondrous strange sight, and this was the historic first voyage of the "Walk-in-the-Water."

The sailing ship still ruled the waves, and would continue to be the queen of the seas for years to come. But Clevelanders knew that day that in seeing the steamship, a strange sight with smoke rolling out of its stacks, they were looking at the promise of the future.

The "Walk-in-the-Water" was 300 tons and could carry 100 cabin passengers and a large number of people in steerage. She was capable of a cruising speed of a steady 8 to 10 miles an hour.

the harbor area were simply too shallow for navigation, thanks to the heavy deposits of silt laid down through the years by the river at its mouth.

It was bad enough that the larger boats were unable to come into the docking area, but standing at anchor offshore in the open lake, as they had to do, exposed them to a terrible battering when the seas were running rough.

A pioneer journalist of the time, Eber D. Howe, described one such experience when he took a trip to Cleveland during a bad weather period aboard the "Walk-in-the-Water."

"We arrived off Cleveland at near the close of the second day (out of Buffalo), under a heavy northwest gale of wind, and a heavy sea. At that time there was no entrance to the harbor, except for very small craft and lighters. It was soon discovered that the boat could proceed no farther against the wind, and could not put back without great peril.

Harvey Rice

Steamship Walk-in-the-Water

The village saluted the new steamship appreciatively with a round of artillery, and a number of Clevelanders rode out into the harbor to board the boat for the rest of its historic trip to Detroit.

It was a fleeting incident, only a few hours out of a summer's day, but it served to focus public attention in Cleveland on one of the settlement's most serious problems: the difficulty of navigation into the Cleveland harbor and the Cuyahoga River.

Few ships of any size were able to make their way into the Cuyahoga because of the sand bars at the mouth of the river. Even moderately-sized vessels had to anchor some distance out in the lake and send their passengers and crewmen into shore on small boats. The lake waters off the river and within

"Finally, all the anchors were cast, with the alternative of riding out the gale or going onto the beach, and I think the latter was most expected by all on board. The gale continued for three nights and two days without much abatement, and on the morning of the third day, the passengers were taken ashore in small boats, among whom were the late Governor Wood, wife and child."

A few years later, a schooner carrying the man who would become Cleveland's most famous educator, Harvey Rice, arrived off the Cuyahoga. The date was Sept. 24, 1824. Rice recalled those first uncomfortable moments in Cleveland in a later writing:

"A sand-bar prevented the schooner from entering the river.

The jolly boat was let down, and two jolly fellows, myself and a young man from Baltimore, were transferred to the boat with our baggage, and rowed by a brawny sailor over the sand-bar into the placid waters of the river, and landed on the end of a row of planks that stood on stilts and bridged the marshy brink of the river, to the foot of Union Lane. Here we were left standing with our trunks on the wharf-end of a plank at midnight, strangers in a strange land..."

Cleveland as a lake port, it can be seen, left something to be desired.

Agitation for remedial measures to eliminate the sand-bar problem and provide for a protected harbor had reached the point where it no longer could be ignored. Shortly after Rice made his haphazard entry, on March 3, 1825, Congress appropriated $5,000 for the building of a pier in Cleveland. It was to be 600 feet long, jutting out into the lake nearly at right angles to the shore, beginning some 40 rods to the east off the east bank of the river at its mouth.

However, this new facility had no effect on the accumulation of sand at the river's mouth. Congress then appropriated $10,000 towards a harbor-river plan prepared by Maj. T. W. Maurice of the U.S. Corps of Engineers. It called for the opening of a new, more direct channel into the lake, west of where the Cuyahoga flowed into Lake Erie at the time, at a point where the bend of the river carried it closest to the lake shore.

history. The great Erie Canal in New York, connecting Lake Erie with the Hudson River, was completed in 1825 and put into full use in autumn of that year.

The Erie Canal opened the gates to a floodtide of immigration from Europe directly into inland America; it was, in fact, the largest mass migration of people in history. It broke through the wilderness wall that had kept humanity outside the richest, most spacious territory on the North American continent.

Millions of people began to race into the Northwest Territory; many came from eastern states where living off the land was difficult, but by far the largest number were from the countries of Europe.

These were the people who would help create the new cities of America. Within a few years after the Erie Canal was cut through, the waters of the Great Lakes were speckled with passenger ships moving their human cargoes from Buffalo into the virgin lands of the Northwest Territory.

Cleveland's harbor and dock facilities were constructed just in time to receive this furious outburst of marine traffic.

This sudden surge meant the beginning of a new and different Cleveland. What it had been until then was a tiny settlement in a picturesque setting, with modest hopes of competing evenly with other lake communities such as Painesville, Ashtabula, Lorain and Sandusky.

Cleveland's lakefront, including its first railroad terminal, circa 1854

The following spring saw the beginning of the building of an eastern pier, and, according to Historian James Harrison Kennedy, "By 1840, over $75,000 had been used in this work, but a good harbor had been secured. The mouth of the old river bed gradually filled up, and the bed itself was used as a place of anchorage and wharfage."

The cutting through a new channel for the mouth of the river also resulted in the creation of that modern anomaly, Whiskey Island; so-called because of the distillery of David and Gilman Bryant.

There could be no way to appreciate fully the importance of the harbor-and-river improvements of that period. They made the Cleveland settlement a leading lakeport at a critical time in

But the success of the Erie Canal gave birth to a new dream: the construction of a counterpart of that great canal in Ohio — one almost as long as DeWitt Clinton's New York miracle — that would connect Cleveland with the Ohio River, more than 300 miles to the south. The route favored would link the city with the Ohio River town of Portsmouth.

The dreamers of the day predicted that such a state canal assuredly would make Cleveland a major city and an important lake port with direct water connection with the Ohio River.

As the idea took hold of public imagination, Clevelanders contracted a severe case of canal fever. It was almost as bad as the malarial fever that once had raged in the river flats. Water

Life on the canal

From dreams to reality — Dreamers of the day predicted that the Ohio Canal, a counterpart to the great Erie Canal, would make Cleveland a major city and important lake port with direct connection to the Ohio River. Life along the canal: at right, at Roscoe, Ohio, circa 1860; far right, near Bolivar, Ohio, 1898; lower right, near Gnadenhutten, circa 1890. The photograph below pictures the Ohio Canal in The Flats of Cleveland, circa 1859.

travel was the only way to go, everybody knew. Conestoga wagons were still lumbering in from the east, and new stage coach lines were beginning to fan out in all directions, connecting Cleveland with such places as Columbus, Painesville and Norwalk and Milan. But land travel was uncomfortable, expensive, and slow. To find the future, Clevelanders looked towards the water.

Gov. DeWitt Clinton, the most celebrated American of the day, gave Cleveland's hope a big boost when he personally encouraged Ohio to proceed with the kind of major north-south canal that had been dreamed of.

Before his own Erie Canal was fully completed, Clinton loaned his engineering genius, James Geddes, to Ohio to direct construction of the proposed Ohio Canal.

The Ohio legislature had authorized a survey of a canal project in January, 1822, and among the men who were named to the canal commission was Alfred Kelley, Cleveland's leading citizen. It was he, more than any one person, who pushed the construction of the canal to a successful conclusion, guaranteeing Cleveland's growth into greatness.

The canal route was established in 1825. Cleveland would be the northern terminus on Lake Erie; Portsmouth would be the southern terminus on the Ohio River. The canal matched the dimensions of the Erie Canal: 40 feet wide, 4-1/2 feet deep. The Erie Canal was 363 miles long; the Ohio Canal would be 307 miles. But the Ohio Canal would be more difficult to build because it would require twice as many locks as the famous New York prototype, and each lock was an engineering challenge.

After the Ohio General Assembly approved the project, Gov. Clinton turned the first spade full of earth in ceremonies held on Licking summit, about three miles west of Newark in Licking County, July 4, 1825.

The New York governor arrived in Cleveland aboard the vessel, "Superior," and was given a grand reception by a delegation of civic dignitaries at the Mansion House on Superior Street.

The first link in the new canal, the connection between Cleveland and Akron, was completed in mid-summer of 1827 and put into use immediately. The entire canal, from river to lake, was finished and in use by 1832.

Cleveland, meanwhile, had felt the effect of the Erie Canal traffic. The village's population in 1825 was only 500 persons. By 1833, there were 2,500 residents in the city.

The fleets of ships carrying immigrants from the Buffalo docks to all parts of the Great Lakes unfortunately brought more than people to the ports they visited.

A cholera epidemic swept Cleveland in 1832 and again in 1834. The blame, in each instance, was laid to the visiting vessels.

The steamer Henry Clay twice brought cases of cholera to Cleveland. The resulting epidemics were so bad that it wasn't uncommon for people to topple over and fall dead in the streets. A hospital for cholera victims was built on Whiskey Island because it was a site removed from the general population, and because it was convenient as a quarantine center to receive sick people on the incoming ships.

The wilderness, nevertheless, was not far removed from the Cleveland of 1833. There were many people in the village who had vivid memories of the Indian days. Most of the inhabitants, though, were newcomers to the west and had never seen an Indian. No wonder, then, that the visit to Cleveland that year of the famous Indian chief, Black Hawk, was a village sensation.

Black Hawk was under federal escort, having just waged his hopeless war against the white invaders. But his stopover in Cleveland was a sentimental one because his family's ancestral home was here.

He had explained to his captors that his mother was buried on the banks of the Cuyahoga and he received permission to visit her grave. Black Hawk went by canoe up the river to the bluff that later was set aside for Riverside Cemetery; it was the site of his mother's grave. There he remained in meditation for several hours before returning to Cleveland and the custody of the federal agents.

Three years after that episode, the number of people living in Cleveland had more than doubled, jumping to a total of more than 6,000; it was enough to qualify for incorporation as a city.

However, it was bitter news when Clevelanders learned that the rival town across the river, Brooklyn, with only about 2,000 population, had beat them to the honor of becoming a city, Cuyahoga County's first, by a matter of days. It was a humiliating experience and it had the effect of deepening the already strong rivalry between the settlements on opposite banks of the Cuyahoga.

The Ohio Canal

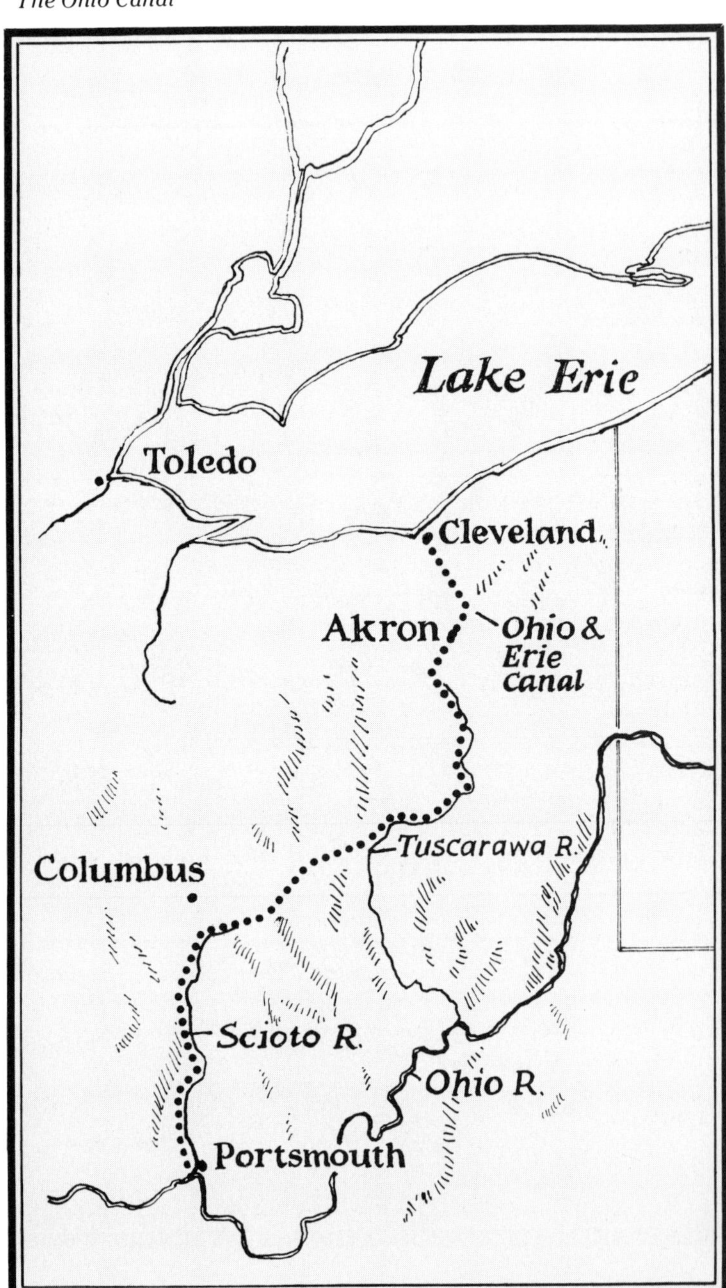

13. The War of the bridges

The Columbus Street Bridge, 1836

The only way the Cuyahoga River could be crossed until 1822 was by boat, by ferry, or by swimming. In that year, the first bridge spanned the river; it was a float bridge that joined the foot of Detroit Avenue on the west bank with the foot of Superior Hill on the east bank.

In 1837, as competition between the opposing cities grew keener, there were several important developments on either side.

On the west, a group of real estate speculators from Buffalo, whose enterprise, indeed, was called The Buffalo Company, moved to develop some 80 acres it had purchased in the Flats. Elaborate plans were announced for the creation of an area of civic importance. The opening moves included the construction of a grand new hotel called the Ohio City Exchange.

Envy glistened in the eyes of Clevelanders as they looked across the river at the new structure. It was more elegant than any hotel in Cleveland. Some travelers called it the finest hotel in the west.

It was impressive — an elaborate 5-story building with a large, bright dome from which lights shone at night, making it the most conspicuous landmark in the Flats; it was a spectacular sight arising out of the dark Cuyahoga Valley. The glowing dome also served as a guide to ships groping through the dark passageway of Cleveland Harbor, looking for the Cuyahoga.

Thanks to the new hotel, some of the most brilliant social functions of the day were shifting to what Clevelanders regarded as the wrong side of the river — a fact that rubbed raw a lot of proud citizens.

But there were momentous plans underway, meanwhile, on the Cleveland side also, thanks to the enterprising daring of some real estate entrepreneurs headed by James S. Clark.

Clark and his associates had acquired a large allotment in Ohio City, to the south of the Buffalo Company development; an area of land they named Willeyville, after Cleveland's first mayor, John W. Willey.

Opposite Willeyville, on the east side of the river and within the great ox-bow, the developers had laid out an ambitious undertaking which they named Cleveland Center. It was meant to be just that: a civic center which, in effect, would be common to both Ohio City and Cleveland.

To draw traffic into the new center and make it the main route of travel between the lake port and areas to the south, Clark routed Columbus Street from the southern edge of Ohio City down into the valley, across a new bridge, and directly into Cleveland Center.

The leaders of Ohio City looked on anxiously as Clark pursued his plans. They appreciated the fact that if Columbus Road became a major avenue of travel for traffic from places like Wooster and Medina, it would divert business from Pearl Road (W. 25th Street) and the main business district of Ohio City.

While Ohio City was fretting over the situation, Mayor Willey of Cleveland and developer Clark played their trump card. Cleveland City Council, at their urging, adopted a resolution ordering the removal of the eastern half of the old float bridge to the north of the new Columbus Road span.

The float bridge was jointly owned by the two cities and Cleveland, legally speaking, had a right to do away with its half of the bridge.

But a bridge is not like a loaf of bread. Half a loaf undoubtedly is better than none, but half a bridge is no good at all.

Cleveland moved swiftly to obey the councilmanic order. One night, as the City of Ohio slumbered, the eastern half of the float bridge was dismantled and removed.

"Bridge War," detail from "Early History of Cleveland," a painting by Fred Dana Marsh

In the early morning, horse-drawn wagons carrying merchandise and produce into Cleveland from the west side went thundering over the wooden roadway of the bridge through the low-lying mists and suddenly had to reign to emergency stops, with horses whinnying in fright and teamsters cursing over the incredible bridgenapping.

The effect of Cleveland's action, to be sure, was to restrict all river crossing to the bridge a short distance to the south — the new Columbus Road Bridge.

The people of Ohio City raged over the perfidy that had been committed by their rivals across the Cuyahoga. A rallying war-cry was raised: "Two bridges or none!"

To implement that fiery slogan, the Ohio City fathers agreed, in councilmanic resolution, that the Columbus Street Bridge was a "public nuisance," and, as such, had to be abated.

The appointed abaters were the city marshal and a number of his deputies. Their method of abatement was to insert a heavy charge of powder under the west end of the offending bridge and attempt to blow it up.

The explosive charge wasn't explosive enough. The blast didn't cause enough damage to halt the use of the bridge, or even reduce the amount of traffic. Clevelanders grinned and the rage in Ohio City rose higher. The embarrassment of the episode fired their determination now, more than ever, to rid the river of the Columbus Road Bridge.

It was no longer a covert operation, however. Ohio City loudly announced this time that the order to abate the bridge nuisance would be carried out by civic volunteers carrying arms, clubs, rocks, and anything heavy they could pick up and swing.

Clevelanders pressed their lips together and prepared for the attack. An ancient cannon, used hitherto only for a few salvos to liven up 4th of July celebrations, was wheeled into place on the east bank of the river. It was loaded to the muzzle and made ready to fire. Behind the cannon, in correct order, was a company of Cleveland militia holding muskets at ready stance.

On the Ohio City side, meanwhile, a Presbyterian minister, Rev. Dr. Pickans, standing before the assault force of nearly 1,000 Ohio City volunteers, invoked divine aid for the attack on the bridge. Then, led by a lawyer named C. L. Russell, the Ohio City army began its march down the hill towards the bridge.

A peacemaker stood on the bridge awaiting the arrival of the west siders. He was Mayor Willey of Cleveland. Those who heard his opening lines said the mayor had prepared a speech whose theme was peace, moderation and cool heads. But the Ohio City army was in no mood for sweet, reasonable talk from Clevelanders. They chased the mayor from the bridge with a volley of stones.

Mayor John W. Willey

Then the apron ramp at the west end of the bridge was raised, and the Ohio City people, protected by the upraised plate, began to rip up bridge planks and to chop support struts with heavy axes.

The sounds of that destructive activity infuriated the Cleveland militia and spurred them into a charge across the bridge, bringing about a general melee in the middle of the river crossing.

The cannon never was brought into offensive use because a man named Deacon House of Ohio City sneaked through the enemy lines during the big mixup on the bridge and spiked the cannon with a file.

The consequences of the engagement could have been a lot more serious in terms of human life and limb if the marshal of Cleveland and the sheriff of Cuyahoga County had not appeared on the scene. They demanded a halt to the fighting and took legal possession of the embattled bridge.

The issue ended in the courts and a settlement of differences was satisfactorily reached. But there was no doubt in anybody's mind that Ohio City, in spite of its valiant resistance, had suffered a grievous loss.

Traffic from the south continued to flow down Columbus Road and through Cleveland Center, up the hill into downtown Cleveland — a significant diversion of business from Ohio City.

To make things worse, the Buffalo Company's west side development faltered and collapsed. The grand Exchange Hotel lost much of its glitter and its patronage. The riverfront simply was not a good site for a first-class hotel.

"...Despite its architecture and size and unrivaled interior," wrote S. J. Kelly in *The Plain Dealer,* "its ascendancy was to last but ten years. It was to become a tenement house for workmen, a stopping place for gypsies, a factory, a storage building, a haunt of birds, including owls. It was to stand on its site for nearly 30 years, when fire destroyed it."

Ohio City itself followed a lacklustre trail after reaching the heights of civic patriotism in the Battle of the Bridge. It grew steadily, but its prosperity and population did not compare with that of the rival city on the east bank of the Cuyahoga.

Finally, in April, 1854, a majority of the voters on either side of the river, indicated their approval of a merger of the municipal corporations.

Annexation of the City of Ohio by the City of Cleveland took place in June of that year, and the western city lost its identity, simply becoming the 8th, 9th, 10th, and 11th wards of the expanded Cleveland.

* * *

The important civic issue that undoubtedly hastened the merger of the two cities was the increasing need for a good water system.

Drinking water had been a problem ever since the city began, even though Cleveland sat on the shores of one of the world's largest bodies of fresh water. Springs, wells, and cisterns still were common sources of water after more than 50 years.

The wells brought up hard water, however, not the kind of water recommended for washing purposes. So it was that in the pioneer days, a one-legged man named Benhu Johnson, a veteran of the War of 1812, earned a good living by stumping about the streets selling soft water at two barrels for 25 cents to the townspeople.

"Benhu, with his wooden leg, little wagon, and old horse," wrote Mrs. George B. Merwin in the *Annals* of the Early Settlers Association, "was in great demand on Mondays, when he drew two barrels of water at a time, covered with blankets, up the long steep hill from the river now known as Vineyard street, to parties requiring the element.

"In fancy I see him now, with his unpainted vehicle, old white horse, himself stumbling along keeping time to the tune of 'Roving Sailor,' which he was fond of singing, occasionally starting 'Old Whitey' with a kick from the always ready leg, especially if he had been imbibing freely..."

Old Benhu apparently did not restrict his imbibing to water. He was, at any rate, something of a civic institution for many years, and his product was deeply admired by the housewives.

Perhaps Benhu wore himself out going up and down the steep hillside, or perhaps old Whitey gave out; whatever happened, there arose in Cleveland in 1833 a new enterprise called the Cleveland Water Company. It was headed by a man named Philo Scovill, whose company supplied fresh water to Clevelanders for about 20 years. But there was mounting awareness that the continuing growth of population would one day soon bring about a water crisis. A waterworks system had to be built. It was an inescapable need.

Surveys of possible systems of drawing water out of Lake Erie had led hydraulic experts to the conclusion that the best site for the waterworks and a reservoir was in Ohio City. The fact probably encouraged merger talks between the two cities.

Soon after Ohio City was absorbed, a tract of land on Kentucky (W. 38th) Street, between Franklin Avenue and Whitman Avenue, was chosen as the site of a 5-million gallon reservoir.

That Kentucky Street Reservoir and a pumping station on the western lakefront supplied the growing city a reliable supply of fresh, clean water by 1855.

But there were problems immediately ahead. Few if any foresaw the geometric increase in population that was occurring, nor the related jump in the rate of lake pollution close to shore. It wasn't long before the city was forced to draw its water supply from a point farther out in the lake.

The solution was to build an intake crib 6,600 feet from shore and sink it in 36 feet of water. Then a tunnel was dug 90 feet below the water's surface from the crib to the lakefront pumping station.

The new system, an impressive example of engineering brilliance, was begun in 1869 and completed in the spring of 1874 at a cost of $320,351.72. The crib served double-duty, being fitted out as a lighthouse manned by a full-time keeper.

A second intake tunnel was connected to the crib in 1890 in response to the increased water demand of the growing city. Another reservoir had been built, meanwhile, in 1885 at the top of Fairmount Hill. It had two basins, one with a capacity of 47 million gallons and the other able to hold 33 million gallons.

Cleveland had come a long way from one-legged Benhu Johnson and his water wagon.

Cleveland's west side (looking northeast) from the walk around the Kentucky Street Reservoir, 1872, and right, Cleveland's lakefront entrance to the harbor in 1865.

14. Bankers on the frontier

Leonard Case, circa 1859, in his office looking out onto Superior Street

Truman P. Handy

The priorities of a new settlement such as Cleveland did not always meet the tests of logic, or convenience, or need.

There are those, for example, who would study the fact that Cleveland had a distillery before it had a grocery store, or a cobbler shop, or a bakery, through narrowed eyes. It would prove to them that first things are not necessarily first.

And no doubt there are others who would openly approve such a sequence of improvements in the life of a frontier town.

It is worth noting, at any rate, that Cleveland got its first bank before it got its first bridge.

The Commercial Bank of Lake Erie opened its doors in August, 1816, with Alfred Kelley as its president and Leonard Case, Sr., as its cashier — two of the village's heavyweights.

The first bridge across the Cuyahoga was not built until 1822. It was the float bridge that caused so much trouble when Cleveland authorities in 1837 dismantled their half of the span.

Again, though, there is raised that question of priorities. During the first 26 years of the settlement on the Cuyahoga River, people were satisfied to splash back and forth aboard one of Lorenzo Carter's ferries or row their own boats across the river. The town was only 20 years old when it was given banking service.

The first bridge lasted 15 years, though; the first bank collapsed after only 4 years. It failed in 1820.

One of the rules of pioneering is: if you fail, try and try again. With this in mind, no doubt, the pioneer bankers reorganized the Commercial Bank of Lake Erie and resumed business as of April 2, 1832 — wisely dodging the handicap of having April Fool's Day as its anniversary.

On the second time around — another short-lived run — Leonard Case served as the bank president and Truman P. Handy as its cashier.

The banking quarters were housed in a part of the Case residence, and a legend of the time had it that Leonard Case, suspecting that a burglar was trying to tunnel his way into the bank with the help of a spade, sat by his hearthstone with a hatchet in his hand, ready to sink it into the skull of the felon as soon as he came up through the floorboards.

The fateful meeting never came about. The bank's 20-year charter expired and Case gave up his vigil because the bank was forced to close its doors again. It is not known if the hapless bank robber was still shoveling or collapsed before the bank.

The sticky financial problem of the time, 1842, was that the Ohio Legislature was refusing to extend the charter of existing banks.

There were some serious flaws in the early banking structure of Ohio. One was that the banks were allowed to issue bank notes for general circulation, and a lot of the paper issued proved to be worthless when put to the test, as it had been by the Panic of 1837 and the depression that followed. The experience left the money market in a notably unsteady condition.

Important legislation reforming banking practices in the state was passed by the Ohio General Assembly in 1845 through the leadership of Cleveland's Alfred Kelley, by then a distinguished state senator.

The Society for Savings Building, 1889

It was not until then that the state again began licensing new banking institutions. Among the first was the City Bank of Cleveland on May 17, 1845. It had its origin in an organization called Fireman's Insurance Co.

Twenty years later, in February, 1865, the City Bank shut its doors, scraped the old name off its plateglass windows, and opened for business the next day as the National City Bank of Cleveland.

Among the other banks that opened after the state freeze was ended was the Cleveland Society for Savings, which began business on April 4, 1849; its president was John W. Allen. Samuel H. Mather was secretary and J. F. Taintor was treasurer. Mather, a direct descendant of one of the original investors in the Connecticut Land Company, eventually became president of the new institution.

By century's end, Clevelanders had their choice of 45 banks altogether. There were others in the period from 1850 to 1900 that failed to make the financial grade. One of the most memorable was the Canal Bank, a short-lived institution that collapsed in November, 1854.

It could not have been the kind of bank that inspired total confidence because the *Cleveland Herald,* in announcing the bank's bust in its issue of Nov. 9th, said that "the failure of this bank excited no surprise in this city."

That could not have been an entirely accurate statement because a lot of the depositors who stormed the bank building on Superior Avenue, near the American House, certainly put up a good impersonation of surprised people when they found they couldn't withdraw their deposits.

One of the customers who was especially astounded was the captain of a Great Lake vessel, a veteran mariner named Gummage, who, the day before the bank failed, deposited his entire season's pay — a total of $1,000.

Capt. Gummage was a direct man. When informed that the bank had failed and that his savings had been swallowed up by the disaster, he stuck a pistol in his belt and forced his way into the bank. There he demanded his money from the startled bank officials.

They explained to him in a straightforward way that, under the circumstances, return of his money was quite out of the question.

The captain shook off their answer.

"It is all the money I own in the world," he said, fingering his pistol, "and I will have it or I will kill you."

Straight talk goes a long way in banking circles. As Capt. Gummage's message sank through, there was a lot of head-bobbing up and down the line and some of the officials scurried hurriedly about, scooping up money. Capt. Gummage got his $1,000 back.

There was still another depositor who refused to give in to the busted bank without a fight. He was a prominent Cleveland physician, Dr. H. C. Ackley.

The doctor had a personal account in the bank that failed, but that didn't bother him as much as the fact that he, as a trustee of the new State Insane Asylum in Newburgh, had deposited $9,000 of public funds in the bank. The money was earmarked for the operation of the institution and the doctor was not about to let that money go by the boards. He pointed out to the bankers that loss of the money would mean that the asylum would be able to open for more than a year, and that during the period it remained closed some 100 insane persons stood to be deprived of care and treatment.

When his arguments failed to produce any results, Dr. Ackley swore out a writ of attachment and turned it over to Sheriff M. M. Spangler, who took it directly to the bank and demanded the money. The bank officials refused.

"The keys of the vault being refused him," said an account of the incident in the *Cleveland Herald,* "he proceeded to break open the vault."

The way the sheriff did that was to summon "several stalwart deputies" and, in the words of another chronicler, James Harrison Kennedy, the sheriff and his men "laid down such lusty blows as had not been heard since Richard of the Lion Heart drove his battle-axe against the castle gates of Front de-Bouef. Sledge-hammers swung in the air, and came down on the brickwork with a crash; clouds of lime and mortar filled the room."

While this was going on, "the officers and clerks of the bank looked on, helpless to prevent, and in no position to aid."

At the height of the bank melodrama, F. T. Backus, an attorney of the bank and a part-owner of the building, rushed in and demanded a halt on the grounds of trespass.

The sheriff turned a deaf ear to the legal plea. The sledge hammers continued to fall heavily on the vault.

It was not until late that night, as ways to break open the safe itself were under serious consideration, that the bank admitted defeat and surrendered the money to the insane asylum.

It wasn't such a crazy thing that Dr. Ackley did, after all.

15. Bridging the big divide

The Cleveland-Columbus Street Bridge, 1835, from a painting by C. H. Hicks, looking east toward Cleveland

If the comic-opera war between Ohio City and Cleveland had no other effect, it did emphasize the need for better facilities in the busy Flats. The confluence of marine traffic — the canal boats from the south and the lake boats from the north — had turned the downtown valley into the busiest neighborhood in the two-city area.

As part of the peace settlement with Ohio City, the Cleveland authorities presumably recognized the hardship that was being visited upon its west side neighbor by the inadequate bridge facilities and immediately launched on a program leading to construction of the Main Street Bridge, the rebuilding of the controversial Center Street Bridge, and the building of still another bridge at the foot of Seneca (W. 3rd) Street.

All of the steps taken helped to alleviate the problem, but the city simply couldn't keep up with its own growth and the needs that the increasing population generated.

The city's first directory, published in 1837, contained the names of 1,339 persons. The census count of 1850 showed a population of 17,034. Ohio City, by that time lagging far behind, had an official count of only 3,950 residents. But they officially would become Clevelanders four years hence, swelling the city total still more.

There were times, it seemed, when Clevelanders on both sides of the river were completely immobilized by the Main

Central Viaduct, second of the high level bridges to span the Cuyahoga River, circa 1900

Construction of Superior Avenue High Level Bridge, circa 1916

Right, the Nickel Plate Railroad Bridge under the Central Viaduct, circa 1880

Street Bridge, which was designed with a central section that pivoted to allow river vessels to proceed through.

Fully as much of a nuisance to the people using the bridge was that it was built at river level and the rapidly growing traffic had to descend and ascend steep hills at either side of the valley. The horse-drawn vehicles, especially those pulling heavy loads, often had a difficult time making the grade. On snowy, icy days during the rugged Cleveland winters, the hills were all but impossible.

The increase in bridge traffic, meanwhile, was more than matched by the increase in the use of the river by commercial vessels of all kinds. The center section of the bridge was pivoted open as much as it was closed. Either the land vehicles were jammed up at either end of the bridge, or the river craft were bottled up and noisily demanding right of way with their loud whistles.

Public clamor for a high-level bridge that would eliminate the descent into the valley and the climb back up finally brought action. Such a major improvement was recommended by Mayor Stephen Buhrer in his annual message of 1870. A bond issue for $1,100,000 to build a high-level toll bridge was approved by the voters.

There was considerable public controversy over the plan to make it a toll bridge, however, and another special election in 1876 rejected that idea and approved a larger bond issue to make the new span a free bridge. When the great project finally was completed on Dec. 27, 1878, after 4-1/2 years of construction work, the cost came to $2,170,000 — an enormous sum of money for the time and the town.

But the Superior Viaduct, as it was called, was the symbol of the city's pride — its signal to the world that it was on the verge of adulthood. All the picture postcards of the city scene immediately alighted on the photograph of the new bridge — and, indeed, it was an impressive sight: 3,211 feet in length, soaring 70 feet over the waters of the Cuyahoga and its high-walled valley. Ten stone arches, reaching as high as 97-1/2 feet into the air, supported the massive span in its reach from Pearl (W. 25th) Street and Detroit Avenue on the west bank to Water Street (W. 9th) and Superior on the east bank.

Among the reasons for local pride was the fact that the grayish-white sandstone used in the construction of the viaduct, totaling more than 2 million cubic feet, came from the Berea quarries.

Cleveland enjoyed one of its greatest civic celebrations on the day the new viaduct was dedicated, Dec. 28, 1878. The day was proclaimed an official holiday and there were speeches around the clock.

Only 10 years later the bridge-fanciers had another big celebration to mark the completion of the Central Viaduct, which connected downtown with the southwest side by spanning the Cuyahoga Valley between Jennings Avenue on the south side and Ohio and Hill streets on the east side.

The Central Viaduct also boasted impressive statistics. While costing only $885,000, it extended for a distance of 3,931 feet, rising as high as 101 feet above the water.

It was, like the Superior Viaduct, a drawbridge, and that proved to be a fatal weakness in both instances. Every time the central part of the span was drawn open, traffic on the bridge was jammed up until the vessels on the river below had cleared passage.

That continual traffic problem disillusioned the public and led to agitation for a replacement bridge, resulting in construction of the Detroit-Superior High Level Bridge in 1915.

The drawbridge feature of the Central Viaduct also had serious consequences. On the night of Nov. 16, 1895, a streetcar of the Cedar-Jennings line plunged through the open draw of the viaduct and fell into the Cuyahoga River, 100 feet below. Seventeen persons died in the disaster.

The river valley that separated the city and kept it divided for so long a time did not surrender easily.

Progression of construction of the Superior Viaduct seen, from top to bottom, in 1871, 1873 and 1875, respectively.

16. Iron rails and iron ore

The midway point of the 19th century was the place where Cleveland teetered in the doorway to the future, casting a last regretful look back at the idyllic settlement that Charles Dickens himself, travel-weary and annoyed by a provocative newspaper piece, had called "a beautiful town."

Dickens, remember, was not given to complimentary descriptions of the American scene.

In 1850, though, it was like the end of childhood in Cleveland — the first fading of innocence. After the rush of events immediately ahead, the city never again would be the same.

Change was the order of the day, but even the most sophisticated found it difficult to grasp the swift sequence of happenings.

It had been only 20 years or so since the community had cheered the building of the Ohio Canal and had hailed the waterway as the channel through which the town would move to greatness. But already the canal was in jeopardy, apparently headed for obsolescence in the face of the developing competition of the railroads.

It took a mighty adjustment for a world in which change of any kind had been a rarity for centuries suddenly to become accustomed to a series of lightning developments.

Cleveland was keenly aware of the urgent need to entice railroads into the city. And, oddly enough, the legendary Alfred Kelley, the pioneer who had been instrumental in routing the Ohio Canal into Cleveland, was the prime mover in putting the city on the railroad mainline.

Kelley was president of the newly-organized Cleveland, Columbus & Cincinnati Railroad Company, a forerunner of the New York Central System's Big Four Route.

Amasa Stone

The line went into operation in 1851. Its first train into Cleveland that year was pulled by a locomotive built in Ohio City.

Among the principals in the building of the railroad was a New Englander named Amasa Stone, who chose Cleveland as his permanent residence and became one of the city's wealthiest citizens.

The first train, from Columbus, was given a tumultuous welcome at the hastily built railroad station, an unprepossessing wooden building at the foot of Superior Street hill, near the river. It was a site that history never got tired of visiting. That first crude station served the city for 15 years before a proper depot was built on the lakefront in response to the needs, by then, of six major railroads.

The first leg of the Cleveland & Pittsburgh Railroad, the forerunner of the Pennsylvania Railroad, was built from Cleveland to Hudson and placed in operation on Feb. 22, 1851. A lakeshore line, the Cleveland, Painesville & Ashtabula Rail-

The Cleveland Union Depot; top 1899, bottom, 1865

Cleveland & Pittsburgh Railroad bridge over Tinkers Creek at Bedford, Ohio, 1865

road, was begun in 1850 and was running by 1852.

It was a time of progress. It also was a time of mingled emotions.

The railroads obviously were boosting Cleveland into a place of importance in the American transportation system and guaranteeing the city's future in the industrial scheme of things.

But the railroads, just as obviously, also were inflicting terrible damage to the little city.

Railroads traditionally have sought out the flat, water-level routes wherever they could. That meant, in Cleveland, the acquisition of the lovely lakefront and its companion riverfront for the tracks of the new rail lines that suddenly came shooting into the city from all points of the compass but north.

The rails criss-crossed the Cuyahoga Valley, laced across the brow of the bluff overlooking Lake Erie, streaked alongside the sandy beaches, and cut a raw, rude swathe through the great stands of forest that still covered large sections of the young city.

A hundred years later, the same city still would be fighting to regain possession of that prime waterfront land for recreational use and, of course, in an effort to restore beauty of the city.

But in the flush of the exciting time in which the silver rails made their first thrilling appearance, beauty was the city's most plentiful asset. It seemed to be a cheap price to pay in those days: a little beauty for a lot of progress.

Railroad locomotive in Cleveland, 1877

Rumors had reached Cleveland over the years about a mysterious area in the wilds of the upper peninsula in Michigan where compasses behaved wildly and where Chippewa Indian legends spoke of a mountain of iron.

Dr. J. Lang Cassels

Finally, in 1846, a prominent Cleveland physician, Dr. J. Lang Cassels, who also was a noted chemist, traveled to the northern region to examine it in behalf of a group of Clevelanders who had formed the Dead River & Ohio Mining Company.

Traveling by foot and by canoe, and led by Indian guides, Dr. Cassels went into the Lake Superior country, to the region of Ishpeming and Cleveland Mountain, and obtained samples of copper and silver ore of the richest content. When he returned to Cleveland and reported his findings of mineral wealth, the reaction was one of delight, but some skepticism.

It was agreed that a second opinion was in order. Another remarkable man of the time, Charles Whittlesey, a leading geologist and, later, an outstanding historian of the city, went into the northern wilds to go over the ground covered by Dr. Cassels. His report confirmed what Dr. Cassels had reported.

Within a few years, the Michigan copper mines were yielding millions of dollars worth of the ore to Cleveland investors.

Meanwhile, another syndicate of Clevelanders was laying the groundwork for the exploitation of the vast iron ore reserves in the Lake Superior region. Their corporate name in the beginning was the Cleveland Iron Mining Company.

A dry goods merchant named W. J. Gordon was president of the company and its secretary was Samuel L. Mather. The investors in the company included Isaac Hewitt, his brother, Dr. Morgan L. Hewitt, H. B. Tuttle, George Worthington, John Outhwaite, Selah Chamberlain, Henry Brayton and John W. Allen.

Out of this group and the original company, which began mining the northern iron ore in 1854 with a modest 4,000 tons, emerged the giant Cleveland-Cliffs Iron Company.

Two other Cleveland companies that joined Cleveland-Cliffs in the extraction of the mineral wealth from the Lake Superior region were Pickands-Mather & Company and Oglebay, Norton and Company.

What those shrewd Cleveland businessmen did, in effect, was build a sluiceway that channeled riches from the remote, largely uninhabited north country into the rapidly industrializing Cuyahoga Valley.

And there were Clevelanders who saw to it that there were boats to carry the ore across the lakes to Cleveland.

And there were facilities in the Flats to receive the ore and to process it — iron works established by such as William A. Otis, Henry Chisholm and Fayette Brown.

And there were railroads now to bring in the coal and the limestone, and to carry away the finished product.

And there was brawny immigrant labor available, and more of it arriving in the city every day.

Cleveland, through the blessing of location and through human design and enterprise, found itself with the firmest of foundations upon which to build an iron and steel industry and to win a high place among the great manufacturing cities of America.

Charles Whittlesey

Mouth of the Cuyahoga River, 1910

Ore docks along the Cuyahoga River, 1889

Interior of the Bowler and Company Foundry in The Flats, circa 1885

Looking west along The Flats of Cleveland, circa 1900

Evolution of lifestyle

17. Down in the valley

The Cleveland Rolling Mills on Broadway and Jones Road, circa 1900

There was no mistaking the fact that Cleveland's commercial life had settled on its twisting Cuyahoga River and its valley that already was being given over to manufactories and industry of the heavy kind.

But the riverfront still presented a picturesque sight until late in the 19th century, when the smoke and the grime had blackened the greenery, sullied the river, and smogged the atmosphere.

Until then, there were the tall-masted sailing schooners and the passenger steamships, vying for dock space, and the wharfs piled high with cargoes bound for distant ports. Even the early-model locomotives, puffing and chugging so earnestly, had a charm of their own.

But it was a busy river and it didn't let anyone forget that the secret of Cleveland's success was the water: Peculiar-looking lake carriers, romantic-looking ocean ships, handsome lakes passenger steamships, and low, squat canal boats — they all mingled in the Cuyahoga River.

Not only was Cleveland one of the busiest ports on the Great Lakes in the second half of the 19th century, the home port of 3 sidewheel passenger steamers and more than 80 sailing schooners, it also was one of the world's great shipbuilding centers.

The construction of boats and ships was an industry that was just entering its most furious years of activity in the 1860s. Cleveland came by the industry naturally. Close by were the forests that still were overwhelming in the size and quality of their trees, ideal for shipbuilding.

Out of the Cleveland shipyards went fleets of sailing ships to carry the grains and the lumber of the Ohio fields and forests through the Welland Canal and across the Atlantic Ocean. In many cases, the ship and its cargo both would be sold overseas and the crew would hitchhike back on other ships.

When the copper and iron ore interests needed fleets of

Riverfront activity — In the second half of the 19th century, Cleveland was one of the busiest ports on the Great Lakes and was also one of the world's greatest shipbuilding centers. Top, the Cleveland Shipbuilding Company dock, circa 1890. Left, the Cleveland Rolling Mills, circa 1873. Right, the busy Cuyahoga River, 1876.

boats to carry the minerals from the Lake Superior region to the Cleveland mills, it was the Cleveland shipyards that built the armadas.

In many instances, the same Cleveland investors who owned the ore and copper mines also bought the boats that carried their rich cargoes, and so Cleveland became the headquarters city in lakes shipping.

As a result of the fortunate combination of circumstances, the city's shipyards by 1890 had made Cleveland the greatest shipbuilding center in the world outside of the yards along the Clyde in Scotland.

The wonder of it all when the golden years that followed 1850 were just getting underway was that there were any number of people on the Cleveland scene who could remember clearly the wilderness, the loneliness, and the isolation that prevailed on this site when they were younger.

There were those who could remember that the city's first small iron foundry had been placed in operation in 1828 by John Ballard & Co.

That year of 1828, it seems, had been a year of special portent, but perhaps the signs were too faint and too vague to be read at the time.

It was the year, at any rate, in which a man named Henry Newberry shipped a few tons of coal into Cleveland and drew a bemused reaction from people who viewed the product as nothing more than a dirty, if combustible, curiosity.

Newberry, a determined man, loaded it onto a wagon and tried to peddle it from door to door as a household fuel. He would have been better advised to carry the coal to Newcastle because Cleveland was surrounded by a forest of wood just waiting to be burned in the town's stoves.

A few householders had accepted some lumps of coal as a gift, but Newberry, by the end of his first day of salesmanship, had failed to make a single sale.

Famous family — In 1854, Mr. and Mrs. William Avery Rockefeller moved to Cleveland from Tioga County, New York, with their five children (left to right) John, Mary Ann, Lucy, William and Frank. One of the sons — John Davison Rockefeller (below) — created the American oil industry and became the richest man in the world.

An inn-keeper, Philo Scovill of the Franklin House, was persuaded by Newberry late that night to buy some of the black fuel to use in his barroom stove, strictly as an experiment.

It was a small beginning, but eventually some business places and factories saw some merit in coal and began to convert to the fuel. Not until the 1840s, however, did an appreciable market for coal develop in Cleveland. Its biggest boost came from the establishment in 1840 by William A. Otis of the city's first important iron works.

The juxtaposition of two important historical happenings in the decade that followed brought coal to the fore as another vital element in the meeting of minerals in the Cuyahoga Valley: They were the development of coal fields in southeastern Ohio, and the completion of two new railroads that made possible the movement of that coal to Cleveland mills in large quantities.

Still another kind of wealth began flowing into Cleveland in those mid-century years whose value is beyond estimate. It was the flood of immigration from European shores that surged into the little lake city.

The immediate effect of the sharp rise in population was to create a severe housing shortage. It wasn't uncommon to see people living out of tents and wagons while carpenters frantically sawed and hammered away, trying to meet the demand for shelter.

The long-range significance of the situation was the contribution of the newcomers to the city. They brought with them the brawn and the brains needed to turn raw minerals into money, to turn dreams into reality.

With so many newcomers streaming into the city from all parts of Europe and the eastern United States, the arrival in 1854 of a family from Tioga County, New York, caused no stir whatsoever. Nevertheless, the appearance on the Cleveland scene of Mr. and Mrs. William Avery Rockefeller and their five children may have been the most important single occurrence in a time crammed with fateful happenings.

The two older boys, John Davison Rockefeller, and his brother, William, were enrolled that year in Central High School, the city's only institution of advanced education; it then occupied a frame building on Euclid Avenue, a few steps west of Erie (E. 9th) Street on the south side of the avenue.

Among the students were a girl named Laura Celestia Spelman and a boy named Marcus Alonzo Hanna. Laura became Mrs. John D. Rockefeller in 1864. Mark Hanna went on to become a millionaire businessman, a United States senator, and a political genius who steered William McKinley into the presidency of the United States.

John D. Rockefeller, on the other hand, became the richest man in the world. The American oil industry was his personal creation. And in his climb to the summit of industry and finance, Rockefeller helped to make Cleveland one of America's golden cities.

The chronology of events tells the vital role that Cleveland played in the development of the oil industry.

The world's first producing oil well was drilled at Titusville, Pa., in 1859 by Col. Edwin L. Drake. By 1863 there were no fewer than 20 oil refineries in the Cuyahoga Valley, and the river already carried the stench of their waste product — which happened to be gasoline. The important main product derived from petroleum was kerosene for lamps, and paraffin.

Young Rockefeller, after a brief apprenticeship in a commission house, went into partnership with an Englishman, Maurice B. Clark, in his own commission merchant business. But he was alert for larger opportunities.

The office of the Rockefeller & Clark firm was on Merwin Street in the Flats, where the smell of oil and gasoline was inescapable. Rockefeller's instincts told him the acrid combination was the smell of success. He decided to cast his lot with the oil business.

Rockefeller's first business headquarters, on Merwin Street and Superior Avenue, circa 1867

Marcus A. Hanna

Samuel Andrews

Rockefeller's start: Standard Oil Refinery Number 1, 1873.

Another young Englishman, Samuel Andrews, was newly-arrived in Cleveland and looking about at that time. His talents integrated nicely with Rockefeller's plans and he shortly became an important member of the Rockefeller team. Andrews was a candlemaker by trade, but he also was a talented chemist, and he had developed a new process for refining oil kerosene from crude petroleum.

Rockefeller appreciated the value of Andrews' discovery as well as his basic knowledge and he drew the Englishman into a new three-way partnership with Clark and himself. The new company was modestly called, Andrews, Clark & Co. It was the forerunner of The Standard Oil Company, which was organized in Cleveland seven years later, in 1870.

Rockefeller's first refinery was in the Flats, at the place where Kingsbury Run connected with the Cuyahoga Valley. Standard Oil Refinery No. 1 at that site was the beginning of a worldwide business empire. It remained in that Flats location until the 1960s.

Among the Clevelanders who joined the Rockefeller tide early, before it crested, were Henry M. Flagler, Henry B. Payne, and Steven V. Harkness — the latter, by the way, being a descendant not many years removed of Nathaniel Doan, the pioneer Clevelander. Payne also served as a United States senator from Ohio, and Flagler probably is best remembered as the developer who created much of modern Florida.

With the addition of petroleum refineries to the city scene, and the intangible, priceless asset of Rockefeller's business genius working in behalf of the community, Cleveland's pattern for industrial and financial success was firmly locked in by 1870.

The Cuyahoga Valley became the phenomenal place where rivers of iron ore, coal, and petroleum came together in one mighty stream — such a confluence of mineral wealth and new industrial zeal as nobody would have dreamed possible a few years before.

The idyllic lake town still could be remembered, and some of the old charm was evident here and there, but a brawny young city had taken its place, and already there were smudges on the face and grime on the hands.

18. Religion on the frontier

Rev. Joseph Badger

Construction workers at the Trinity Episcopal Cathedral project, circa 1906

One of the early missionaries to the Western Reserve, Dr. Thomas Robbins, a stern man, visited Cleveland in 1803 and found the people to be "loose in principles and conduct."

"Few of them," he added, "had heard a sermon or a hymn in eighteen months."

An even earlier missionary visitor, Rev. Joseph Badger, a Presbyterian, had formed a similarly displeased impression of the loose-living Clevelanders and their close neighbors in Newburgh. After visiting the only two families in Cleveland in 1802, he went on to Newburgh to preach.

"There were five families here, but no apparent piety," he wrote in his diary. "They seemed to glory in their infidelity."

It wasn't until 1816 that the situation took a turn for the better. In March of that year, organized religion finally entered the frontier picture with the establishment of Trinity Parish of the Episcopal Church in the house of Phineas Shepherd in Brooklyn Village.

Lay readers conducted the services at Trinity most of the time, but occasionally a traveling clergyman would visit the town and officiate. It was not until 1826 that a rector, Rev. Silas C. Freeman of Virginia, could be employed, and even then only on a part-time basis.

Rev. Freeman was shared with an Episcopal parish in Norwalk, which agreed to pay part of his $500 yearly salary. Services in Cleveland were held in the courthouse.

Cleveland's first church building was erected by Trinity in 1829 at Seneca (W. 3rd) Street and St. Clair Avenue. The following year the parish persuaded Rev. Mr. McElroy to accept the Trinity pulpit on a full-time basis.

The original parish was divided in 1834 with the creation of St. John's Church in Ohio City. An edifice to serve the new parish was built on Church Street, a block west of Pearl (W. 25th) Street.

Catholic missionaries from the diocese of Quebec moved through the Ohio country when it still was exclusively Indian territory. The last of the Canadian missionary priests to visit Northern Ohio and the Cuyahoga valley was Rev. Edmund Burke in 1796, the year of Moses Cleaveland's arrival.

Bishop Edward Fenwick of Cincinnati sent Dominican

Above, the Eagle Street Synagogue, 1875; right, St. Mary's on the Flats, 1875, inset, Bishop Amadeus Rappe; below, St. John's Episcopal Church; bottom, looking east, 1860, the City Hotel, and the First Presbyterian (Old Stone) Church

fathers from Perry County to visit Cleveland at regular intervals in the late 1820s as numbers of Irish Catholic canal workers began to settle in the town. Rev. Thomas Martin made Cleveland one of his stops in 1826. Another Dominican who became acquainted with Cleveland, succeeding Father Martin, was Rev. Stephen Badin, the first priest ordained in the United States.

Cleveland's first resident pastor was Rev. John Dillon, assigned to minister to the Catholics of the area in 1835. There was no church. Masses were said in private residences until Father Dillon rented Shakespeare Hall for services.

The death of Father Dillon at the age of 29 left Catholics without a pastor until September, 1837, when Rev. Patrick O'Dwyer was assigned to Cleveland. One of his first acts was to begin construction of a small church at Columbus and Girard streets in the Flats. But difficulties were encountered. The congregation could not raise enough money to complete the building, and, to make matters more complicated, Father O'Dwyer was reassigned at that time.

Not until Bishop Purcell of Cincinnati came to Cleveland and personally supervised the project was the first Catholic Church here completed. Its formal name was Our Lady of the Lake, but so many parishioners persisted in calling it St. Mary's-on-the-Flats that its name was changed to the common usage. The first mass was said in the church in October, 1839.

Cleveland was chosen as the seat of a new diocese covering all of Northern Ohio in April, 1847, and the bishop of the new see was Father Amadeus Rappe, heretofore an active missionary. The Catholic population of the diocese was estimated then to be about 10,000.

Bishop Rappe bought several lots at Bond (E. 6th) Street and St. Clair and established his residence there in a brick house. Behind the house, he began the diocese's first seminary in a one-story frame building.

In the same year, 1848, Bishop Rappe bought property at the corner of Erie (E. 9th) Street and Superior as the site of Cleveland's first cathedral.

The cornerstone was laid in October, 1848, and the St. John Cathedral was consecrated and opened on Nov. 7, 1852. The only discordant note sounded were the complaints of some Catholics that the church and the diocesan headquarters were too far out in the country.

With the completion of the cathedral, St. Mary's-on-the-Flats mainly served the large German Catholic population. Likewise, Bishop Rappe in 1854 directed the establishment of a new parish to serve the Irish immigrants in Ohio City. The new church was named St. Patrick's.

So swiftly was Cleveland growing, and so large was the influx of Catholics, that in a period of nine years, from 1848 to 1857, some 26 churches were built in the diocese.

The Jewish community in Cleveland began slowly. The first formal organization was the Israelitic Society, formed in 1839. At that time, it was estimated that there were not more than a dozen Jewish families in the city. The society purchased a burial ground in Ohio City in 1840.

The Anshe Chesed congregation was organized in 1842. It was united with the Israelitic Society in 1846, forming the Israelitic Anshe Chesed Society, the city's oldest Jewish congregation. Its first synagogue was built on Eagle Street downtown. The edifice was enlarged and rededicated in 1860.

A second Jewish congregation, Tifereth Israel, conducted services in a house on Lake (Lakeside) Street until its first temple on Huron Street was completed in December, 1855. It occupied that building until its new temple was built at Wilson (E. 55th) Street and Central Avenue in 1894. This had the distinction of being the first "open temple" ever established anywhere by the Jewish people; it was open in the sense that it offered programs of a cultural nature to the community at large. Its direct descendant is The Temple in University Circle, whose "main" location is now in Beachwood. Its most distinguished spiritual leaders were Rabbi Moses J. Gries (1892-1917) and Rabbi Abba Hillel Silver (1917-1963).

The city's first Methodist church was organized in 1818 on the west side of the river, in Brooklyn. Cleveland's earliest Methodist Episcopal services were performed by a circuit preacher, Rev. Ira Eddy, in 1822. The city's first Methodist society was formed in 1827, but not until 1841 was a Methodist Episcopal church built. It was erected at the corner of St. Clair and Wood streets. It served until 1869, when it gave way to a new stone chapel erected on Erie (E. 9th) Street, near Euclid Avenue.

The first Presbyterian Church, better known as the Old Stone Church, grew out of a Union Sunday school established in 1820, with Elisha Taylor as superintendent. Its first permanent building was erected on Public Square in 1833. Rev. Samuel C. Aiken became its pastor in 1834.

Even though Rev. Joseph Badger preached in Cleveland as early as 1800, a Baptist society was not organized in Cleveland until 1833. The first Baptist church was built at the corner of Seneca (W. 3rd) and Champlain streets in 1835. It became the Euclid Avenue Baptist Church, whose edifice was erected at E. 18th Street and Euclid Avenue in 1871. Its most prominent worshipper was John D. Rockefeller.

The large German immigrant colony organized the first Lutheran church here in 1835. Services were held in a meeting house at the corner of Hamilton Avenue and Erie (E. 9th) Street, built in 1842. The congregation, known as Zum Schifflein Christi, or "The Ship of Christ," moved to larger quarters on Superior Street in 1875.

Zion Evangelical Lutheran Church was founded in 1843, with David Schuh as first pastor. It was formed by families who seceded from Zum Schifflein Christi.

Lutherans on the West Side organized their first congregation, the Evangelical Lutheran Trinity, in 1853, with Rev. J. C. W. Linderman as pastor.

An historical sidelight on Zion Evangelical Lutheran Church is that a candle-lighted Christmas tree was set up in the little church sanctuary during the holiday season in 1852. It is believed to have been the first Christmas tree to appear in a church or to be allowed in a church ceremony.

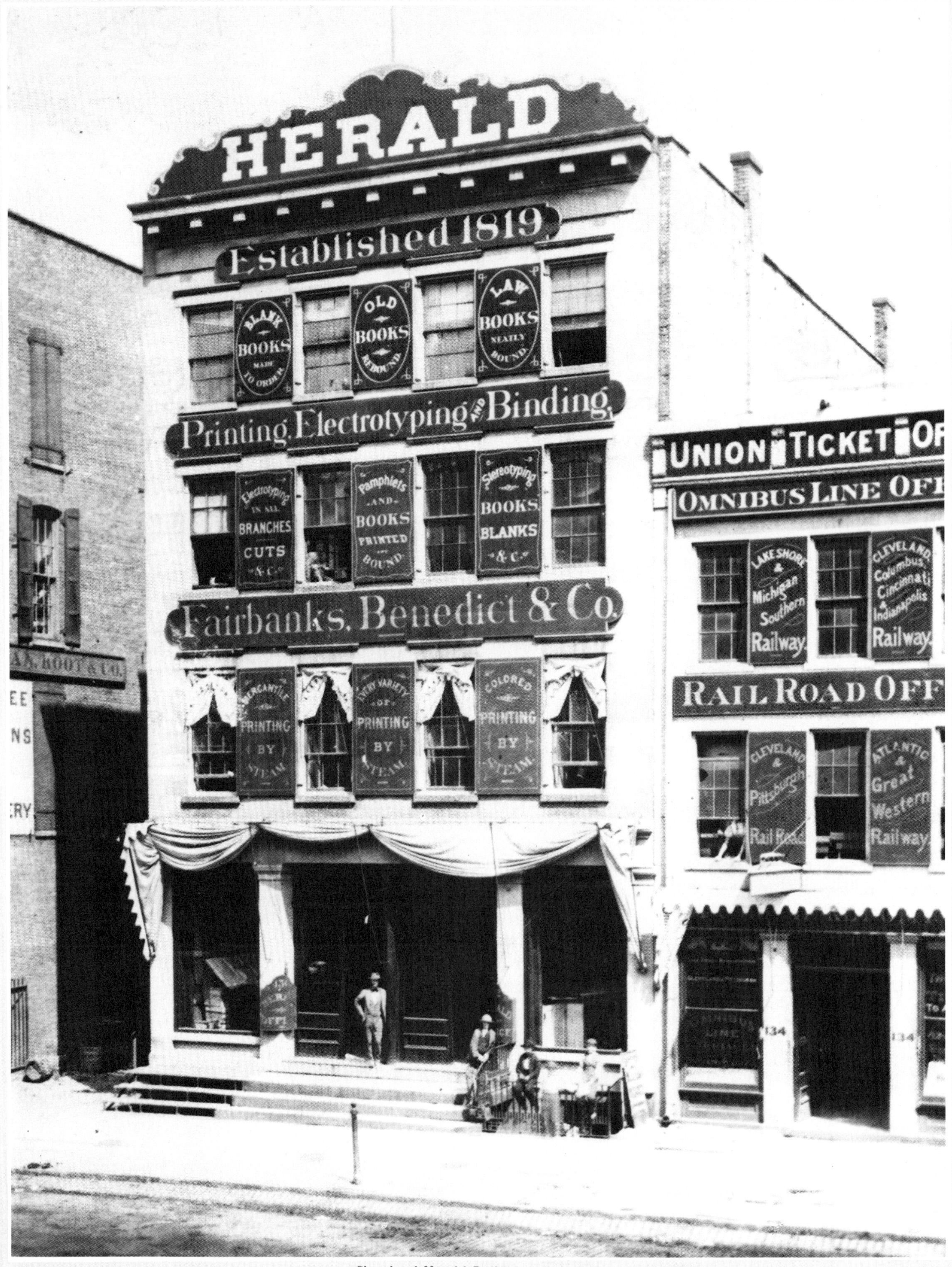

Cleveland Herald *Building, circa 1873*

19. Early journalism

The complexity of the new modern media, and the surfeit of information that is thrust on people today, stands in sharp contrast with the situation that prevailed when the Western Reserve was in its opening stages.

Frontier travelers, especially those freshly arrived from the sophisticated east, were eagerly sought out in taverns and inns of early Cleveland as the carriers of news from the outside world.

Isolation was not total in those days, but it certainly meant an exasperating time lag in the relay of current history.

One of the real shortcomings in the word-of-mouth relay of news, apart from its slowness, was that it had a tendency often to mangle the facts beyond recognition.

An attempt to remedy the situation was the establishment on July 31, 1818 of Cleveland's first newspaper: *The Cleveland Gazette and Commercial Register.*

It was a formidable, topheavy name for a small, frail publication presented under the editorial direction of Andrew Logan of Beaver, Pa. He, in some ways, was more interesting than his newspaper because it was rumored that he was descended from the famous Mingo Indian chief, Logan. The fact that he was swarthy of complexion didn't discourage the rumor in any way.

That first edition of the *Gazette and Commercial Register,* offered at a subscription price of $2 a year, was small in format and slight in size — only four pages, each four columns wide. The big news was all about trouble in Chile and other South American unrest. But Logan was an editor with insight and an understanding of the universal weakness of readers: his main story was all about a sea serpent that did battle with a giant whale somewhere off the Altantic coast, while the captain, crew and passengers of a packet named Delia looked on and gave the occurrence, one can guess, their full attention.

It was a fine journalistic opener, and it had the people of the small town — all 500 of them — buzzing, no doubt. But Logan had many problems to command his attention, as editors usually do, as he struggled for a foothold. The *Register's* office was in a building on the south side of Superior, just west of

Office of Cleveland Herald *business manager William Perry Fogg, circa 1873*

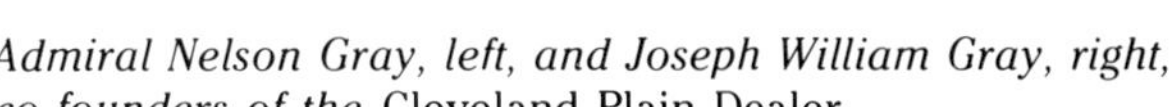
Admiral Nelson Gray, left, and Joseph William Gray, right, co-founders of the Cleveland Plain Dealer

E. W. Scripps, founder of The Cleveland Press

Seneca (W. 3rd) Street. The building, interestingly enough, also served as a hay-weighing station.

"Its roof projected at the front like a modern gasoline station," wrote S. J. Kelly, describing the old newspaper in *The Plain Dealer.* "Four chains suspended from this porch were attached to the wagon hubs and a big counter-balance raised the load. The beam end swung in the office so that the printer could attend to the weighing."

It wasn't enough that Editor Logan had to weigh the stories of the day; he also had to weigh hay. He also had to work as his own printer, advertising salesman, pressman, and, probably most trying of all, be his own carrier.

Advertisments were payable in cordwood and produce; editors have to stay warm and eat. One of Logan's chief difficulties was obtaining paper, ink and type. Publication of his newspaper would have to be suspended frequently while he traveled long distances to other towns in search of supplies.

The name of the newspaper was shortened on Oct. 6, 1818 to the more manageable *Cleveland Register.* The following year, on Nov. 9th, the name of Carlos V. Hickox appeared on the masthead as a co-owner with Logan. Then, in March, 1820, it was announced that Hickox had purchased the *Register* and would discontinue its publication for a few weeks while regrouping his journalistic forces.

But the discontinuance of the *Register* settled into permanence. The little newspaper never did reappear.

Meanwhile, however, a second newspaper had appeared on the Cleveland scene. It was the *Cleaveland Herald,* and its editor and publisher was Eber D. Howe from Erie, Pa. His newspaper was "printed and published weekly by Z. Willes & Company, directly opposite the Commercial Coffee House, Superior Street" during its first year of existence, which began on Oct. 19, 1819.

Howe, in his "Autobiography of a Pioneer Printer," later recalled some of the "difficulties and perplexities" he encountered in publishing the *Herald:*

"Our Mails were then all carried on horse-back. We had one mail a week from Buffalo, Pittsburgh, Columbus and Sandusky. The paper, on which we printed, was transported in wagons from Pittsburgh, and at some seasons the roads were in such condition that it was impossible to procure it in time for publication days.

"Advance payments for newspapers at that time were never thought of. In a few weeks our subscription list amounted to about 300, at which point it stood for about two years, with no very great variation. These were scattered all over the Western Reserve, except in the County of Trumbull.

"In order to extend our circulation to its greatest capacity, we were obliged to resort to measures and expedients which would appear rather ludicrous at the present day. For instance, each and every week, after the paper had been struck off, I mounted a horse with a valise, filled with copies of the 'Herald,' and distributed them at the doors of all subscribers between Cleveland and Painesville, a distance of thirty miles, leaving a package at the latter place; and on returning diverged two miles to what is known as Kirtland Flats, where another package was left for distribution, which occupied fully two days.

"I frequently carried a tin horn to notify the yeomanry of the arrival of the latest news, which was generally forty days from Europe and ten days from New York. This service was performed through the fall, winter, and spring, and through rain, snow, and mud, with only one additional charge of fifty cents on the subscription price; and as the number of papers thus carried averaged about sixty the profits may be readily calculated."

After doing some calculating himself, Howe in 1821 must have come to the conclusion that the profits were not sufficient. He sold his interest in the *Herald* that year and moved to Painesville, where he founded the *Painesville Telegraph,* which is still a thriving newspaper today.

A new Cleveland publication begun in 1827 was called the *Independent News-Letter;* a name that was dropped in 1832 in favor of the *Cleveland Advertiser.* Another name change occurred in late 1841 when the *Advertiser* was acquired by two brothers, Admiral Nelson Gray and Joseph William Gray. They

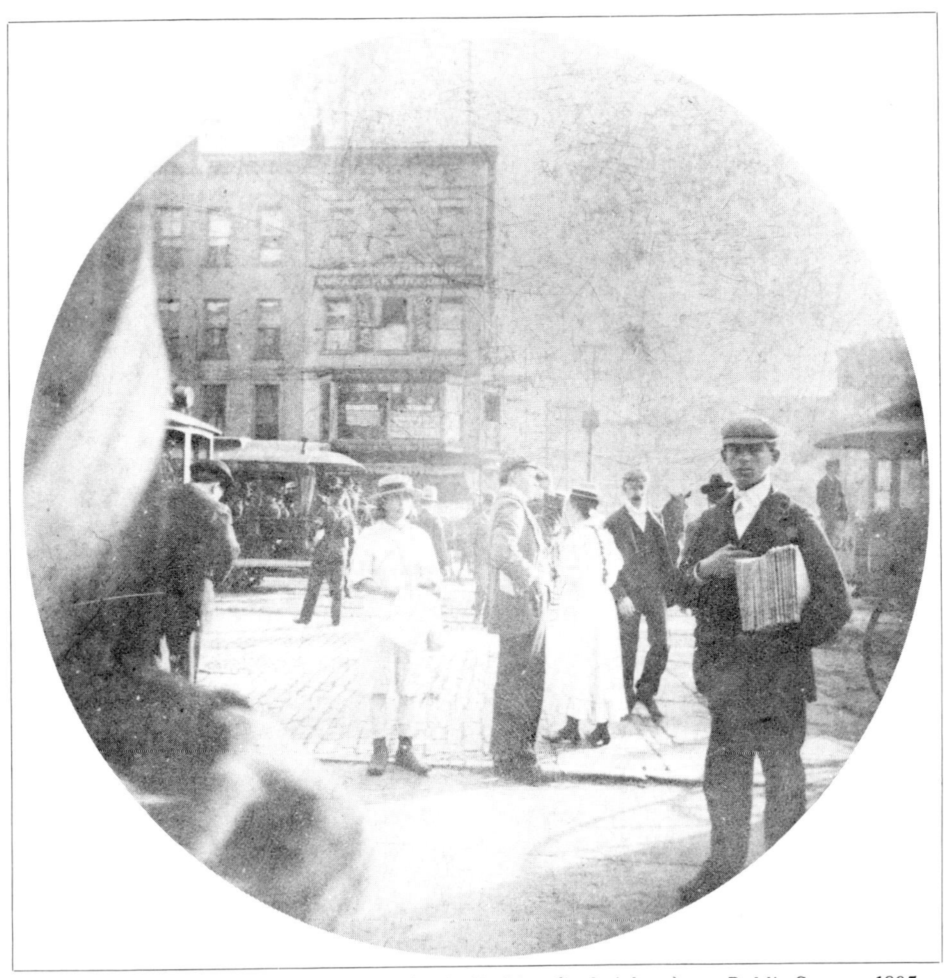

Newsboys and Cleveland's newsgirl Annie Perkins (in knickers) on Public Square, 1895

called the newspaper the *Cleveland Plain Dealer,* a name out of the old English lexicon, frequently used by Shakespeare. In its popular use, it was a kind of slang expression. A "plain dealer" was an honest sort of fellow; a square shooter.

The publication with the odd name found favor among Clevelanders. It is still the city's morning and Sunday newspaper.

The other survivor in the long list of journalistic efforts in Cleveland is *The Cleveland Press,* begun in 1878 by one of the giants of American journalism, Edward W. Scripps. He founded it under the name of the *Penny Press.* Out of this venture grew the large Scripps-Howard chain of newspapers, radio and television stations in the United States.

The journalistic trail leading to the present is littered with the bleached bones of newspapers that strove to become a permanent part of the Cleveland scene, but failed. They include the remains of the *Morning Mercury,* the *Eagle-Eyed News Catcher,* the *Commercial Intelligencer,* the *Cleveland Gatherer,* the *True Democrat,* the *Forest City,* the *Leader,* the *Forest City Democrat,* the *Times,* the *Sunday Voice,* the *News,* and the *News-Leader.*

Two brothers from Coshocton, Ohio — Joseph and James Medill — were the publishers of the *Forest City,* which they started in 1852. When, after a series of mergers, it was renamed the *Leader,* Joseph Medill withdrew from the front office and went to Chicago, where he founded a newspaper called the *Chicago Tribune.*

For a while, in the early 1920s, Cleveland was the home office of the national news weekly magazine, *Time.* Henry Luce and Briton Hadden were the publishers of the magazine, then only two years old, when in 1925 it moved from New York to Cleveland. What Cleveland offered were the advantages of lower cost printing, lower office expenses, and better postal distribution.

After two years of enjoying the Cleveland economies and increasing its national circulation, *Time,* spurred on by Hadden, who missed New York, returned to the nation's largest city in 1927.

Following the death of the morning *Times* at the outset of the depression of the '30s, the Cleveland newspaper field became stabilized for three decades — until the *News,* then owned by the *Plain Dealer,* sold out to the *Press* in 1960, leaving Cleveland with but two daily newspapers.

The foreign-language press flourished more fully in Cleveland than in most American cities because of a large cosmopolitan population. There were, at one time, daily newspapers serving Polish, Hungarian, German and Italians, although the passing of the immigrant generations has made the foreign-language publications a dying branch of journalism. Among the major survivors in Cleveland are such weekly publications as the *Slovenian Daily News,* the *Szabadsag,* the *Waechter und Anzeiger,* the *Amerikanski Slovenec,* and the *Magyar Ujsag.*

The Cleveland *Call and Post,* serving the city's black population (Circulation: 28,000), marked its 50th anniversary in 1979. The weekly, however, reaches back to an earlier date, to the beginning of the *Cleveland Call* in 1913; the *Post* was founded in 1919. The two newspapers merged in 1929 to form the *Call and Post.* Publisher W. O. Walker has served the newspaper in that position for 48 years.

Of increasing importance in the sprawled-out metropolitan community is a chain of suburban weeklies called the Sun Newspapers, which experienced a period of considerable growth in recent years.

20. Idealism and institutions

"An Evening at the Ark," an 1856 painting by Julius Gollman, shows the men who met every week for discussions of natural history. Originally known as the Arkites, the group later changed its name to The Kirtland Society of the Natural Sciences.

There was a remarkable continuity in the surnames of leading families in Cleveland through the city's first century. Contrary to the usual order of happenings, the pioneers somehow managed to breed a lot of capable civic leaders.

The modern city owes a major debt to the second and third generations of the old families for their philanthropic support of culture and intellectualism in such measure as to make Cleveland a leading center of the humanities.

The core group of intellectuals in the early city would have included, certainly, Alfred Kelley, Charles Whittlesey, Harvey Rice, Dr. J. Lang Cassels, and Dr. Jared P. Kirtland.

Kelley was the civic genius, Rice the great educator, Whittlesey the great geologist and the great historian, Dr. Cassels the leading physician and chemist, Dr. Kirtland an outstanding medical doctor and one of the great naturalists of the 19th century.

There would be no accurate way to measure the extent of the contributions of such men, or to weigh their significance in the analysis of the civic sum total. But it is possible to trace their influence in the creation of certain institutions that glorify the modern city. In such a study, it becomes obvious that the dreams of the intellectuals would not have become marble and mortar without the generosity of civic leaders who were able to appreciate their lofty aims.

Among the old pioneer names that played a prominent part in the 19th century history of the city, and whose influence in the city's cultural life is still strong today, is that of the Case family.

The first member of the family to make his mark in Cleveland was Leonard Case, who was among the early settlers. He moved to Cleveland in 1816, served as president of the village from 1821 to 1824, acted as agent of the Connecticut Land Company from 1827 to 1855, served as the county's first auditor, became a leader in banking circles, and stayed active in civic affairs until his death in December, 1864.

Leonard Case had two sons, William and Leonard, Jr.; both successful businessmen and followers in their father's civic footsteps. William Case served as mayor for two terms beginning in 1850.

Exterior of the Case homestead, also known as The Ark, in 1859. The building, built in 1826, was once the Case Land Office. Below, interiors of the Case home, dining room, left, and Leonard Case's desk, right.

University Circle 1906 panorama with Western Reserve College, Case School of Applied Science and The Western Reserve Historical Society

He took over the helm of the city at a time when it was just on the verge of an incredible time of growth. He, like many far-sighted men of the time, could sense that the little city was headed for greater things. He wrote in his diary on Dec. 31, 1850:

"The prospects for our city are now brighter than at any former period, real estate having risen in value this last year 20 percent; outlying lots, 50 to 100 percent. People abroad begin to look more to us. Two railroads are now completed and three plank roads are in operation."

Leonard Case, Jr.

Mayor Case was an unusual person — certainly a rare type to fill political office. Born to a wealthy family, his health was so poor as a child that, in desperation, he took to the outdoor life to build up his constitution.

In his years of traveling through the unspoiled fields and forests of Ohio, Michigan and the northwest country, he became a fierce lover of nature and all wild life. Among the people he met in his travels was the great Audubon, whom, for a period, he served as an assistant.

Case wasn't able to dismiss his experiences from his mind when he finally returned to Cleveland and settled down. He and some friends who were interested in the mysteries and beauty of the natural evnironment would come together frequently for discussions and exchanges of experiences. When, in 1835, his father, Leonard Case, Sr., gave up the use of a one-story frame building on the northeast corner of Public Square that had served as his office, young Case and his friends took over the building as a permanent home for their collections of birds and mammals and geologic specimens. They named it, for obvious reasons, "The Ark." And the members of their group who met there every week for discussions of natural history became known as the "Arkites."

A painting of the original Arkites, commissioned by William Case in 1858, included the following Clevelanders:

William Case, Leonard Case, Dr. Elisha Sterling, Stroughton Bliss, Col. E. A. Scoville, George A. Stanley, Bushnell White, Capt. B. A. Stannard, Dr. A. Maynard, D. W. Cross, Henry G. Abbey, R. K. Winslow, J. J. Tracy and John Coon.

Among the original discussion group was Dr. Kirtland, whose reputation as a great naturalist already was well established. In his honor, the Arkites changed the name of their group to The Kirtland Society of the Natural Sciences. It remained a thriving organization until age overtook its close-knit membership and dissolved the society through natural attrition of the years.

The Ark itself was torn down to make way for the new postoffice building some years later.

Leonard Case, Jr., who survived his brother, made a bequest to the city that was, in a real sense, an extension of the Ark and its high-minded purpose. His will left property worth more than a million dollars to be used to establish an institution of higher learning to be called Case School of Applied Sciences. He died in 1880. The new school, incorporated and organized in 1881, was built on some open meadows off Euclid Avenue, beyond E. 107th Street.

In the same year, another prominent Cleveland millionaire, Amasa Stone, who had gained great riches building railroads, offered $500,000 to Western Reserve College in Hudson, Ohio, if that old institution would transfer to Cleveland and occupy a selected site which happened to be adjacent to that chosen by Case School of Applied Sciences.

There was more to this curious juxtaposition of new universities than a whimsical fate. There had been a fierce personal rivalry between Leonard Case and Amasa Stone. The funding of the two universities, coming so closely together, adjacent in time and space, simply represented a furtherance of the contest between strong personalities.

The old, but impoverished, Hudson institution accepted Stone's offer and moved to the Cleveland site in 1882. It was the beginning of Western Reserve University. It also was the beginning of the area called University Circle, now world-famous for its cluster of cultural institutions.

* * *

Besides the great universities, which merged into one under the name of Case Western Reserve University in 1967, the area takes in the Western Reserve Historical Society, the Cleveland Museum of Art, the Cleveland Museum of Natural History, Severance Hall (home of the Cleveland Orchestra) and, more recently, private research organizations.

It may be the most outstanding example of a cultural chain reaction. As Western Reserve began to grow into an important center of learning, for example, a distinguished faculty member, Francis H. Herrick, noted biologist, urged the establishment of a natural history museum.

The idea was taken up by Harold T. Clark in 1906 and his promotional endeavors culminated in the organization of the Cleveland Museum of Natural History on Dec. 13, 1920. The new museum found a proper home when, in December, 1921, it moved into the great mansion at 2717 Euclid Avenue that formerly had been the home of Leonard C. Hanna. Once again the Hanna name had been brought back into its favorite field of natural science. The wheel turned full circle when the museum in 1927 became the legal successor to the Kirtland Society of Natural Sciences.

William Case

Art patrons : With the financial help of Mrs. Adella Prentiss Hughes (above), the Cleveland Orchestra progressed under the baton of Nikolai Sokoloff (upper photograph, 1922). In 1931, the orchestra was given a grand new hall by John L. Severance (right), who broke ground for the palatial performing arena on Euclid Avenue

John L. Severance with Nikolai Sokoloff, Charles Martin Loeffler and Dr. Walter J. Barlow, November 1924

Jeptha Wade and his son, Randall

Construction of the Inner Belt Highway through the downtown area in the 1950s cut a swathe through the Euclid Avenue neighborhood and the Natural History museum and its two buildings, the Hanna house and the Harvey Brown mansion, were right in the path of the interstate road. The museum in 1958 moved to Wade Park in University Circle. Its complex of buildings there now represents one of the finest natural history museums in the world.

* * *

Among the Wade Park neighbors in this unique grouping of cultural facilities are the world-renowned Cleveland Museum of Art and the equally celebrated Cleveland Orchestra's magnificent home, Severance Hall — all the outgrowth of idealistic vision and philanthropic largesse.

An earlier organization of the Cleveland Orchestra in 1895 had failed after two struggling seasons, but, thanks to the encouragement and financial help of Mrs. Adella Prentiss Hughes (an aunt of Howard Hughes), the symphony was given a new beginning in 1918 with Nikolai Sokoloff as its musical conductor.

Commendable progress was made under Sokoloff, and still more under his successor in 1933, Artur Rodzinski. But the most brilliant moment in those early years of the orchestra unquestionably was on the night of Feb. 5, 1931, when the grand new home at 11001 Euclid Avenue, Severance Hall, was opened officially. It was built with a gift of $2,500,000 from John L. Severance.

Once settled in this palatial hall, the Cleveland Orchestra began its serious and uninterrupted march towards greatness. Erich Leinsdorf held the orchestral baton briefly, from 1943 to 1946, when he turned it over to George Szell. It was the beginning of the orchestra's most brilliant period of growth in performance and world esteem. Szell's tenure as conductor, lasting until his death in 1970, was nothing short of epochal.

Lorin Maazel, following the toughest act in town, became conductor in 1972. The sound of the orchestra reflected the change, but critics the world over generally have conceded that quality of the highest kind remained the keynote of the Cleveland Orchestra.

* * *

The Cleveland Museum of Art, perhaps second only to the New York Art Museum in the United States, traces its origin to 1881, when a Clevelander named Hinman B. Hurlbut left a generous bequest in his will to finance an art museum. It was the seed money.

Then Jeptha H. Wade, the prominent Cleveland businessman who put together 13 different telegraph companies into one organization called Western Union Telegraph Company, left the city in his will a great forested tract of land for use as a park — Wade Park.

The will specifically reserved four acres of the land, however, for a civic use to be determined later. His grandson, also named Jeptha H. Wade, decided 10 years later that an art museum would be the perfect civic fulfillment for that four acres of unspoiled parkland.

Two other wealthy Clevelanders had died, in the interim, and had made provision in their wills for the financing of the art museum. They were John Huntington and Horace Kelley.

The result of all that unprecedented philanthropy was the erection of a monumental structure in Wade Park to house the new Cleveland Museum of Art. Construction began in 1913 and

Rockefeller Boulevard in Rockefeller Park, 1906

The Spring at Wade Park, 1885

Wade Park Lagoon, circa 1905

the museum was opened on June 6, 1916.

Even during those years of building effort, other generous Clevelanders were contributing to the future institution. Among them were Delia E. Holden, wife of the *Plain Dealer* owner, Liberty E. Holden; Mr. and Mrs. John L. Severance, and Mrs. Dudley P. Allen.

The tradition of museum support has been continued in recent years, but the most outstanding contributions, by far, came from Leonard C. Hanna, Jr., grandnephew of U.S. Senator Mark Hanna. After a lifetime of philanthropy, Leonard Hanna, Jr., left the museum an endowment of some $20 million, plus a private art collection valued at $1,400,000.

The Art Museum, now doubled in size, stands today as one of the most highly endowed institutions of its kind anywhere. Its endowment is estimated at $100 million and its annual income is in the vicinity of $3 million.

* * *

The Western Reserve Historical Society, another member of the University Circle cultural cluster, arose out of the same earnest group of young Clevelanders who pondered the intellectual issues of the day in William Case's Ark in the middle of the 19th century.

A frequent member of that meeting group was the highly-respected Col. Charles Whittlesey, geologist and historian. He was the author of the first authoritative history of Cleveland.

Thanks mainly to Whittlesey's prompting, 21 Cleveland civic leaders met on May 28, 1867 and organized the Western Reserve Historical Society as a branch of the Cleveland Library Association. Whittlesey was the first selected president of the society, which in the beginning occupied a third floor room in the Society for Savings Building on Public Square as of November, 1867 — a room only 29 feet by 125 feet. It served mostly as a storage room for pioneer and military relics and books relating to the Western Reserve, and was not opened to the public as a library and museum until 1871.

In 1890, as the Society for Savings prepared to move into its new 10-story building on Public Square, the historical society was offered the financial institution's old 3-story structure.

Western Reserve Historical Society complex

St. Ignatius College (now John Carroll University), 1889

Daguerreotype of plan for Cleveland University, circa 1855

The society, still a department of the Public Library, accepted.

John D. Rockefeller eased the organization into its new quarters by making a substantial contribution to the conversion of the building to its new purpose. The state chartered the historical society as an independent organization in March, 1892. But it had no sooner settled in its new home than the Cleveland Chamber of Commerce bought the building and its site for the construction of a new C. of C. headquarters building, forcing the historical society to move to Euclid and Fairmount St. (E. 107th) and a new 3-story building in 1898.

In 1938 the society purchased the old Price McKinney mansion at 10825 East Boulevard, originally built for Mrs. John Hay, widow of the former U.S. Secretary of State, and in May, 1940, acquired the adjoining Leonard C. Hanna mansion. The two magnificent homes were joined in 1957 to make up the present Western Reserve Historical Society quarters. More recently, a wing to accommodate the Frederick C. Crawford Auto Aviation Museum was added to the society's growing complex of attractions.

* * *

The first Cleveland University was on a high promontory on the South Side, overlooking the Cuyahoga River, where it was begun in 1850. That part of the city in which it was located was given the name at the time of University Heights.

It was a short-lived educational venture, lasting only a few years. The university had as president a distinguished educator named Rev. Asa Mahan, who previously had been president of Oberlin College. But the city was not ready.

In the same decade of the 1880s in which Case School of Applied Science and Western Reserve University came into existence in the University Circle area, still another institution of higher learning was added to the Cleveland scene. It was St. Ignatius College, created by the Cleveland Catholic Diocese and the Society of Jesus religious order.

It began as a West Side college, with a building at W. 30th Street and Carroll Avenue, in 1886. It was, at first, a combination high school and college. A separation of names came about in 1923; the high school continued to be called St. Ignatius, but the institution of higher learning was named John Carroll University, after experimenting for a few months with the name, Cleveland University.

The West Side lost John Carroll in 1935, when it moved east to University Heights and a large campus at Miramar Drive and North Park Boulevard. The high school remained in the old building.

* * *

The collegiate picture in the city was rounded out in 1965 with the creation of the new Cleveland State University under the leadership of Gov. James A. Rhodes, whose administration acquired 135 acres in downtown Cleveland as a campus for the new university.

The site extended from E. 18th Street east to the new Inner Belt Freeway along a part of Euclid Avenue that once was the beginning of Millionaires Row and included, indeed, the old Samuel Mather mansion, which became one of the first buildings of CSU.

The new university incorporated the old Fenn College, a YMCA-sponsored institution, and the Fenn Tower, a 22-story building, became the central facility of Cleveland State.

While the university was new, the name was very old.

Besides John Carroll's brief use of the name back in the summer of 1923, there had been also a Cleveland College in downtown Cleveland from 1925 until after World War II. It became part of Western Reserve University, which decided to close the downtown institution, then a tenant in the old Chamber of Commerce Building, and the name was swallowed up by the University Circle complex of the institution and eventually died.

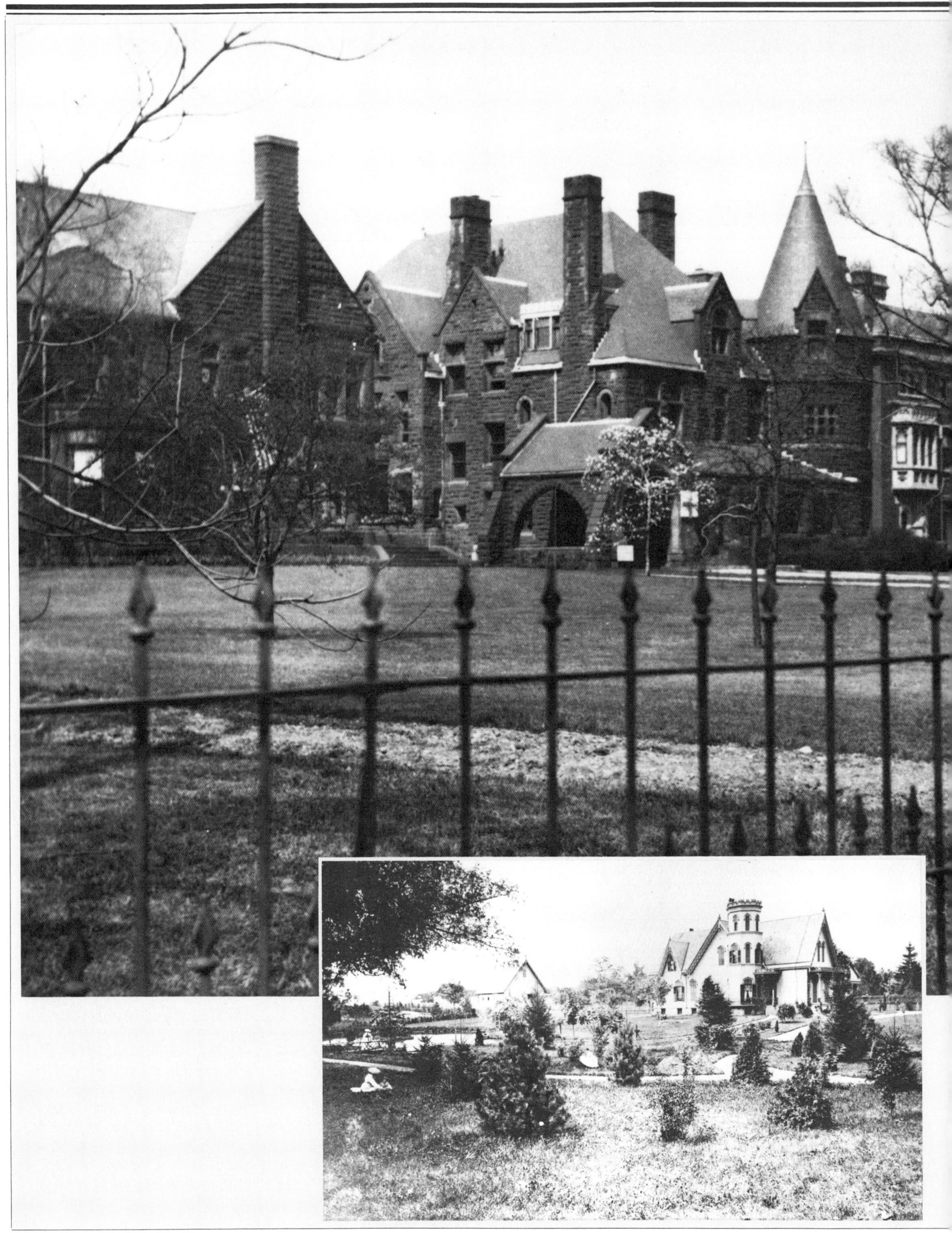

21. Euclid Avenue

The ancient lake ridge radiating eastward from Public Square was given official certification as a sensible way to travel in 1815 by surveyor Moses Warren. He added the trail, long used by the Indians, to the township plat because it connected Cleveland with the township of Euclid.

The trail, which led onward to such distant points as Erie in Pennsylvania and Buffalo in New York State, was more familiarly known to travelers as the Buffalo Road. Its new, official name gradually came to be accepted, and Euclid Avenue, to the surprise of the early planners, came to be the settlement's main street instead of Superior Avenue, which was much wider and grander in concept.

Several other new streets were added to the plan for the village as afterthoughts in that same year of 1815; among them were St. Clair, Bank (W. 6th), Seneca (W. 3rd), Wood (E. 3rd), and Diamond streets (Diamond bounded Public Square). The name given St. Clair at the outset was North Highway.

"Millionaires Row," residences of the ultra-rich along Euclid Avenue.

Left, home of Captain A. P. Winslow

W. S. Tyler home, circa 1870

Residences of John D. Rockefeller, lower left; Rollin Charles White, circa 1890, upper left; and the Samuel Mather mansion, right, last of the great homes built along Euclid Avenue.

The original plans called for the main residential section of the young town to develop in the area just east of Erie (E. 9th) Street; Superior Avenue would serve as the connection with that section and Public Square. But, by the time Payne Avenue was created in 1853, industry already was making that area less desirable for residential purposes.

Prospect, Superior and Kinsman (formerly known as South Highway) all were favored with beautiful residences in the city's first half-century, but it was Euclid Avenue that took the lead as the most elegant, most fashionable street of all.

There were, by the 1860s, impressive homes from Erie (E. 9th) Street as far as Dodge (E. 17th) Street, and the promise of an even grander future could be read in the scramble of wealthy families for property along the length of what was becoming the golden avenue.

Before the century had ended, the mansions of the rich commanded two miles of Euclid Avenue, on either side of the street, all the way from Erie Street to Willson (E. 55th) Street. It was Millionaires Row with a vengeance: showy, ostentatious, extravagant, flamboyant, but also spectacularly beautiful. The avenue became the city's pride, a display of grandeur in which even the poor could take vicarious pleasure.

Euclid Avenue was more than a local phenomenon. It was such a concentrated grouping of mansions, in such a beautiful setting, that its wonder became known all over the world.

A reporter for the *New York World,* when the street was still in its first stage of development, wrote in 1863 that it was "perhaps the finest avenue in the west, a double row of villas and gardens where one might sigh to dwell."

By the time that John D. Rockefeller and his family joined the fashionable drift and bought a home on the southwest corner of Case (E. 40th) Street and Euclid Avenue in 1868, the thoroughfare represented wall-to-wall, curb-to-curb money; perhaps the greatest single concentration of family wealth of any street in America. Cleveland's rich people never since have been so close.

Rockefeller, as a matter of fact, was not among the in-people of Cleveland society. It was rather appropriate that his home should have been at the easternmost limit of really important residences. Case Avenue was sort of a line of demarcation, separating the ultra-fashionable from the very-fashionable, which would have been the families living in the big homes between E. 40th and E. 55th streets.

During all his years in Cleveland, Rockefeller, at his own wish, stayed on the fringe of society. He was polite and proper, friendly in a reserved way, but he was no mixer. Frivolity was something that puzzled and offended him. If life were a popularity contest, John D. was a dropout. He did not have time for the ordinary recreational pursuits of bluebloods, most of which he regarded as empty, inane, foolish and wasteful. The world's richest man was just as frugal with his time as he was with his money.

There were many things about Euclid Avenue, however, that appealed to John D., and among the pluses was the wintertime fun when the residents raced their horsedrawn sleighs down the street on a snowy afternoon, or under the pale glow of the gaslights.

Rockefeller's own stable of horses included some of the best blooded animals in the country. His brother Frank also was an active horseman. Some of their Euclid Avenue neighbors, like

Porte-cochere of the Sylvester T. Everett mansion, circa 1890. Inset, rear view of the Everett home on Euclid Avenue and Case (now East 40th) Street, circa 1889.

Col. William (Billy) Edwards and Harry K. Devereaux, and Charles A. Otis, were among the country's leading amateur drivers.

To live on Euclid Avenue in the years from 1850 to 1910, or 1915, was a distinction in itself, of course, but it also mattered which side of the street one lived on. Either side featured elegant homes, but the north side was deemed more desirable. People on that side of Euclid Avenue were called the "nabobs," while those on the opposite side were known as the "bobs."

That kind of social separation made for a natural rivalry that found expression in the sleigh races, among other things. But the competition was kept within the exclusive circle of aristocratic peers. There was no denying that snobbishness had its principal residence on Euclid Avenue. Most of the families were nouveau riche, and some of them had not had time to adjust to the heady experience of being wealthy.

No doubt the families on Millionaires Row were envied for their good fortune, and no doubt a lot of Clevelanders grumbled when the Euclid Avenue streetcars were barred from that length of avenue from Erie (E. 9th) Street out to Case (E. 40th) Street, so as not to disturb the millionaires with their noise and so as not to mar the neighborhood with their presence. The trolleys, and the horsedrawn streetcars before them, had to turn south on Erie Street to Prospect, and detour eastward on Prospect to Case Avenue, before being allowed back on Euclid Avenue.

But it also was a fact that the entire city took a measure of deep pride in the avenue of beautiful mansions, and most people seemed to understand, and agree, that it was much too beautiful a neighborhood to be subjected to the corrupting invasion of mundane utilities, such as streetcars.

Artemus Ward, who, as a writer for *The Plain Dealer,* set the pattern for American humor writing, conceded in one of his pieces that Euclid Avenue was "a justly celebrated thoroughfare."

"Some folks go so far as to say it puts it all over the well known Unter der Sauerkraut in Berlin and the equally well known Rue de Boolfrog in Paree, France," he wrote. "Entering by way of the Public Square and showing a certificate of high moral character, the visitor, after carefully wiping his feet on the 'welcome' mat, is permitted to roam the sacred highway free of charge.

"The houses are on both sides of the street and seem large as well as commodious. They are covered with tin roofs and pain and mortgages, and present a truly distangy appearance..."

Euclid Avenue was not too good to be true, but it was too good to last. There would be other mansions built after 1900 on the avenue, like the magnificent residence of Samuel Mather which was constructed between 1906 and 1910, but the turn of the century also marked the turning point for Millionaires Row.

The commercial city could not be held back from invading the sacred precincts of Euclid Avenue. The streetcars, like the ongoing city, could not be detoured forever. It was plain by the time of World War I, that the palatial homes and the great estates were too close to the center of the city to survive as an exclusive enclave. The workaday world was closing in and the end was in sight.

Coaching on Euclid Avenue, at the turn of the 20th century.

The end of an era

Triumphal Arch erected by Cleveland's German population celebrating the German victory in the Franco-Prussian War, 1871

22. The newcomers

Immigrants helped build the city, including laborers on the Belt Line Railroad (left), a number of which were Irish, and the Women's Welsh American Club (above), in a 1913 centennial parade.

New Connecticut held its ground in the Western Reserve with stout determination for a long time. It was able to come to terms with the thousands of Irish who became part of the Cleveland home population beginning in the late years of the 1820s, and with the Germans and the Bohemians who traveled the canal highway into the Cuyahoga Valley in large numbers in the 1840s and the 1850s.

But the dilution of the New England stock could not be denied once the city began its period of phenomenal growth at the middle of the 19th century.

The census takers had to work at peak speed to keep up with the multiplication of numbers in Cleveland during that time of population explosion.

The official census figures tell the story:

1850 — 17,034
1860 — 43,417
1870 — 92,829
1880 — 160,146
1890 — 261,353
1900 — 361,768

As sensational as those statistics were, the period of greatest growth still was ahead, to be found within the first three decades of the 20th century. Cleveland's population during that time could be reckoned only in terms of geometric progressions, as follows:

1910 — 560,663
1920 — 796,841
1930 — 900,429

The development was more than just a story of numbers. Cleveland suddenly had become a babel of tongues, in sharp contrast to the recent time when the prevailing sound was the New England twang with no more than an occasional intrusion of gutteral German or the Irish brogue.

The rush of immigration brought with it the sounds of 48 different nationalities, turning Cleveland into one of the most cosmopolitan cities in the nation. What had been an outpost of Connecticut now could be described as an outpost of the world. By 1860, nearly half (44.76 percent) of Cleveland's population was of foreign extraction.

The Irish, as has been mentioned, tended to congregate on the lower West Side, in old Ohio City, and in old Newburgh. The Germans were slower to discover Cleveland. Their numbers were not consequential in the first half of the 19th century. Only 10 persons of German descent could be counted among the 1,000-or-so Clevelanders of 1832. But the Germans made up for their earlier slow foot in the second half of the century. By 1900, the number of German immigrants in Cleveland had shot up to the incredible total of 100,000, and they constituted an influential element in Cleveland society generally, and in Cleveland politics particularly.

The most illustrious of Cleveland mayors, Tom L. Johnson, who had firm control of City Hall from 1901 into 1909, was topped in his bid for a fifth term as mayor by an unknown in political circles whose name was Herman Baehr. His German name was enough to topple Mayor Johnson.

Another Clevelander of German descent who came to prominence at that time was Johnson's chief of police, Fred Kohler. He, too, became mayor.

The Germans were most numerous on the West Side. St. Mary's Catholic Church on Carroll Avenue was their church, just as St. Patrick's, not far away on Bridge Avenue at Fulton, was the church of the Irish families. Sermons at St. Mary's were delivered in German and the parishoners spoke German in the confessional.

Many thousands of Germans chose to live on the East Side, to be sure, and their influence was felt heavily in that part of the city also. The effect of the traditional German love of music was especially noticeable in community life.

Clevelanders of German descent came to civic prominence: Herman Baehr (above, with relatives), who served as mayor; and Fred Kohler (right), who was chief of police and mayor.

The Mendelssohn Singing Society was formed in 1851 and a "gesangverein" was in existence even earlier than that. Oratorios and singing festivals sponsored by the Germans became a delightful part of city life.

One of the great achievements of the German population in the incorporation of their music into the Cleveland culture was the construction of a large auditorium, Saengerfest Hall, financed by a stock company into which Cleveland Germans poured $60,000.

The large structure, which seated 9,000 persons in its auditorium, and which had a capacity of 1,500 on its stage, was erected in 1874 on Willson Avenue (E. 55th Street) from Outhwaite Street to Scovill Avenue, on a site later to be occupied by East Technical High School.

The 19th annual Saengerfest, which drew thousands of music lovers from all parts of the country, was held in the great German Hall from June 22 to June 29, 1874. Orchestral and vocal music by German orchestras, bands and singing societies gave the city a musical festival such as it never before had experienced.

One of the main streams of immigration after the Civil War came from Italy. Like the other ethnic groups, the Italians clustered together in their own colonies. They established a Little Italy on Mayfield Road hill, off Euclid Avenue, on the East Side, and built that neighborhood's West Side counterpart in the vicinity of W. 69th Street, north of Detroit Avenue, just to the west of the predominantly Irish area known as the Cheyenne territory. It won the Indian name, incidentally, because some of the Irish thought it was just about as far west as anyone could go.

With the passing of the years, at any rate, there was a harmonious mingling of Irish, Italians and Romanians in the Detroit Avenue area.

* * *

The Bohemians already had made their presence felt in Cleveland by 1850, but the number of Czechs and Slovaks steadily increased through the second half of the 19th century.

It was estimated at the time of World War I that nearly 70,000 persons of Czech nationality lived in the south side district bounded by Kingsbury Run, E. 55th Street, and the length of Broadway.

Within that district there were five private Bohemian language schools and a population served by four Bohemian newspapers.

Concurrently, a stream of Jewish immigrants had taken over a neighborhood bounded by E. 30th Street to E. 70th Street, Scovill Avenue and the Nickel Plate Railroad tracks. About 70 percent of the people within that area were Jewish at the time of the first World War. A new element of black population already was beginning to move into the area at the time, however, and the Jewish population was gradually shifting towards the area around E. 105th Street.

A third large pocket of foreign population was to be found within the area east of E. 55th Street to East Boulevard, and from Superior Avenue north to Lake Erie.

It was estimated in 1918 that 85 percent of the people living

German culture was evident in Cleveland: a Saengerfest Hall (left) was built for a German singing festival; editors (below) produced a newspaper, The Wachter am Erie, in German.

Italian immigrants settled in a section of Cleveland which came to be known as "Little Italy," including lower Woodland Avenue, above circa 1910. Italian groups gathered (left) on the Hiram House Settlement Playground for Columbus Day, 1923. The Italian construction firm of Joseph Carabelli built the Wade Memorial Chapel (right) in Lakeview Cemetery, 1898.

CAFÉ
39

Central and Eastern Europeans established homes in Cleveland: Bohemian National Hall (upper left) was built in 1896; a statue to Slovak hero Milan Stefanik (lower left) was placed in Wade Park; and an immigrant family (above), perhaps Greek or Syrian, settled on Bolivar Road.

in that area were foreign-born. Among them were 19,000 Slovenians, 6,000 Croatians, 10,000 Poles, and a sizeable number of Lithuanians and Slovaks.

The largest concentration of Poles at that time, however, was from Union Street south to the city limits, from E. 54th Street to the C. & P. Railroad. Within that general area were some 50,000 persons of Polish nationality.

Approximately 20,000 Slovaks, Croatians, Slovenians and Romanians lived in the neighborhoods extending from E. 40th Street to Superior Avenue to E. 20th Street and north to Lake Erie, and from E. 60th Street to Payne Avenue.

The 1918 survey, undertaken by the Federated Churches of Cleveland, found the near South Side to be favored by newly-arrived Slovaks, Poles and Lithuanians, with Pilgrim Congregational Church at W. 14th Street and Starkweather Avenue a popular nationalities center.

About 85 percent of the people living in the district bounded by E. 70th Street and E. 130th Street, between Quincy Avenue and Kinsman Road, were foreigners at the time of the survey. They were, in the main, mostly Hungarians, Bohemians and Slovaks.

The survey of Cleveland's foreign-born population at the time showed the city to be host and home to the following large nationality groups:

Bohemians	46,296
Italians	23,000
Hungarians	31,628
Russian Jews	30,000
Croatians	6,000
Slovenians	19,000
Slovaks	18,977
Poles	49,000
Lithuanians	5,640
Romanians	2,456

Curiously enough, the Germans and the Irish were not listed among the foreigners; a sign, perhaps, that those two nationalities had been in the city long enough to have been accepted as a standard part of the urban scene, like the founding New Englanders.

What the 1918 survey verified, however, was what everybody in Cleveland already knew: the overwhelming influx of new residents from all parts of the world had brought about a social metamorphosis — a basic change in the character of the city and the nature of its population.

Immigrants shared various social arenas: recruiters for the Polish Volunteer Army (below), assembled in 1917 in front of the Polish Falcon Hall on Broadway Avenue; salesmen at the publishing office of The Monitor Clevelandzki (lower left), 1930, a daily newspaper published in Polish; and in a saloon on St. Clair Avenue (right), 1905, in the Slovenian neighborhood.

The city's Hungarian community dedicated the Louis Kossuth Monument (above) in 1902; and the Hungarian Ladies Charity Club (below) prepared relief packages during the Depression in 1933.

23. The black beginning

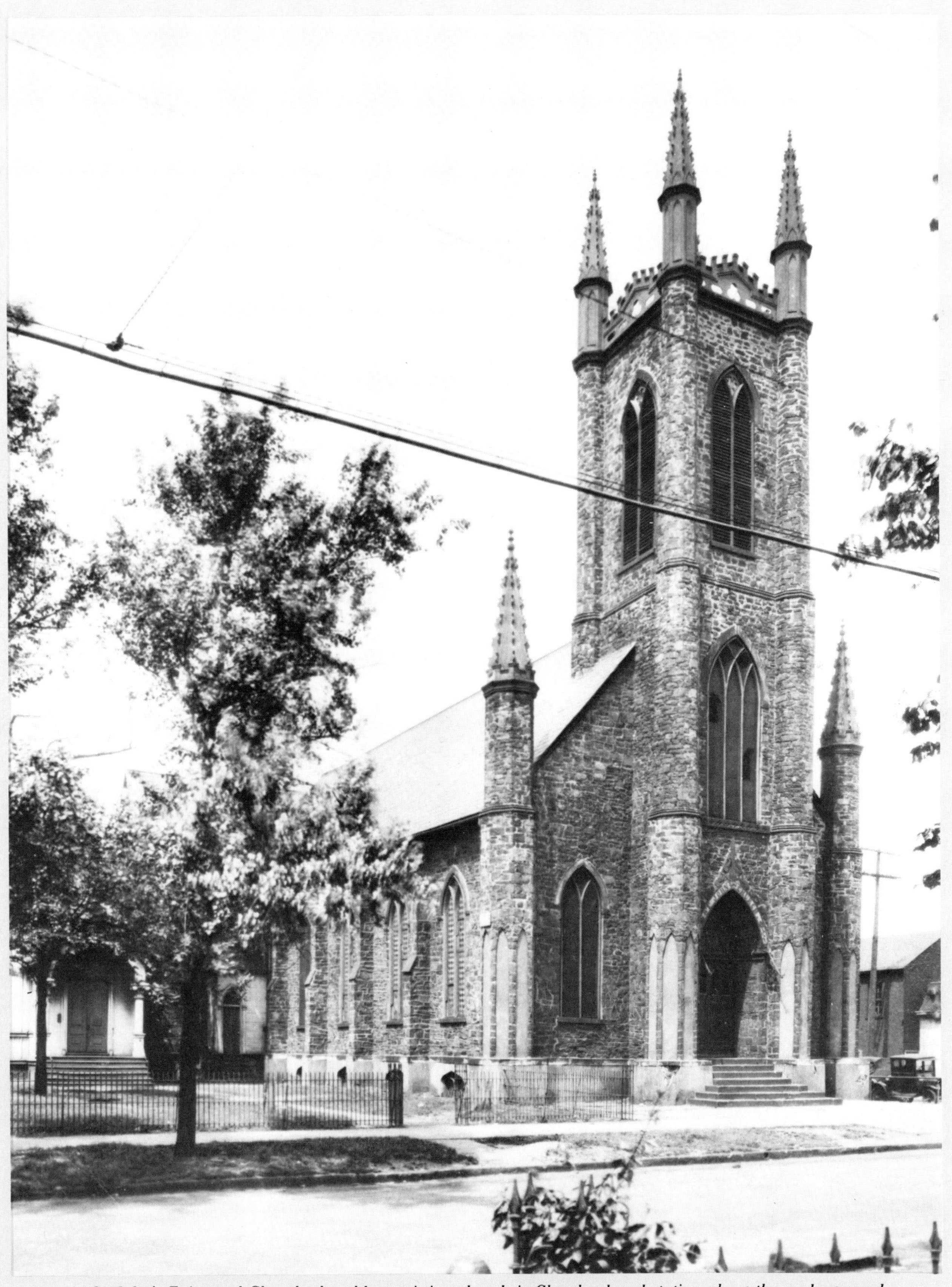

St. John's Episcopal Church, the oldest existing church in Cleveland and station along the underground railroad before the Civil War.

It took a long time before there were enough black people in Cleveland to become an influential force in the city's social composition, but they appeared on the scene early. Cleveland's first black immigrant was George Peake, who, with his family, settled in the western part of Rockport Township, later to be named Rocky River, in 1809.

The history of the family in that pioneer time is sketchy, but it is known that Peake and his four sons, James, Henry, George and Joseph, built the first grist mill in Rockport Township.

More actually is known about the earlier years of the remarkable George Peake. He was a white-haired man of 87 years when he arrived in Cleveland in the spring of 1809 with his furniture-laden wagon, his wife, and two of his sons. He was a trailblazer at an age reached by few men — especially in that distant day — even in a rocking chair.

The stories about this pioneer say that he was born in Maryland in 1722, ten years before the birth of George Washington. It is believed that he was a slave, but that he escaped to Canada, where he is said to have enlisted in the British armed forces and fought with Gen. Wolfe in the decisive victory over the French at the heights of Abraham. When Quebec fell, he marched into the city with the victorious English troops.

Following his Canadian adventure, Peake returned to the United States and took up residence in the Pennsylvania wilderness. There he lived until, feeling hemmed in by the increasing population of the area, he decided to move his family into the empty reaches of the glamorous new Ohio country — specifically, into the Western Reserve.

Although, except for the Peake family, there was virtually no black population in Cleveland during the town's early years, the slavery issue was a major subject of discussion and controversy in the town in the first half of the 19th century, as it was everywhere in America.

In 1827, for instance, there was formed in Cleveland an organization named the Cuyahoga County Colonization Society, with Samuel Cowles as president. This group, a branch of the National Colonization Society, had as its aim helping freed blacks to leave the country. And there were enough black people in the town at the time to support St. John's African Methodist Episcopal Church, the first Negro house of worship, formed in 1830.

In 1833, the Cleveland Anti-Slavery Society was organized with Dr. David Long as president. Six years later, in 1839, newspapers noted the forming of The Colored Men's Union Society.

As mid-century approached, the slavery issue was reaching a feverish level, and the so-called "underground railroad" was especially active in the Oberlin-Cleveland axis.

Cleveland, because of its position on Lake Erie, was an effective embarkation point for escaped slaves being helped to Canadian sanctuary. Many citizens and institutions covertly cooperated in the movement and concealment of the fugitive blacks.

Among the most notable of the agencies involved in the secret, illicit operation was St. John's Episcopal Church, the city's oldest church, just west of W. 25th Street on Church Avenue.

Cleveland then was a red-hot abolitionist center. The evil of slavery frequently was the subject of discussion and protest in large public rallies. On Sept. 10, 1853, for example, there was a protest meeting in Empire Hall at which a Judge Hitchcock and a Dr. Aiken denounced the Fugitive Slave Act before a large, demonstrative audience.

Earlier that year, in April, William Howard Day edited and published an edition of Cleveland's first Negro newspaper, *The Aliened American.* Another edition followed in August. And in 1857, the city's Melodeon Hall was the scene of a national emancipation convention.

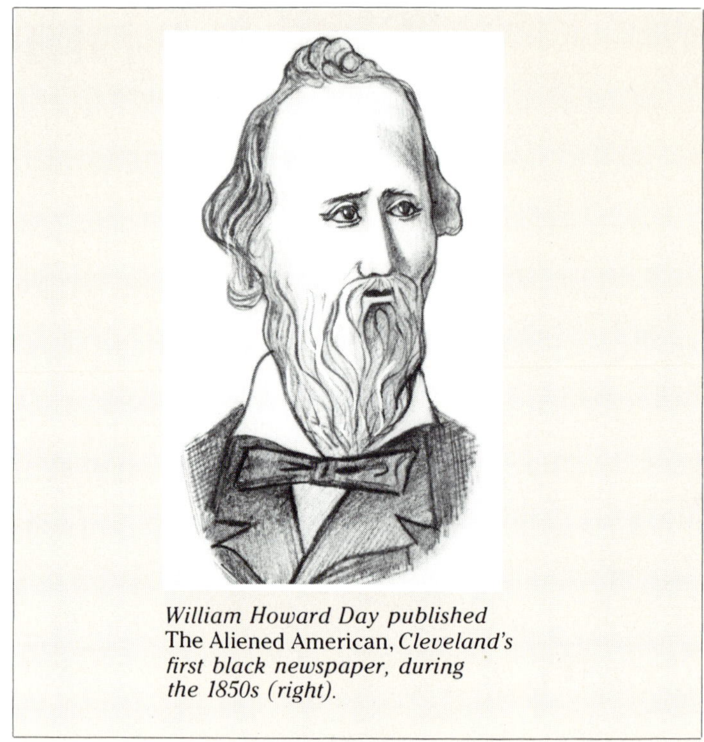

William Howard Day published The Aliened American, *Cleveland's first black newspaper, during the 1850s (right).*

Violations of the federal law barring aid to escaped slaves were common in that tense time as sympathetic people in Cleveland and surrounding communities insisted on giving aid and succor to the fugitive blacks in spite of the law of the land. Court cases involving prosecution for such illegal assistance were numerous.

One of Cleveland's most sensational cases was tried on April 7, 1859 and won national attention. It was the trial of Simeon Bushnell, one of many who, in September, 1858, had joined in rescuing a fugitive slave named John Price from the hands of slave-catchers who had abducted the escapee and were holding him prisoner in a hotel in Wellington, Ohio, while they awaited a train to take them to Columbus.

Involved in the rescue, it seemed, was a large number of students and faculty of Oberlin College; indeed, the slave was once hidden in the home of a professor, and later in the home of the college president, while his rescuers awaited a chance to slip him across the lake and into Canada.

A fair representation of that group was to be found among the 24 residents of Oberlin and 13 residents of Wellington who were indicted for the crime in December, 1858, and arraigned in U.S. District Court in Cleveland. All pleaded not guilty and were dismissed upon their own recognizance pending trial the following spring.

Simeon Bushnell, the first to be brought to trial, was found guilty and sentenced to pay a fine of $600 or serve 60 days in county jail. Legal complications and determined resistance by the other defendants led to the mass jailing of all of them from the middle of April into July, sparking mass protest meetings throughout the state. A large platform was built in Public Square near the jail so speakers could address the imprisoned martyrs to the cause and the demonstrators in the Square.

The Cleveland scene was a sensation in the midst of the national uproar over the slavery issue.

"Meantime," wrote historian Elroy McKendree Avery, "the men behind the walls of the Cuyahoga County jail were doing propaganda work, writing to the newspapers, issuing pam-

THE ALIENED AMERICAN.

To furnish News: To favor Literature, Science and Art: To aid the development, Educational, Mechanical and Social, of Colored Americans: To defend the Rights of Humanity.

VOLUME I. CLEVELAND, OHIO: SATURDAY, APRIL 9, 1853. NUMBER 1.

THE ALIENED AMERICAN,

WILLIAM H. DAY,

Poetry.

THE OLD FARM GATE.

Original Tale.

CHARLES AND CLARA HAYES.

Ohio State Convention of Colored Freemen.

The Family Opposed to Newspapers.

CONSTITUTION.

phlets and advising the preachers of the North to make sermons on the case.

"The fire they started extended throughout all the states in the North. The railways carried relatives and friends to Cleveland at reduced rates and the prisoners were bountifully supplied with all the delicacies of the market by the sympathizing public. Sheriff Wightman and the jailor treated the prisoners as guests and friends rather than criminals."

In one classic demonstration, the Oberlin Sunday school class of Prisoner Fitch paid a visit to the county jail to cheer its superintendent instead of having its usual picnic.

By the way of counter-action, the grand jury of Lorain County, that included Oberlin and Wellington, indicted the four men "slave-catchers" on a charge of abducting the Negro in violation of Ohio laws.

After it became evident that the kidnappers would have to stand trial for their crime if they appeared to testify against the rescuers of the slave, the government's case collapsed and the prisoners were freed. There was national rejoicing over the result of the Cleveland case.

* * *

Shortly before the outbreak of the Civil War, a runaway slave case in Cleveland again attracted national attention.

The slave was a girl named Lucy who had escaped from her owner, William S. Goshorn of Wheeling, Virginia.

Lucy was captured by federal officials in Cleveland on Jan. 19, 1861, in a house on Prospect Street, where she was employed as a maid by the L. A. Benton family.

Anti-slavery feelings were running so high in Northern Ohio by that time that by nightfall a mob of angry abolitionists had gathered around the county jail on Public Square, demanding the release of the girl.

Judge D. R. Tilden ruled that the sheriff had no right to hold Lucy and ordered her release. The sheriff complied, but a United States marshal took her into custody immediately and took her before the U.S. commissioner in the Federal Building. Having to take the escaped slave girl through a Public Square jammed by now with angry whites demanding her release, the marshal hired 150 special deputies as an escort.

The court, after a hearing, reluctantly ordered the girl to be turned over to her owner, Goshorn. He then was offered double her market value by the abolitionists if he would release the girl, but he refused to sell. Lucy and her master were escorted to the train by an armed guard and returned to Wheeling.

Lucy was the last slave to be returned to the south under the Fugitive Slave Law. Lincoln already had been elected president at the time of the Cleveland incident, and shortly thereafter the Civil War broke out.

During the bloodiest of all American wars, some 10,000 Clevelanders were drawn into military service. Many of them were immigrants recently arrived on American shores, including a large number who had fled the Old World to escape military service. It was for them an unfortunate introduction to the Promised Land. And, in the case of many of them, it was the end of the promises altogether.

Residents of Oberlin and Wellington banded together to rescue fugitive slave, John Price, from slave-catchers in 1858.

Blacks were counted in small numbers in Cleveland during the 19th century, but one young black man who won public attention and admiration after the Civil War was a native Clevelander named Charles W. Chesnutt.

Chesnutt, who became a teacher at the age of 16, worked briefly as a journlist in New York before returning to Cleveland in 1883 to begin the study of law while working in the office of Judge Samuel Williamson. He graduated at the head of his class and was admitted to the Ohio bar.

Even while immersed in his law studies, Chesnutt had begun writing for the McClure Syndicate and for the *Atlantic Monthly*. The pieces published by the magazine were collected and published by Houghton, Mifflin & Co. in 1899 under the title, *Conjure Woman*.

Chesnutt led a double life, working as a court reporter and continuing to write stories and articles for leading magazines and newspapers. Among his best-known books was *The Life of Frederick Douglass*.

Perhaps Cleveland's best-known black, outside the fields of politics and literature, was an inventor named Garrett A. Morgan.

Morgan, who moved to Cleveland before the turn of the century from his native Claysville, Kentucky, began his career as a janitor in a sewing machine factory. It was there that his genius for invention first manifested itself when he devised a belt fastener for the drive belt of the machines, an improvement that simplified their operation.

By 1912, he and his brother Frank had developed a breathing apparatus that was an early prototype of the gas mask. There was little interest in the device and the invention of the Morgan brothers might have gone unnoticed had it not been for a disastrous explosion in a tunnel being dug under Lake Erie for the city's water intake system. The date was July 24, 1916.

Eleven men were trapped in the shaft which rapidly had filled with noxious fumes and smoke. Ten would-be rescuers who went down the shaft died in the attempt to save the workers.

It wasn't until somebody remembered the Morgan gas mask that the crisis would be met. The two Morgan brothers, carrying a dozen of their devices, went into the tunnel and rescued two of the victims and recovered four bodies.

A gold medal for heroism was presented to Garrett Morgan by the International Association of Fire Chiefs, which also made him an honorary life member.

But Morgan's talent for invention was to branch out in other fields. In 1923, he was granted a patent for a tri-colored traffic signal, hand-operated, that was the prototype of the modern traffic light. His first working model was installed at Vine Street and Mentor Avenue in Willoughby. The General Electric Co. bought rights to the light for $40,000.

Other Morgan inventions were an electric curling comb and a pellet to be put in cigarettes to extinguish them when they had been smoked down to a certain size, thus preventing fire in case the smoker fell asleep.

Almost forgotten among the many Morgan accomplishments was the fact that he founded a tabloid newspaper, *The Post,* which merged with *The Call* in 1929 to form the modern *Call & Post.* The inventor died in Cleveland on July 26, 1963 at the age of 86.

24. The way it was

Weddell House Hotel, circa 1859 — Abraham Lincoln slept here

There never was a dull moment in Cleveland between 1850 and 1900. Life was a steady stream of exciting events, but occasionally a happening would rise high above the others.

One of these was the stopover in Cleveland of President-elect Abraham Lincoln on Feb. 15, 1861 on his way to his inauguration in Washington, due to take place less than three weeks later.

Lincoln spoke some carefully-worded thoughts from the balcony of the Weddell House on lower Superior Avenue, at the corner of W. 6th Street.

Little more than four years later, Lincoln made a return trip to Cleveland, in the spring of 1865; this time as the martyred president. He was displayed in state under a pavilion hastily erected on Public Square. It was estimated that 100,000 persons moved past his coffin, and that of his son, Willie, which lay at his feet.

Sixteen short years after that sorrowful scene, another martyred president lay in state on Public Square. This time it was James A. Garfield, a native of Mentor, nearby — close enough to Cleveland that the city thought of him as a native son. President Garfield, in office only a few months, was shot by an assassin on July 2, 1881 and died on Sept. 19.

The news of Garfield's death put Cleveland in mourning. Most of the downtown buildings and the statuary in Public Square were draped in black. Cannons placed along the lakefront bluff boomed intermittently through the night following his death.

Garfield's body arrived by train in Cleveland on the morning of Saturday, Sept. 24. It was borne, with the measured tread of military escort, to the high catafalque underneath a flowered and draped pavilion on Public Square, where it remained on public display for two days, attended by an honor guard of the Cleveland Grays. Two ex-presidents, Ulysses S. Grant and Rutherford B. Hayes, came to pay their respects. Generals Sherman, Sheridan and Hancock were among the mourners.

The president's burial was in Lake View Cemetery, near the Forest Hill estate of John D. Rockefeller. Not until 1890, nine years after his death, was the late president permanently entombed in an imposing 180-foot high stone memorial built at a cost of $225,000, contributed mostly by schoolchildren of the 44 states.

The dedication of the Garfield Memorial was attended by many celebrities led by President Benjamin Harrison, another Ohioan. That great memorial quickly became one of Cleveland's most attractive tourist sites. In more recent times, a tall obelisk was erected near the Garfield Tomb, over the grave of John D. Rockefeller.

Public Square always has served as the center of city life in Cleveland, but never more actively than it did in the late years of the 19th century, when it also was the center of considerable controversy.

Abraham Lincoln's body lies in state in Cleveland on Public Square, 1865. A Cleveland-built locomotive, "The Nashville" (inset), pulled the funeral train of the country's slain president.

Catafalque of James A. Garfield, U.S. president and Cleveland's adopted native son. From nearby Mentor, Ohio, young Garfield, left, and his cousin William Boynton (inset) were students at Hiram College in 1852.

There were those, on the one side, who claimed that the intent of the city's founders had been to create a 10-acre park, free of vehicular traffic. In opposition were others, especially merchants, who held that the Square ought to be a practical and utilitarian piece of land criss-crossed by two important thoroughfares, Superior Avenue and Ontario Street.

The park proponents had won the upper hand and placed a fence around the Square by 1860, when a handsome memorial to Oliver Hazard Perry, the hero of the Battle of Lake Erie, was erected in the geographical center of the downtown commons. An iron picket fence with gas lamps at each corner surrounded the 25-foot high statue chiseled out of Italian marble.

But the commercial interests on August 21, 1867 won their fight to extend Superior Avenue and Ontario Street through the public park, dividing the area thereby into four quadrants. Commodore Perry's monument was moved from its central location to the southeast quadrant — but not for long. Proponents of a large Civil War monument succeeded in evicting the hero of the War of 1812 from Public Square altogether in favor of a giant Soldiers and Sailors Monument that was erected in its place at a cost of $280,000.

Garfield Monument in Lakeview Cemetery, circa 1895

Lithograph of the Soldiers and Sailors Monument, dedicated July 4, 1894

The new Soldiers and Sailors Monument, designed by Levi Scofield, was dedicated on July 4, 1894. The Perry Memorial was shifted to a site in Wade Park, then to a lakeside site in Gordon Park, and, finally, left the city to take up an honored position in Perry, Ohio.

Even criss-crossed by busy streets, the Public Square retained some of its beauty and held an honored place in a city that had not lost as yet all of its small-town charm. An eyewitness of the city scene in those days, S. J. Kelly of *The Plain Dealer,* described the Public Square of the 1870s and the 1880s in a story of reminiscence printed by the newspaper on Jan. 9, 1948.

"Cleveland was a different city then," wrote Kelly. "The Square, with its shading trees, surrounding buildings and

The 1880s in Cleveland, with horse-drawn streetcar (above) and Forest City House Hotel

blackened Post Office, standing proudly on the site of the ponderous sculptured Federal Building of today, might be termed almost rustic.

"With easy moving, tinkling horsecars drawn mostly by small, black mules (they would stop anywhere at the raising of your finger, except on upgrades), with Superior Street from Water Street (W. 9th) to Erie (E. 9th) dotted here and there with buggies drawn by trotting horses, the town resembled an enlarged county seat.

"Even the long Forest City House, with its cupola tower and fancy iron two-storied balcony entrance, lent an air of a shady breathing spot so common to small Ohio towns.

"Many will remember the two-way iron stairway where the hotel cornered on Superior that led to justice courts; Downie's Wallpaper store that faced the Square; Likly, McDonald & Rockett's trunk store; the narrow wooden stairs that led up to Dr. Thayer's office; Theodore Closse's tailor shop; King's harness shop, and Diebolt's Alley, running south through to Champlain Street. These stores were in the hotel that stood on the southwest side of the Square facing east.

"A model like steamer revolved in a pool across the street from the main entrance (to the hotel). Its wooden figures of captain, crew and passengers standing on the deck jerked backward and forward at each tip of its walking beam. The model is said to have been constructed by Capt. Lorenzo Kelsey, mayor of the city in 1848, in his later days. Its worn hull is on exhibition now in the museum of the Western Reserve Historical Society."

Leading downtown business establishments in the 1870s included Chandler & Rudd's, Smith & Curtiss's store, Babcock & Hurd, wholesale grocers; Bendict & Ruedy, purveyors of fine furs, with sealskins a specialty; department stores like Mabley & Hull (forerunner of Hull & Dutton), and Hower & Higbee, forerunner of the Higbee Company.

"Professor" D. Mayer had a "select" conservatory of dancing and deportment in the Weisgerber Block at Prospect and Brownell (E. 14th) Street, and one of the leading shoe dealers downtown was Smith, Dodd & Co.

Downtown would not have been complete, of course, without saloons and places of entertainment. A man named Andy McHugh had just opened (in 1876) a new billiard parlor and saloon at Euclid and Sheriff (E. 4th) Street, and it was hailed as "a superb place" by a reporter who covered the big premiere.

"Money has been lavishly expended," raved the newspaper piece. "The parlors occupy the first floor of the Waverly Block and the whole of the second floor of the Windsor and Waverly Blocks," and "those who have traveled extensively had never seen anywhere so superb an establishment."

McHugh's billiard parlor and saloon had settled in a strategic location at Euclid and Sheriff because it was the heart of Cleveland's restaurant and theatrical district in those years. Largest of all the entertainment facilities in the city was the Euclid Avenue Opera House, which, when completed in 1875 on the southeast corner of the intersection, was acknowledged as one of the finest theaters in the United States.

The new Opera House, a 4-story blue-sandstone-front building with a central tower over an arched entrance, was almost a direct copy of Edwin Booth's Theater in New York. The entrance was two stories high and featured heavily carved folding doors. The stage opening proscenium arch was 45 feet wide and 39 feet high. The frescoed ceiling was 77 feet from the orchestra floor, and a center dome rose 20 feet higher.

One of the marvels of the Opera House and a sight that townspeople never got tired of admiring, was the theater's great chandelier. It was, in its time, the largest prismatic fixture in the United States — 25 feet in length, 14 feet in circumference; two tons in weight, with countless glass chains, festoons and pendants stretched upward in tiers. It carried 325 gas jets. Here was another wonder of the time: an automatic dial control regulated the 325 gas jets, turning their lights on or off, up in intensity or down low.

The moving genius behind the construction of the Euclid Avenue Opera House was John A. Ellsler, the leading pioneer of Cleveland's theatrical life. Ellsler, nicknamed "Uncle John," first came to prominence in the city as actor-manager of the Academy of Music on Bank (W. 6th) Street, just north of Superior, in the early 1850s. It was, at the time, the city's leading theater, and possibly the best dramatic school in the United States. Regular players at the Academy of Music were John Wilkes Booth, Edwin Booth, and James O'Neill, a great actor in his own right and the father of playwright Eugene O'Neill.

After more than two decades running the Academy of Music, Ellsler won financing for the new Euclid Avenue Opera House.

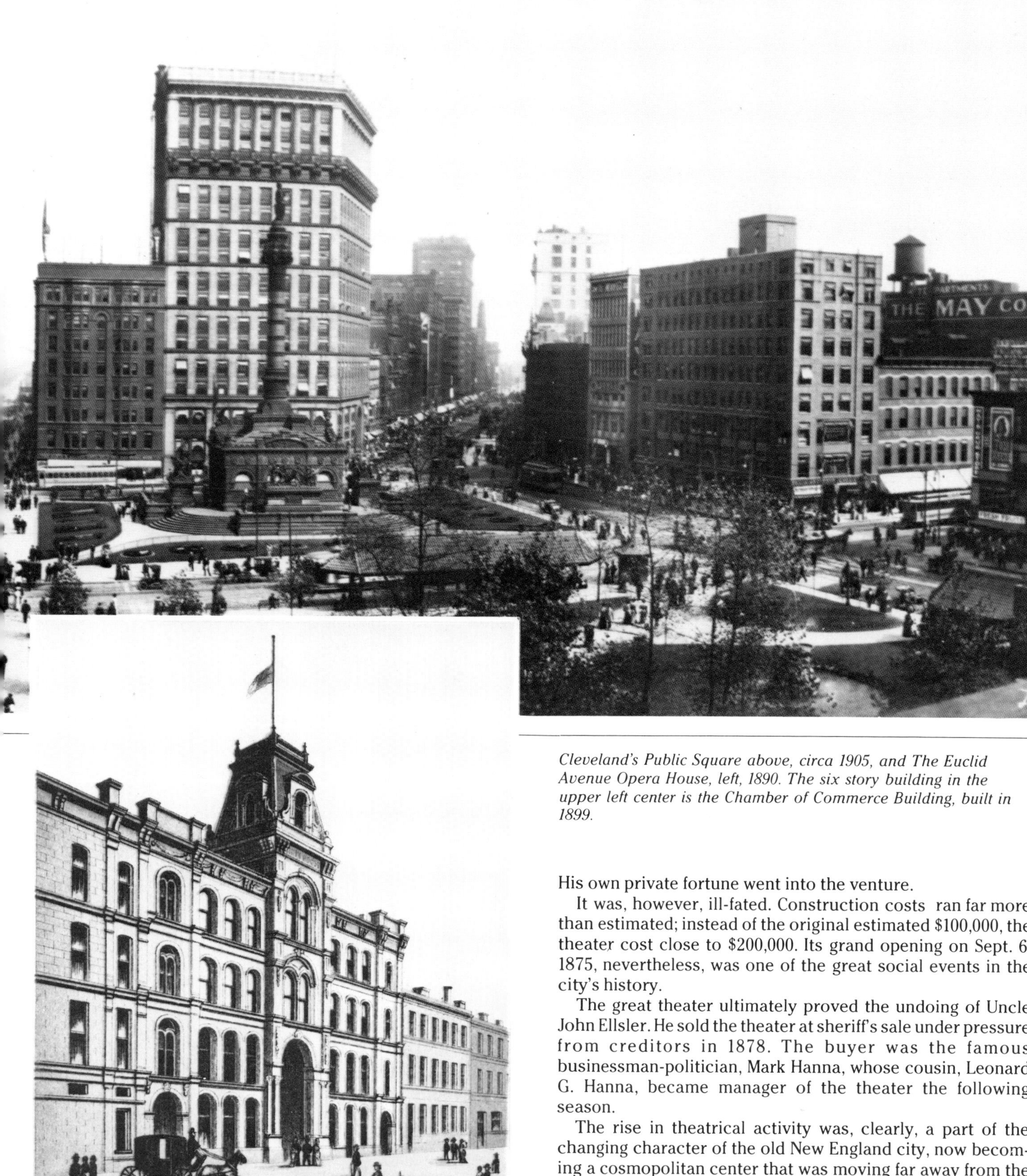

Cleveland's Public Square above, circa 1905, and The Euclid Avenue Opera House, left, 1890. The six story building in the upper left center is the Chamber of Commerce Building, built in 1899.

His own private fortune went into the venture.

It was, however, ill-fated. Construction costs ran far more than estimated; instead of the original estimated $100,000, the theater cost close to $200,000. Its grand opening on Sept. 6, 1875, nevertheless, was one of the great social events in the city's history.

The great theater ultimately proved the undoing of Uncle John Ellsler. He sold the theater at sheriff's sale under pressure from creditors in 1878. The buyer was the famous businessman-politician, Mark Hanna, whose cousin, Leonard G. Hanna, became manager of the theater the following season.

The rise in theatrical activity was, clearly, a part of the changing character of the old New England city, now becoming a cosmopolitan center that was moving far away from the old Puritanical principles that so long had dominated life in the Lake Erie port.

Cleveland's first professional entertainment had come about in 1820, when the town of some 500 population was visited by its first theatrical troop led by an actor named Blanchard. Performances then were given in the ballroom of the Cleveland House on Public Square, which, in the absence of a theater, served as the center of entertainment.

Academy of Music on Bank (now West Sixth) Street and (left) John A. Ellsler, pioneer leader of Cleveland's theatrical life

The first real theaters were a second-floor facility in a building at the corner of Superior and Union Lane (W. 10th) and a place called Italian Hall on the top floor of a 3-story building on Water (W. 9th) Street, built in the 1830s. They were followed by Mechanics' Hall at Prospect and Ontario Streets in 1839; the Water Street Theater in 1848, a fine 1,000-seat auditorium that was destroyed by fire in 1850; Watson's Hall, built in 1840 on Superior Street — renamed Melodeon Hall in 1845; and Brainard's Hall in 1860, which became Brainard's Opera House and the Globe Theater before it was torn down in 1880.

Among the unsuccessful theaters of the time in Cleveland, incidentally, was one opened by master showman P. T. Barnum in the 1860s. It stood in the Kelley Block on Superior Street, opposite the end of W. 6th Street.

The Academy of Music was partly destroyed by fire on June 30, 1889, but was rebuilt. Three years later, on Sept. 8, 1892, it was all but destroyed by fire again. It was rebuilt a third time, but it was no use; the theater was dead.

Fire also claimed the great Euclid Avenue Opera House in 1892. Sen. Hanna rebuilt the theater and it continued for a while as a center of the city's theatrical life. Its successor was today's Hanna Theater, built by Mark Hanna's son, Dan R. Hanna, on E. 14th Street, south of Euclid, in the budding Playhouse Square district. It continues as the city's leading legitimate theater.

25. Out of the mud and dark

A White Streamer on a road in Bay Village, a western suburb of Cleveland, 1910.

There was a time when travel within Cleveland proper was more difficult than a long distance trip to another city.

To go to Buffalo by steamship, say, was to enjoy a certain leisure and comfort on the lake cruise. Or to go to Cincinnati was to experience a rather attractive, slow-paced journey through picturesque countryside aboard a smooth-riding canal packet.

But to go across town on the hard seat of a jouncing, jolting hard-wheeled wagon that shook and swayed, bucked and bounced, as it made its way over rutted, dusty, muddy streets! Ah, that was what brought the pinched look of discomfort to the faces of the city's people through so many years as the community strove for maturity.

Efforts to improve the main streets by spreading gravel on them were undertaken and did offer temporary relief before the gravel sank into the mud and disappeared.

Macadamizing was another alleviant, but no solution. The best solution seemed to be the building of plank roads. After all, the greatest stand of trees the world ever had known was all about, free for the taking.

With the half-century mark approaching, the young city in 1842 began the job of laying planks on its main thoroughfares to ease the travel situation. The two most heavily-traveled streets were Superior Street and the River Road and they were the first to be planked. A Cleveland journalist, James Harrison Kennedy, described the operation.

"The plan pursued," he wrote, "was somewhat primitive in character. The 'paving' consisted of the laying down of heavy planking crosswise of the street. These planks were of use when new and while held firmly in place, but when worn out or loosened, the condition of those who travelled over them was not one to envy. Down on River Street, the floods would sometimes rise and float the paving off into the Cuyahoga."

It was not until the use of cobblestone pavements in the

streets, begun after 1850, that the city began to emerge as a reasonably easy place in which to get around. But even with the best of conditions underfoot, nighttime movement was very much a matter of groping and thrashing about in the dark.

The big innovation of the time was the lighting of streets by natural gas lamps, but this improvement was slow to come, even though the Cleveland Gas Light & Coke Company was organized on Feb. 6, 1846. It was not until 1848 that the laying of gas pipes began and the installation of the gas lights got underway.

As weak as the gaslight illumination was, the improvement was notable and beneficial. The street lamps did cast a light that was better than no light at all, and the pale, yellow glow of the gaslights in the streets was a cheerful sight to the people of the time.

Even better lights were in store in this old battle of man against the darkness, to be sure. They came about in Cleveland not many years after the gaslights first split the nighttime barrier, thanks to the works of a brilliant Cleveland engineer named Charles Francis Brush.

Brush, a graduate mining engineer and analytical chemist, had become deeply interested in the possibilities of electricity; his experiments, in time, probed deeply into the mysteries of the subject, especially as they related to theories of illumination through electricity.

By the springtime of 1879, Brush's attempt to develop an arc light and dynamo had reached the stage where he was willing to perform a public demonstration of his invention in operation.

The Cleveland Telegraph Supply Company, with whom Brush was associated, installed several 150-foot-high poles, each topped with twelve lamps of 2,000 horsepower, around

Paving Broadway (near East 55th Street) with granite blocks, November 1919, left.

Charles F. Brush, above right, a pioneer in the field of electricity, developed an electric generating windmill, seen in his own yard in 1889.

Public Square. It was announced well in advance that the lamps would be switched on after sunset on the night of April 29th.

The news was received incredulously for miles around the city, but, skeptical or not, thousands of people decided not to take a chance on missing a miracle. Public Square was crowded with people from as far away as southern Ohio and Pennsylvania long before the magic moment arrived. Newspaper stories had warned of the blinding light that might be expected, and many of the spectators carried pieces of smoked glass to shield their eyes from the man-made glare.

Inventor Brush gave the signal for the lights to be turned on at 8:05 p.m. One of the lamps immediately gave off a purplish flickering light. Then, one by one, each of the other lamps turned the same colorful glow. And as the minutes ticked by, the lights grew stronger and brighter and white, gradually losing their purplish tint and taking on a strength that cast a perceptible illumination over the entire Public Square below while the crowd of upturned faces audibly murmured its appreciation and awe.

Finally there was a spontaneous outburst of cheers and applause from the onlookers. The people knew instinctively that they had been witnesses to one of the truly historic moments in man's upward struggle out of darkness.

The band of the Cleveland Grays played a rousing series of musical numbers and cannons that had been lined up on the lakeside bluff fired a long series of salvos in celebration.

The electric light at last had arrived, and the first streets in the world to receive its illumination were the ones on Cleveland's Public Square.

26. The Centennial

The cannonading in celebration of the first outdoor electric light in Cleveland was in the best tradition of a happy humanity; one which compels people in the throes of rejoicing to make as much noise as they possibly can.

Outside of a few spirited New Year's Eve parties here and there, the best example of noisy celebrations in America is to be found in the annual 4th of July program, which usually runs the gamut from loud orators to loud fireworks.

The Independence Day of 1876 was no ordinary 4th of July. It was the 100th anniversary of the Declaration of Independence, and the whole nation, still young and bright-eyed, was caught up in the convulsion of patriotic emotion that guaranteed one of the noisiest celebrations within the capability of the aroused people.

The capital of New Connecticut was determined not to be outdone by any city anywhere in expressing its love of country. The rented City Hall on Superior Street was bedecked with red-white-and-blue bunting from the sidewalk level to the rooftops. Flags flew everywhere.

But Cleveland was not about to wait until the dawn of Independence Day to begin celebrating. A proper welcome was arranged to greet the historic anniversary at midnight of July 3rd. What happened at that critical moment is described by the journalist-historian, James Harrison Kennedy.

"On the stroke of twelve," he wrote, "the steam whistles all over the city, broke into one vast chorus of echoing notes. A great cauldron of oil on the Public Square was set ablaze and the deep boom of the guns was heard. Before the echo died away, a perfect tornado of sound swept in from all quarters, and made the very foundations of the earth seem to shake. The alarm of the fire bells cleft the air with sudden sound, and a dozen church towers gave answer, while the hoarse voices of the steam monsters, the banging of the firearms, the popping of firecrackers, and the shouts of thousands of excited people, were added to the chorus, while every now and then the deep boom of the cannon came in as a heavy accompaniment."

The Independence Day celebration itself had to be something of an anti-climax after that midnight outburst, although it did feature an unusual event: the dedication of a newly-installed steel flagstaff on Public Square. It was the gift of one of the city's leading industrialists, Henry Chisholm, on behalf of his Cleveland Rolling Mill Company.

A poem written especially for the occasion by F. T. Wallace was read at the dedication ceremony:

The banner that a hundred years
Has waved above our good ship's keel,
Upheld by oak or mast or pine,
Now proudly floats from staff of steel.

Soon Lakeview, Woodland, Riverside
Will keep the graves where kindred kneel —
Of all who now salute the stars
That wave above that staff of steel.

And in remoter ages still,
The antiquary's worthy zeal
Will note the tombs and mural stones
Of those who gave that staff of steel!

The heightened observance of the special Independence Day was, in a sense, a kind of warming up for another big anniversary celebration just ahead — the centennial of Cleveland itself.

There was much to celebrate.

Cleveland, by 1896, had become the nation's 10th largest city! And it had gained this important position from a standing start; from a clearing in the forest, far from the amenities of civilization, ringed by wild animals; a wilderness settlement whose founder had gone so far as to predict in ponderous manner that the new town someday could have a population as great as that of Windham, Connecticut (Population: 1,400).

The Cleveland of 1896 already boasted more than 250,000 people within its fold. It gloried in a skyline that already was pierced by a few prototypes of modern skyscrapers like the Perry-Payne Building and the Williamson Building.

It was a boomtown that exulted in its smoke-darkened industrial valley, that cheered the noisy trains whose tracks scarred the whole city, and turned approving eyes on the tall, belching smokestacks that had sprung up everywhere in replacement of the trees.

It was a city that was ripe and ready to celebrate its rare

Early Settlers Association at the log cabin erected in 1896 on the Public Square during the city's centennial.

good fortune, and the anniversary of Moses Cleaveland's landing, July 22nd, was the perfect excuse. The city's 100th birthday party would begin on that date and continue until September 10th.

The focal point of the celebration, as usual, was the Public Square. A large log cabin was built on the northeast quadrant by a citizen named Bolivar Butts as a reminder of the city's pioneering past, while, more impressive, a great centennial arch not much smaller than the Arc de Triomphe was erected straddling Superior Avenue.

The great arch, some 75 feet high, was outlined in electric lights even though they still were an uncommon luxury in American life. And with a touch of 20th century showmanship, it was arranged that President Grover Cleveland, a distant relative of Moses Cleaveland, would join in the opening of the centennial celebration by turning on the electric lights of the anniversary arch.

When the magic moment arrived, President Cleveland, at his summer home in Buzzard's Bay, Massachusetts, pressed a button that switched on the hundreds of lights.

Thousands of people gathered in Public Square roared with appreciation when the mighty arch burst into light. There hadn't been a moment like that since Brush's first display of outdoor electricity several years before.

It was the beginning of a centennial in which Clevelanders set new high marks for oratory and self-congratulation — a warm, happy look backwards and a confident, optimistic look forwards.

Unloading ore on the Cuyahoga River, 1889

Into the twentieth century

Mayor Tom L. Johnson and son Loftin (above) lead a 1902 parade in a Winton "Red Devil" automobile. Johnson pitched the first ball at Brookside Park, 1903.

27. Giants at work

Marcus Alonzo Hanna in Washington, D.C.

The old riddle about cause and effect is especially perplexing when any attempt is made to determine whether great men are the product of their times and their environment, or whether it is the outstanding people who bring about the extraordinary climate in which they thrive and grow great.

Whatever the answer — and it probably is a mixture of both schools of thought — it is an unarguable fact that in Tom L. Johnson and Marcus Alonzo Hanna, Cleveland could claim two of the greatest men of America at the turn of the century.

They were adversaries, these two, and yet they were similar in many ways.

Each was the product of distinguished lineage. Each was an outgoing personality. Each was a highly successful businessman. Each had become a tycoon in the field of streetcar transportation. Each had achieved national recognition in politics.

It was the streetcar system connection that first brought the careers of these two giants into a headon collision.

Even as Cleveland was struggling through the muddy streets and the primitive plank roads of 1859, the city's first street railway was making ready to give Clevelanders their first really comfortable mode of in-town transportation.

It was the East Cleveland Railway Company, organized in 1859 and placed in operation in 1860. Its first line was between Bank (W. 6th) Street and Willson (E. 55th) Avenue.

Electric streetcars on the East Cleveland Railway: the City's first (right), on Garden Street, 1884; and on Euclid Avenue 1890.

This system of horse-drawn streetcars was the outgrowth of earlier, cruder attempts to transport city residents through streets that were hardly traversible by foot. The Cleveland & Newburgh Railroad in the 1830s had operated over wooden tracks on Euclid Avenue, between the Newburgh stone quarries to Public Square.

Omnibus lines, whose vehicles were heavy wooden wagons with hard benches for the passengers, did their best to meet the transportation needs of the city through the 1850s and into the 1860s.

But the East Cleveland Railway Company, operating horse-drawn streetcars rolling on iron rails, was the actual forerunner of the streetcar systems that served Cleveland so efficiently into the middle of the 20th century. The mode of transportation it offered was so much more comfortable and reliable than any hitherto developed that it won immediate acceptance.

By the time Tom L. Johnson arrived in Cleveland in 1879, there were many competing streetcar lines in the city and their routes criss-crossed in a web of confusion. The mess was made to order for his genius.

Johnson's credentials were impressive. At the age of 17, he was the superintendent of the street railway in Louisville, Ky., and had invented the world's first coin fare box. At 22, he was owner of the transit system in Indianapolis, Ind. By the time he was 25, he was a millionaire with transit holdings in St. Louis, Detroit, and in Brooklyn, N.Y. And, withal, he was restlessly looking for new worlds to conquer.

When a business trip brought him to Cleveland in 1879, he was immediately taken by the pretty, booming city with a confusion of streetcar lines. He concluded immediately that this was the particular world he wanted most to conquer. He bought one of the troubled transit lines, the Brooklyn Street Railway on the West Side, and became a Clevelander.

Even as Johnson was expanding his streetcar line from a neighborhood service into a citywide operation, a major innovation in street surface transportation was about to be unveiled in Cleveland.

It was the world's first electric streetcar, and it was placed in service by the East Cleveland Street Railway Company on July 26, 1884. The tracks of the new kind of self-powered vehicle were strap rails laid on wooden stringers about 8 inches deep. A brush arc light generator in the Euclid Avenue car barns was the source of the system's electrical power.

The electric streetcar at once revolutionized city rail transportation everywhere, and it threw the highly competitive Cleveland situation into a fierce gang fight for survival.

A direct result was the consolidation of the several competing systems and, eventually, thanks to Johnson's determination, the emergence of the biggest transportation bargain in the country — a street railway system that offered its customers 3-cent fares.

During this quarter-century of transit wars, Johnson's system and his personal philosophy conflicted with the streetcar system and the political beliefs of the famous and powerful Mark Hanna. The rivalry between Johnson and Hanna widened, deepened and became a personal duel.

Johnson, as he moved closer to the political field, had become a disciple of economist Henry George and had espoused his single tax theory. He turned away from his business career, finally, and set out to apply the idealistic economic and social principles of Henry George from a political base. In effect, he was determined to beat Hanna at his own game.

The people of Cleveland found Johnson a new kind of politician and a most appealing public figure, straightforward and idealistic. They elected him to the U.S. House of Representa-

Real estate developers Oris Paxton Van Sweringen (far left) and his brother, Mantis James Van Sweringen developed city-suburb Shaker Heights. Above, construction of Shaker Square in the late 1920s.

tives in 1890. After a single term, he decided to make a bid for the job of Cleveland mayor. He was elected on April 1, 1901.

It was the first of four successive terms in City Hall for Tom L. Johnson — a career in which he set the all-time high standards for political performance and demonstrated a civic statesmanship that caused Cleveland to be hailed nationally as "The City on a Hill." It was a recognition of the high ideals, honesty, and dedication of the businessman-turned-politician.

One of the lasting achievements of the Johnson Administration was the physical renaissance of the central city, which was blighted by tenderloin districts, congestion, and tumbledown neighborhoods.

Mayor Johnson commissioned the illustrious Daniel Burnham, architect and civic planner, to replace Cleveland's urban ugliness with utilitarian beauty. The result was The Group Plan, a grand design for the central city which called for the replacement of the hovels and ramshackle business establishments from Ontario Street east to Erie (E. 9th) Street, from the bluff north of Lakeside Avenue south to Superior Avenue.

Within this large area, the Burnham plan called for the creation of a 40-acre commons to be known as the Mall. It was to be flanked by classic structures of civic importance, such as the Public Hall and the Board of Education Building along the east side of the park-like area. To the south of the Mall would be the new Federal Building, a new Public Library, a building for *The Plain Dealer*. Along Lakeside Avenue would be the new County Courthouse and the new City Hall. Between these two would be the centerpiece of the ambitious plan, a new railroad terminal.

The long-term plan was never completed, but even in its unfinished state it turned much of downtown into a place of enduring beauty. The plan was frustrated by two Cleveland real estate developers, O. P. and M. J. Van Sweringen, who were launched on an enterprise unique in American urban history: the creation of a new city-suburb, Shaker Heights.

In the course of achieving their goal, the Van Sweringen brothers were drawn into so many side ventures that they emerged as two of America's leading business tycoons. At one time they controlled as many as 24 railroads with 27,000 miles of track. Altogether, their empire included some 231 companies with assets of $4 billion.

The fantastic network of railroads in the Van Sweringen system grew out of a very simple need essential to the success of Shaker Heights — the building of a rapid transit streetcar line from the suburb to Public Square.

Automobiles were not common in 1906 when the Vans purchased the 1,366 acres of land (formerly a Shaker sect colony) to the southeast of the City as the site for their new suburb. Good rail transportation was a must if the suburban development was to succeed.

To acquire the right-of-way for the Shaker rapid line, the brothers were compelled to purchase the ailing Nickel Plate Railroad. Then, as the dominoes began toppling in earnest, they had to acquire other railroads to make the Nickel Plate a profitable operation. Eventually they had to provide a downtown terminal to take care of the rapid transit line and the railroads.

The result was a Van Sweringen plan for a downtown union terminal complex on the southwest corner of Public Square

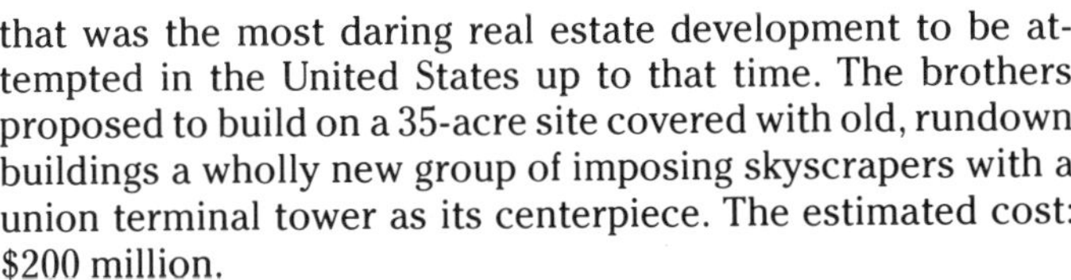

that was the most daring real estate development to be attempted in the United States up to that time. The brothers proposed to build on a 35-acre site covered with old, rundown buildings a wholly new group of imposing skyscrapers with a union terminal tower as its centerpiece. The estimated cost: $200 million.

Not until Rockefeller Center in New York was built a few years later would the Van Sweringens' Cleveland development be outdone in size or cost.

The Union Terminal itself, originally planned as a 25-story building, gradually evolved on the planning board into a 52-story Terminal Tower, 708 feet high; the tallest building in the world outside of New York City for a long time.

Some 2,200 separate structures had to be razed to clear the site for the new union terminal, the Higbee Company store, the Cleveland Hotel, the Medical Arts Building and the Republic Building. Old streets such as Chaplain, Hill, and Diebolt's Alley were swept away. Portions of three cemeteries had to be purchased and the bodies transferred to new sites.

Among the buildings razed were such historic structures as the American House on Superior Avenue, and the Forest City House on the corner of Superior and the Public Square. The Diebolt Brewery and the Gehring Brewery both went down the

Above, pavers work on Euclid Avenue, in front of the old Sullivan Hotel, 1902. Middle, a traffic tower stood in the center of the intersection of East Ninth Street and Euclid Avenue in 1918, a policeman in the tower controlled the lights. Left, a streetcar strike hit Cleveland in 1899.

Cleveland Terminal Tower under construction in 1927

drain. The main building of the Ohio Bell Telephone Co. was torn down. So was Stein's Cafe, the Palisade Hotel, and even the Central Police Station on Champlain Street.

Supporters of Tom Johnson's Group Plan fought the Van Sweringen placement of the railroad station on the Square, but when the New York Central Railroad endorsed the Van Sweringen proposal, the victory went to the brother-developers.

Clearing of the terminal site began in 1920. Actual construction work began in 1923. The entire complex was not completed until 1930.

The effect of the unprecedented building venture was to change the face of the Public Square and its adjacent neighborhood to the south and east just as radically as the partially-completed Group Plan had altered more than 100 acres to the northeast of the Square.

Each of the plans, while in conflict, contributed greatly to the creation of the modern downtown. What was built, in either instance, was of high quality and was certainly enduring.

Surprisingly enough, the City Hall that was erected on Lakeside Avenue as part of the Group Plan is unique as the only one ever to be owned by the city.

Until Tom Johnson directed construction of the classic building that still serves as the seat of government, Cleveland had gone along using rented quarters for more than a century!

28. Sports in the spotlight

Sneaking a peek at the 1920 World Series at League Park's Lexington gate

It is a matter of record that the first professional baseball team in America was the Cincinnati Red Stockings, who abandoned their amateur status in 1869 — but Cleveland's baseballers were not far behind.

The Forest City club, representing Cleveland, was one of 10 teams that made up the first national baseball league, organized under the formal name of the National Association of Professional Baseball Players on March 4, 1871.

The first professional baseball game played in Cleveland was part of that pioneer league's opening play. The Forest City team played the Chicago White Stockings on May 11, 1871, at the corner of Willson Avenue (E. 55th Street) and Garden Street.

The Forest City club actually dated to 1865, when the team was formed for amateur play, and that date generally is accepted as the beginning of organized baseball in Cleveland. But the game itself had caught the fancy of the city's youngsters as early as 1841, when makeshift baseball diamonds were laid out on Public Square and were used until 1856. By that time the games were drawing such large crowds that the sport was considered a public nuisance by many and the police chased the players to more remote fields of play.

The historic professional opener in May, 1871, was an uproarious one that set the tone for the future of the sport in Cleveland.

The trouble, as it so often does in baseball to this day, centered about the umpire.

The names of five possible choices for umpire had been submitted to the Cleveland team captain, left fielder Pabor, and he unfortunately had selected a man named James L. Haynie.

Mr. Haynie, it turned out, was a writer for the *Chicago Times* and had more than a passing affection for the hometown White Stockings. There was no doubt, as the game progressed, that he was willing to let his personal bias influence his umpiring judgment to a scandalous extent.

After six consecutive decisions by Umpire Haynie went against the Forest City team, the outraged Clevelanders walked off the playing field in the 8th inning, announcing they were going to appeal the game.

It had been a close game up to that point, in spite of the umpire (or perhaps because of him), with Cleveland leading

The Cleveland American League Baseball Club — 1920 world's champions. The team wears black armbands to mourn the death of fellow player Ray Chapman (inset), first player to die from injuries on the field in the 50-year history of the game.

most of the way. But the official forfeit score that went into the books gave the contest to Chicago by a tally of 18 to 10.

In the decades following the organization of the National League in 1871, professional baseball — and its Cleveland representatives — went through an unstable formative period. The membership of the league and its rival, the American Association, changed from year to year.

Cleveland dropped out of the National League in 1872 because of financial problems, returned to the league in 1879, dropped out again in 1884, joined the American Association in 1887, and returned to the National League again in 1888.

That latest affiliation with the National League saw Cleveland represented by a team named the Spiders, certainly an unusual identification, even in sports. Two years later, in 1890, Clevelanders could root for two teams: the Spiders in the National League and a team in the Brotherhood League, also known as the Players League. The latter association was an interesting, but short-lived, experiment in profit-sharing by players and management.

That was a time of success and glory in Cleveland baseball history. The Spiders fielded a powerhouse team in the National League from 1891 through 1896 and won the Temple Cup, forerunner of the World Series, in 1895. The team that Cleveland defeated in the post-season playoff that year represented Pittsburgh, and its manager was a very young Cornelius McGillicuddy — better known as Connie Mack.

The glory trail turned into a cul-de-sac in 1898 when the Cleveland owner, Frank DeHaas Robison, broke up the powerful Spider team by transferring some of its best players to a new franchise that he had acquired in St. Louis. Two of the stars who were removed from the Cleveland scene were the immortal Denton True (Cy) Young, perhaps the greatest baseball pitcher of all time, and his outstanding catcher, Chief Zimmer.

The sorry Spiders, stripped of their best talent, staggered through the 1899 National League schedule in such gloriously inept style as to merit consideration as perhaps the worst professional baseball team of all time. The final record of the Spiders that year was 20 victories and 134 defeats.

Cleveland sports fans obviously were ready for a new deal by the time that season ended, and they got it from a pair of young businessmen of the city, Charles W. Somers and John F. Kilfoyl. Those two financed the organization of a new ball club and entered it in the newly-formed American League. The team was known initially as the Cleveland Blues, but the name was changed in 1903 to the Cleveland Napoleons, or "Naps," in honor of the club's great second baseman, Napoleon Lajoie.

It was a good baseball team that wore the livery of the Naps. The players included such stars as Elmer Flick, Bill Bernhard and Addie Joss, and their field performances thrilled the fans and left their mark in the record books. But the team had one serious failing: it couldn't win a pennant. The closest the Naps came to that glorious goal was in 1908, when the team lost by four percentage points.

With the departure of Napoleon Lajoie in 1915, the team was renamed the Cleveland Indians. One story is that it was given that name because one of the players was an Indian named Sockalexis, but it is not verified by the records.

A new owner, Sunny Jim Dunn, took over the team that year and one of his first moves turned out to be his very best — the purchase of the holdout star center fielder of the Boston Red Sox, Tris Speaker.

Speaker, nicknamed the Gray Eagle, became the playing manager of the Indians in 1919, and led the club in 1920 to Cleveland's first American League pennant, followed by a victory over the Brooklyn Dodgers in the World Series.

It was a spectacular season that left the baseball world gasping, and the post-season championship playoff was fully as incredible. Three teams — Cleveland, New York and Chicago — staged such a close race for the pennant that the issue was not decided until the very end of the season.

The most sensational on-the-field occurrence of the season happened in New York on the afternoon of August 16th, when Ray Chapman, star shortstop of the Indians, was killed by a pitched ball thrown by Carl Mays of the Yankees. The pitch struck Chapman in the temple. He died in the hospital the following morning — the first player to die on the field in the 50-year history of the game.

The following month, on Sept. 28th, with the race still undecided, a Chicago grand jury returned indictments against eight White Sox players for complicity in the fixing of the 1919 World Series. The scandal all but destroyed the Chicago team and, in the few games that remained, the Indians went on to win the 1920 pennant.

Pitcher Jim Bagby won 31 games that year. Pitcher George Uhle jumped from the Cleveland sandlots to a starring role with the Indians. Pitcher Ray Caldwell, a victim of alcoholism, made a sensational comeback to win 20 games. Shortstop Joe Sewell, fresh from the University of Alabama campus as a replacement for the dead Ray Chapman, proved superb, and 10 team members sported season batting averages over .300.

The World Series put the cherry on top of the whipped cream. The Indians' Elmer Smith, the right-fielder, hit a grand slam home run over the fence of League Park in the fifth game of the series; it was the first grand-slam homer in World Series history. And in the fifth inning of the same game, Cleveland's second baseman, Bill Wambsganss (better known as "Wamby"), made a sensational catch of a line drive by Brooklyn Pitcher Clarence Mitchell, and turned it into an unassisted triple play — another first in World Series history.

First grand slam homerun in world series history, in Cleveland in 1920, scored Jamieson, Wambsganss, Speaker and Elmer Smith, the batter.

Not until 1948 did the Indians win another American League pennant. That one came under the ownership of Bill Veeck, one of the most colorful and enterprising executives baseball ever has known, who acquired control of the Indians in the middle of the 1946 season.

It took Veeck less than two years to produce a big winner and to set new baseball attendance marks. One of his first moves was to establish the Indians as full-season tenants of the enormous Cleveland Municipal Stadium: capacity, 82,000. Although the Stadium had been available since it was opened in 1933, the Indians had used it only occasionally in a regular season because it was so big that it swallowed up a 10,000 crowd, or even a 20,000 crowd. League Park (also named Dunn Field for some years), an intimate ball park at E. 66th Street and Lexington Avenue, was the regular home of the team.

Veeck changed that, abandoning League Park, and fielded such colorful teams that the fans descended on Cleveland Stadium in record numbers. Baseball's high mark for single game attendance up to that time was set by the Indians with a crowd of 82,781 on June 20, 1948. The 1947 Indians drew 1,521,978 customers. The 1948 team followed with a major league attendance record of 2,620,627. Cleveland, without question, was the baseball capital of the nation in those rapturous postwar years.

The basic reason for the popularity of the Indians, to be sure, was not Veeck's showmanship but the appealing nature of the outstanding baseball team that he had put together in such a short time. The Indians, a fourth-place team in 1947, won the American League pennant in 1948 over the course of such a thrilling season that the World Series victory over the Boston Braves was almost an anti-climax.

Lou Boudreau was the manager and star shortstop of that 1948 team, which included such stars as Joe Gordon, second baseman; Ken Keltner, third baseman; Bob Kennedy, right field; Thurman Tucker, center field, Bob Feller, one of the greatest right-handed pitchers of all time; Dale Mitchell, left field; Eddie Robinson, first base, Jim Hegan, catcher.

There were two other players whose presence on the 1948 squad was important, even though their contributions to the team's winning of the pennant were relatively minor. They were Larry Doby and Satchel Paige, two of baseball's black pioneers.

Doby was the American League's first black player. Veeck, who was determined to break the color line in the junior circuit, in 1947 followed the lead of Branch Rickey, who had hired Jackie Robinson, by putting Doby into an Indian uniform in July of that year.

Paige, already a legendary baseball figure because of his long career and record-setting accomplishments in the Negro baseball leagues, joined the Indians in July, 1948, as the team was pressing ahead towards its first pennant in 28 years.

Victory came hard, just as it had in 1920. The regular 1948 season ended in a stalemate, a dead tie between the Indians and the Boston Red Sox. For the first time in the history of the American League, the pennant had to be decided by a playoff game, which the Indians won behind the heroics of pitcher Gene Bearden and Boudreau himself.

Only a handful of the 1948 champions were members of the Indian team that swept on to a record-setting pennant victory in 1954. Manager-player Boudreau had been replaced in both

Lou Boudreau at bat

his capacities. The new manager was Al Lopez. Al Rosen was the star third-baseman; Jim Hegan, catcher; Bobby Avila, second baseman; George Strickland, shortstop; Dale Mitchell, left fielder. Pitching was the team's strongest point, with three hurlers in the 20-victory group: Early Wynn, Mike Garcia, and Bob Lemon. Bob Feller, still one of the winningest pitchers in baseball, rounded out the staff that included the two best relief pitchers in the game, Don Mossi and Ray Narleski.

Those 1954 Indians racked up the highest total of victories, 111, in American League history, while losing only 43 games. The World Series competition with the New York Giants figured to be a cakewalk for the Indians. Instead, it turned out to be a rout as the Giants unbelievably won four straight from the Cleveland A.L. champions, confounding all the experts.

In the 25 years that followed the 1954 World Series debacle, the Indians dropped from the top rung of baseball competition down to a disappointing level of play. There usually was a lot more action in the executive offices of the club than there was on the diamond as the team ownership passed through a series of hands.

The effect of the changes in ownership on the team was generally debilitating. As the financial structure of the club steadily grew weaker, the farm system shrank almost to nothing, and it became the usual thing for the team to sell off star players to get money. There were so many trades as the management desperately tried to regain its competitive footing that the fans hardly had time to get acquainted with a lineup before it changed.

When the Indians in 1978 came under the ownership of Steve O'Neill, a trucking executive, it was seen as the turning point for the club at last. Gabe Paul, who had left Cleveland to become president of the New York Yankees several years before, returned as general manager of the Indians under the new regime.

By late summer of 1979, the Indians were showing signs of respectability again and a hopeful mood was rising in the ranks of the patient fans. But watchful waiting still was the order of the day.

* * *

One of the most outstanding success stories in the history of the city's professional sports is found in the phenomenal achievements of the Cleveland Browns football team during its years under its founding genius, Paul Brown, coach and general manager. His name, of course, was the inspiration for the team's nickname.

Brown was on military leave from his post as coach of the Ohio State University football team in 1944 when he was approached by a Cleveland taxicab magnate, Arthur B. (Mickey) McBride, and asked to become the general manager and coach of a Cleveland team in the All-America Football Conference.

Interestingly enough, no such team existed, nor was there any such league in operation. The All-America Conference was a loop that was being formed under the direction of Arch Ward, sports editor of the *Chicago Tribune,* as a rival to the National Football League. Ward had stirred McBride's interest in entering a Cleveland team in the proposed league.

One thing that was real was Mickey McBride's ability to finance a professional club, and he proved it at the outset by putting Paul Brown on his payroll at a monthly salary of $1,000 for the duration of the war. The salary would be jumped to $25,000 a year once the war was over and Brown could devote his full time to the job of recruiting players and putting a team on the field.

Brown was assured that he would have full authority and all the money he needed. In return, McBride wanted the best team in football. And that's exactly what he got.

It was a case of perfect timing. Professional football in the postwar period was on the verge of the greatest popularity it ever had known, thanks to television. It was the ideal moment for the appearance of a new type of glamorous, disciplined football team such as the Cleveland Browns.

Paul Brown himself was a new kind of football coach; in contrast with the burly, muscular, rough-hewn types who had dominated the coaching ranks in the earlier, cruder days of professional football, he was slight, dapper, reserved, brilliant, and as articulate as a professor of philosophy.

It didn't take Brown long to put together a team. McBride's money proved to be a great convincer. The club's first game was played in late summer of 1946 in Akron's Rubber Bowl and it was an augury of things to come. The brand-new Browns beat the Brooklyn Dodgers in that exhibition contest 35 to 20.

The All-American Conference lasted only four years, 1946 through 1949. It perhaps would have lasted longer had it not been so completely dominated by the Browns. In four seasons of AAC play, Cleveland won 52 games, lost 4, and had 3 ties.

The conference never knew any other champion than the Cleveland Browns in those four years. It was an unhealthy situation for the AAC itself, of course; the inability of the other teams in the league to compete on an even level discouraged attendance and ultimately caused the AAC to collapse.

The National Football League and its followers were highly skeptical of the AAC's wonder team, the Browns, but the Cleveland club was eagerly accepted as an important addition to the old league. Not only was it a glamorous, highly publicized team, but its power to draw fans was impressive.

Most national grid experts expressed respect for the caliber of play demonstrated by the Browns in the AAC, but many of them prophesied that results would be drastically different once the Browns got on the field with the big boys of the sport.

The opening game of the 1950 NFL season enjoyed wide national attention. The schedule fortuitously called for the Browns, champions of the AAC, to play the Philadelphia Eagles, champions of the NFL. It was a world series of football right at the beginning of the season.

Some 85,000 fans in Philadelphia's Municipal Stadium that day looked on in dismay and disbelief as the upstart Browns showed, with consummate skill and strength, that their AAC success had been no fluke. They flattened the Eagles, 35 to 10.

The stars of that early Browns team were football legends in the making. They included Otto Graham, the quarterback; Lou ("The Toe") Groza, the great placekicker; Mac Speedie and Dante Lavelli; Lou Saban, Dub Jones, Marion Motley and Bill Willis.

An important point is that Motley and Willis were black.

Just as Bill Veeck's Cleveland Indians broke the color line in baseball's American League, Paul Brown and Mickey McBride cracked the color line in professional football right at the outset of All-America Conference play.

The sensational performances on the field by Motley and Willis, though, did more to erase the color line than any sociological preaching possibly could have. Football suddenly realized it had an untapped treasury of talent in black players, and, after an initial hesitation, every team in professional football scrambled to catch up with the Browns.

They had their work cut out for them. The quality of Cleveland football was such that in their first 16 seasons in the NFL, the Browns won the Eastern Conference title 9 times and copped the national football championship 4 times. In the same period, they were establishing the best won-lost record in professional football; 142 victories, 54 losses, 6 ties.

Professional football, it ought to be remembered, was an old tradition in Cleveland by the time the Browns arrived on the scene. If Canton, only 50 miles away, was the birthplace of the pro game, as is generally acknowledged, Cleveland was part of the pioneering effort. The city was among the charter members of the American Professional Football Association when it was formed, with Jim Thorpe as president, in 1920. Out of that association grew the modern National Football League, a name adopted in 1921.

The first Cleveland team in that original league was called the Indians. Other names of Cleveland NFL teams in the years that followed were Bulldogs, Panthers, Rams, and, of course, Browns.

The Cleveland public took only desultory interest in the professional game in the 1920s and 1930s. High school and collegiate football were in high popularity. Fans especially enjoyed games involving the collegiate Big Four: Western Reserve's Red Cats, the Case Rough Riders, John Carroll's Blue Streaks, and the Baldwin-Wallace Yellow Jackets. The football heroes were the stars of the home gridiron, and their names are still remembered — Jud Platz, Vic Ippolito, Benny Friedman, Speed Gaul, Eddie Finnigan, Gomer Jones, Les Horvath, Chet Adams, Flash Eredics, Steve Sabath, Ted Bosequist.

Professional football had a difficult time wooing the fans away from their collegiate favorites. Cleveland won the NFL title in 1924, but the victory wasn't enough to sell the play-for-pay game. Cleveland won again in 1945 and interest began to mount, but attendance at professional games still made the sport a precarious investment.

It did seem that the pro game was catching hold in Cleveland in 1945 as the Cleveland Rams fielded an outstanding team that drove to the NFL title under the quarterbacking leadership of Bob Waterfield. Some 32,178 fans turned out for the championship contest with the Washington Redskins in spite of zero weather that December. The Rams' 15-14 victory sent their rooters home chattering about the prospects for the next season.

But there would be no other season for the Rams in Cleveland. Owner Daniel F. Reeves announced that he was moving the team to Los Angeles even as Cleveland fans were cheering the team's title game victory.

Quarterback Otto Graham, in sneakers, against the Rams

The departure of the Rams had the psychological effect of setting the stage perfectly for the Paul Brown era. Cleveland sports fans had been rejected, spurned, jilted by the Rams and the National Football League. Paul Brown's team and the new All-America Conference would serve as a vehicle for vengeance.

Mickey McBride sold the Browns in 1953 for $600,000 to a combine headed by Homer Marshman, whose group resold the team in 1961 to a young New York advertising man, Arthur B. Modell, and a group of investors, for $3,925,000.

Modell, 36, was to be no absentee owner. He was a football fan and he had strong opinions on the sport. It was his intention to be the owner in every sense of the word. Paul Brown, meanwhile, was Paul Brown — proud, distant, reserved, jealous of all the authority that had been in his hands from the very beginning of the Cleveland club. They were the Browns in more than name. They were Paul Brown's Browns.

A conflict between the new owner and the famous coach was inevitable. The relationship between the two strong-willed men started out at the basement level and then steadily went downward until finally, in January, 1963, Modell fired Brown, putting black headlines on sports pages all over the country.

It was an expensive gesture by Modell. Brown, probably the highest-paid coach in football at $82,500 a year, owned a 10-year contract with the Browns, and there were six years remaining on the contract.

Blanton Collier, a Brown protege, succeeded as coach of the Cleveland team. Under his direction the Browns won the Eastern Conference title and the NFL championship in 1964, beating the Baltimore Colts for the title. Again, in 1965, the team won the Eastern Conference title, but lost the championship game to the Green Bay Packers.

After Collier retired from the Browns head coaching job, Nick Skorich, one of his assistants, was named to the post in the early '70s. But the fortunes of the team that had been the most successful in professional football were plainly taking a downward turn and could not be checked. Skorich was replaced, after three dreary years, by Forrest Gregg, a former Green Bay Packers star, who held the top job only two years before Modell brought in Sam Rutigliano as head coach in 1978.

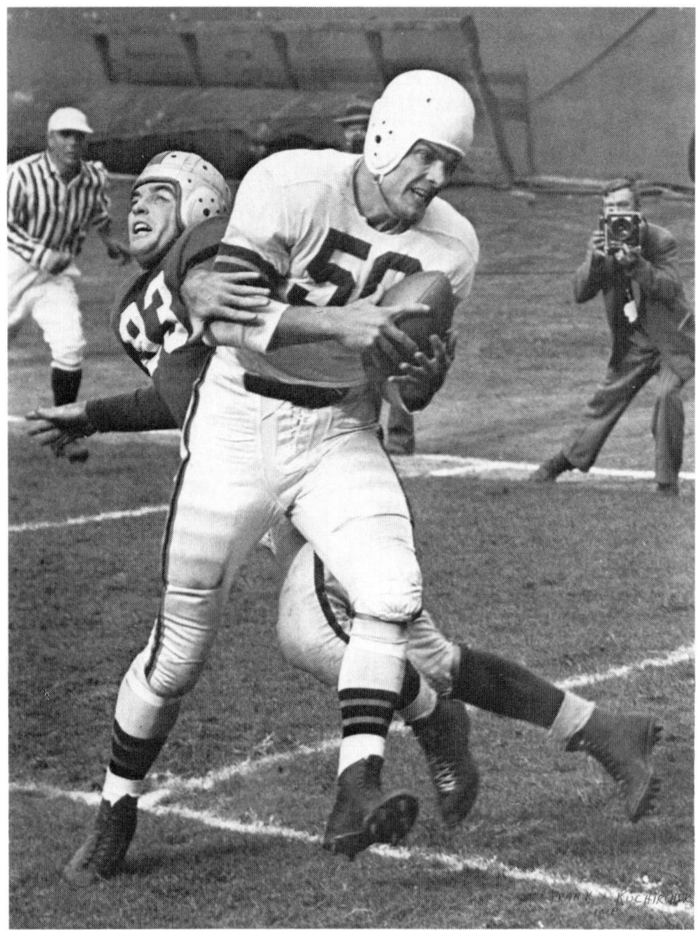

Dante Lavelli backs across the goal line

It was the beginning of the slow, painful process of rebuilding on the shaky foundation of shattered fortunes.

But it was something that Cleveland sports fans had come to understand. Their baseball Indians had acquainted them with the hard facts of life, and they were aware that whatever goes up, no matter how high or how gloriously, someday must come down.

* * *

Among the most frustrating of all the sports experiences in Cleveland has been that which involves professional hockey, once thought to have a brilliant future in the city.

Ice hockey of the minor league variety flourished for more than five decades in Cleveland, and it was confidently expected that one day the city would have a major league team. That day arrived finally in the 1970s, but it brought stormy weather and a quick nightfall.

The beginning was in 1907, when Dudley S. Humphrey, who made a fortune out of popcorn and Euclid Beach Amusement Park, built an ice rink, the Elysium, on the site of his first popcorn stand at E. 107th Street and Euclid Avenue. The rink, built at a cost of $150,000, was said at the time to be the largest and most elaborate skating facility in the United States. Shortly after the rink opened, Cleveland entered a team in the United States Amateur League, and competed in that circuit until professional hockey crossed the border into the United States in the 1920s.

The professional game quickly became dominant and in 1929, Harry (Hap) Holmes, himself an outstanding goal tender, entered a team called the Cleveland Indians in the International League, using the Elysium as the home rink. Because of the confusion of identities with the baseball Indians, the name shortly thereafter was changed to the Cleveland Falcons.

Introducing a new sport at the beginning of the Depression almost proved fatal. The Cleveland franchise was tottering in 1933 when Albert C. Sutphin, an ink company executive and sports enthusiast, bought the faltering Falcons.

It was Sutphin whose faith in the game and generous financial support raised professional hockey in Cleveland to the level of a popular entertainment and gave it status as a competitive sport. Sutphin, like football's Mickey McBride, insisted on quality performance and one of his first acts was to recruit high-class hockey talent. In 1937, he made headlines by hiring one of the game's most famous players, Bill Cook, formerly of the New York Rangers, as coach of the Cleveland team. Later, in 1943, he put together a brother combination, with Bill Cook as general manager and Bun Cook as coach. Alex (Bud) Cook was the star center.

In that same red-letter year, with the Depression steadily deepening, Sutphin took the big gamble by building the Arena at 3700 Euclid Avenue as an all-purpose facility to accommodate basketball, circuses, boxing, wrestling, track, and general entertainment shows, including 6-day bike races.

The new Arena cost $1.5 million, but it gave the sport just the lift it needed at that critical time. It had a seating capacity of 10,000 compared with the 1,900 who could watch games in the old Elysium. Indeed, the new facility was so impressive that the National Hockey League immediately began to make overtures to Sutphin, inviting him to move his team into the big time. He rejected the invitation, saying the time was not yet ripe for such a move. But he did opt for a new name. A public contest came up with the Cleveland Barons.

The Barons blazed a brilliant path across the ice as the winningest team in the International League and the American League. They were the New York Yankees of minor league hockey. Their league record of titles stretched over 20 plus years.

It was the beginning of the end for the Barons when the team and the Arena were acquired by Nick Mileti, a sports speculator, in 1968. It was his first acquisition in a sports sweep that saw him win control also of the Cleveland Indians, briefly, and launch the city's National Basketball Association team, the Cleveland Cavaliers. At the same time, he was putting together plans to build a sports palace, the Coliseum, which would serve as the home of the Cavaliers and Mileti's new hockey team, the Cleveland Crusaders, who were enrolled in the World Hockey Association. The WHA, it was hoped, would be a second major league in hockey, in opposition to the NHL.

When the Crusaders began play in 1972-73, the city, for the one season, had two hockey teams to enjoy. But the old Barons, trying unsuccessfully to find a new home the following year, finally disbanded. The Crusaders, meanwhile, were finding the icy going to be treacherous. The team lasted only four seasons.

The 1976-77 season brought new hope to Cleveland hockey fans as the National Hockey League's California Seals were purchased and transferred to a new home in Cleveland to play in the NHL under the familiar old name of the Cleveland Barons.

The team's play was undistinguished, the Coliseum was too far out in the country, and a lot of hockey fans had become disaffected by all the changes. It's hard to root for strangers, even when they wear the hometown jersey. After two financially disastrous seasons, 1976-77 and 1977-78, the Barons were merged with the Minneapolis North Stars and once again disappeared from the hockey scene as a separate entity. And Cleveland, for the first time in 50 years was without a professional hockey team.

The Cleveland Cavaliers

Greg Pruitt, runningback

* * *

Basketball was another sport that belonged almost exclusively to the college teams and the amateur leagues in Cleveland until the current century was well underway.

A downtown merchant, Max Rosenblum, and his business associate, I. S. (Nig) Rose, probably did as much to stir public interest in the semi-pro and professional game as anyone.

Rosenblum was an enthusiastic supporter of all sports and usually is credited as one of the principal forces in the growth of amateur baseball in Cleveland to a point of such popularity as to make the city the center of the game shortly after World War I.

Basketball also fascinated Rosenblum and Rose. The Rosenblum store on Euclid Avenue began to sponsor teams in city leagues with such favorable results that the clothing merchant in 1923 brought the famous original Celtics to perform in the new Public Hall.

The turnout was incredible. Some 23,000 Clevelanders paid their way into the huge auditorium to watch the Celtics play a double-header with the Indianapolis Omars on February 22 — one game in the afternoon; the other one at night.

The city's surprising reaction understandably fired Rosenblum's enthusiasm for the sport and four years later, 1927, he officially adopted the Celtics as his own team, giving them the name of the Rosenblum-Celtics. The players included such legendary notables as Joe Lapchick, Dutch Dehnert, Pete Barry, Nat Holman, Davey Banks, Nat Hickey and Carl Husta.

It was the greatest team basketball ever had seen up to that time and the Rosenblum-Celtics thrilled thousands of Clevelanders through the early years of the 1930s with their play.

Following World War II, with the college teams still dominating the basketball scene in Cleveland, several attempts were made to give the city representation in the semi-professional and professional leagues struggling for a foothold in the United States.

Late in the 1950s, the owner of a plumbing supply business, Ed Sweeney, entered a team called the Cleveland Pipers in the National Industrial Basketball League. Mike Cleary was general manager of the semi-pro team. Its coach was John McLendon, one of the first black coaches in American basketball.

The Pipers were not able to make a go of it under the Sweeney banner and folded after a few years, but the name continued when George Steinbrenner, Cleveland sportsman who later became owner of the New York Yankees, entered the Pipers in the new American Basketball League. The team played only the 1960-61 season before calling it a day.

Not until 1970 was Cleveland again to have its own professional basketball team. In that year, the ubiquitous Nick Mileti won a franchise for the city in the National Basketball Association.

The team, given the name of the Cleveland Cavaliers, was an immediate favorite of the fans, mostly because of an initial losing streak that drew public sympathy. Under Coach Bill Fitch, formerly of the University of Minnesota, the Cavaliers quickly achieved respectable status and surprised everyone in 1975 by winning the division title before losing in the final playoffs.

There was a long wait between the Celtics and the Cavaliers, but the Cleveland public loved the newcomers. In the heat of the Cavaliers' winning season, the team set a new single-game attendance record for the NBA as 21,130 fans turned out for the game between Cleveland and the Washington Bullets in the home stretch of the victorious year.

Following that one exhilirating season, however, the Cavaliers slumped back into the also-ran category and seemed to lose much of the appeal that had made them a Cinderella club. Attendance declined and popular Coach Bill Fitch resigned at the end of the 1978-79 season. He was replaced by Stan Albeck as the team prepared for its 10th year in an atmosphere of uncertainty.

29. The exciting city

Cleveland's war effort: The Cleveland Trust Company (above), seller of Liberty bonds; a scene on Euclid Avenue (upper right), in 1918.

The glory years in Cleveland continued with unchecked vigor through the first three decades of the current century. They constituted the time of growth, the time of building, and the time of lofty idealism. Not even World War I could interrupt the forward lunge that was taking the city onward, towards some shimmering, indistinct, but wonderful, future.

A Cleveland that had embarrassed itself by allowing the statesmanlike Tom L. Johnson administration to be defeated, mostly through voter apathy, sought to retrieve lost ground by installing one of Johnson's brightest proteges, Newton D. Baker, as mayor.

Baker, a brilliant young lawyer, had served as law director in Tom Johnson's cabinet. As mayor himself, he guided the Group Plan towards realization and had the immense satisfaction of seeing some of its classic buildings and its broad expanse of Mall arising out of the rubble of the tenderloin district which formerly had disgraced the site.

Another Johnson protege, William Stinchcomb, became the head of the Cleveland Metropolitan Parks System when it was created in 1918. He was the guiding force in the remarkable program to save much of the city's precious greenery and unspoiled beauty spots. Under the Stinchcomb leadership, lasting 36 years, until 1957, Cleveland gained the greatest

Pier at Gordon Park (above), 1905, and Edgewater Park (inset), in 1900. Mayor Newton D. Baker (right, center with eyeglasses), with Cleveland Charter Commission.

urban parks system in the United States. Starting with 109 acres in 1919, it has grown to some 18,500 acres of parkland that loop around the metropolitan area, from Rocky River on the west to Euclid on the east, traveling by way of Berea and Bedford to the south. It has become known nationally as Cleveland's "emerald necklace."

And though the railroads, the ore docks, and the mills of heavy industry had sequestered much of the lake shoreline and the riverfront in the rough-and-tumble years past, Clevelanders still were able to enjoy lakefront parks such as Edgewater on the West Side and Gordon Park on the East Side. And the philanthropic generosity of John D. Rockefeller and Jeptha P. Wade provided large links in the chain of city parks leading from Lake Erie to University Circle.

While smaller than its East Side counterparts, Edgewater Park on the West Side was more picturesque than the others, with its basin for the Cleveland Yacht Club, its baseball diamonds, breakwater for fishing, its wide sandy beach, and, most impressive of all, an astonishing bathhouse whose byzantine design was worthy of some exotic port. Its three-story white stucco building, topped by a red tile pavilion for picnic lunchers, was a lakefront landmark until after World War II, when the vandalized remains finally were demolished.

Progress always claims its casualties, of course. The most

prominent victims of downtown change as the 20th century got underway in Cleveland were the wealthy Nabobs and their opposing Bobs on Euclid Avenue's Millionaires Row. The handwriting already was on the wall, legible as early as 1900, but some of the families in that privileged manorial cluster from E. 18th to E. 55th Streets mistakenly dismissed the messages they read as so much graffiti, not to be taken seriously.

The threat posed by the creeping encroachment of commercial establishments into the exclusive residential area was a real one, however. Even the streetcars began running on Euclid Avenue, offering another sign that the world was moving in where hitherto only millionaires had dared — or had been allowed — to tread. The retreat to other, more exclusive, residential retreats began in earnest.

Some of the rich people forsook Euclid Avenue for the lovely lakefront communities of Bratenahl and Glenville. Some looked to the higher elevations to the east and began to build their mansions on Fairmount Boulevard and Fairhill Road. Cleveland Heights and East Cleveland were among the popular refuges for the scattering well-to-do. It was the latter suburb that John D. Rockefeller chose as his home. Others favored the University Circle area close to Wade Park and Rockefeller Park, or Gates Mills, Little Mountain, Waite Hill, Pepper Pike, Shaker Heights, Lyndhurst, Chagrin Falls, or even Lakewood and Rocky River on the West Side.

But if, by the end of World War I, Euclid Avenue had lost its residential character, it was taking on new glitter in the area around E. 14th Street. There, where Huron Road joined Euclid, was the beginning of a spectacular theater district called Playhouse Square.

As the motion pictures moved out of the novelty stage and were being coupled with vaudeville to form an entertainment combination that won instant popularity, large theaters had to be built to accommodate the new form of show business. The

Theatrical activity started in Playhouse Square on Euclid Avenue in the 1920s (below), and continues to thrive today throughout the city.

ERDAY'S
1415
AND LOUNGE
THE PLAY HOUSE

Firestone

Great Lakes Exposition on Cleveland's lakefront, 1936

Street scene (left) on Euclid Avenue, 1928. Cleveland's disastrous blizzard (right), November, 1913.

new movie houses reflected the profitable nature of the business. They were big, baroque, gloriously gaudy, beautiful and palatial.

Three of the new theaters that made Playhouse Square an outstanding concentration of theatrical delight were created almost simultaneously: the Ohio Theater, the Allen Theater, and Loew's State Theater. All were built in 1920. The greatest of all the movie-vaudeville houses was B. F. Keith's Palace, erected in a skyscraper at the corner of E. 17th and Euclid and described by the great showman as "the achievement of my life." It opened in late 1922 under the management of John F. Royal.

Close by, on E. 14th near Euclid, the Hanna Theater was erected by Dan R. Hanna. It opened in March, 1921, to give the legitimate stage another outlet in Cleveland besides the old Colonial Theater on Superior Avenue, near E. 9th Street. The Colonial, a distinguished house for almost 30 years, rang down the final curtain early in the Depression and was demolished in 1932.

Another addition to the Playhouse Square grouping was the Stillman Theater on the north side of Euclid, near E. 12th Street. The Stillman Hotel previously had stood on the site, and, before that, the mansion of the Stillman family.

The largest motion picture-vaudeville theater of all, the imposing Hippodrome, was built on Euclid Avenue to the west of E. 9th Street, close to the old site of the Euclid Avenue Opera House.

The beautiful theaters with their glittering, moving marquees gave Euclid Avenue a life of its own at night and contributed greatly to the downtown area's big city look. Euclid Avenue, of course, had become the central avenue for shoppers, and the big stores during the 1920s and the 1930s were The May Co. and the Bailey Co., close to Public Square; Wm. Taylor & Son Co., west of E. 9th Street; Halle Bros. Co., at E. 12th Street; the Higbee Co. at E. 13th; Sterling & Welch and the Lindner Co'y. near E. 14th Street.

The Higbee store shifted from its site on upper Euclid during the early 1930s to become part of the Van Sweringen complex on Public Square. Sterling & Welch combined with Lindner's to form Sterling Lindner Co. after the war, but the merger failed to step up business and the store failed. So, also, did the big department stores of Taylor's and Bailey's.

But, in the short time between the wars, and in spite of the Depression, there was a magic moment when Euclid Avenue could claim its place among the liveliest and busiest of America's main streets.

J.W. GROVER & SON
SHIP CHANDLERS
J.W. GROVER & SON
SHIP CHANDLERS/SAIL MAKERS
J.C. McWATTERS

30. A time of change

Cleveland's port (left), is busy, now as then (inset), in 1900. Alexander Winton (above), points out the assets of his first experimental vehicle (above), 1901.

Alexander Winton, a maker of bicycles, gave his fellow-Clevelanders (and people everywhere, for that matter) something to think about one day in 1896 when, with grand aplomb, he sputtered up and down the city's streets at the tiller of his first gasoline-powered automobile.

What Winton had created was one of the world's first motor cars, and while it had the immediate effect of setting dogs to barking, horses to shying, and of drawing mingled looks of wonder and annoyance, there was a serious touch of the future in the half-comic public commotion.

The Winton Motor Car Company shortly became an important part of the industrial scene in Cleveland. It led the way for a number of companies in the city to enter the automotive field, including such well-established corporations as the White Sewing Machine Co., which branched out into White Motors.

By 1904, Cleveland was the world's leading manufacturer of automobiles. It relinquished its lead in the important field to Detroit after a number of years, but it continued to be an important auto parts supplier through the three-quarters of a century that followed.

During the industry's proudest years in Cleveland, some 80 different makes of automobiles were produced by Cleveland factories. They included such well-known makes as the Winton, the White Stanhope Steamer, the Jordan, the Stearns-Knight, the Templar, the Rollin, the Chandler, the Cleveland,

Winton "U.S. Mail" truck

Rollin White, on the White tractor

the Baker Electric, the Rauch & Lang Electric, the Hupmobile, and the Peerless.

The last to be wholly manufactured in Cleveland was the Peerless. The plant in which it was manufactured on Quincy Avenue was converted into a brewery for the Brewing Corporation of America, makers of Carling's Beer. The facility later was taken over by the C. Schmidt & Sons, Inc., Brewing Co.

Even after abandoning its role as a maker of automobiles, Cleveland continued to be the largest supplier of automotive parts. Companies such as Thompson Products (TRW), Midland Steel, and Eaton Axle (Eaton Corp.) provided the vital innards of the Detroit product, while the huge Fisher Body plants in Cleveland turned out the steel bodies to wrap around the parts on the Detroit assembly lines.

Following World War II, Cleveland experienced a strengthening of its auto parts industry as General Motors, Ford and Chrysler all built plants in the metropolitan area, making auto parts manufacture the largest employer in Greater Cleveland.

Cleveland from the beginning has had to fight off the stereotype of an iron-and-steel town that keeps a plug of iron ore in its cheek and spits out ingots and nails and screws.

The city actually is a center of such varied industry — paints, machine tools, textiles, chemicals, printing — that economic experts pointed to its diversification as one of Cleveland's chief strengths. They were confident that the city would be able to sustain a period of depression better than most other cities. The theory was that when one element of the Cleveland economy sagged, another element would prop it up.

It was a commendable theory and a source of much cheer in corporate board rooms until it was put to the severe test in the 1930s. In spite of its industrial diversification, Cleveland was badly hurt, staggered and knocked to one knee.

The postwar recovery was slow. The city for the first time was having doubts about its own invincibility. Basic changes were in the works. Reappraisal and reassessment was the order of the day. And out of this painful period of doubt is gadually emerging a new kind of economy in Cleveland.

The heavy manufacturing center, which Cleveland remains — with some 365,000 people engaged in the making of durable goods — is becoming just one side of the overall economy. There is showing in recent years a perceptible growth in non-manufacturing, white-collar employment.

While Cleveland is the 6th largest manufacturing center in the United States, it also has become the third leading corporate headquarters center, behind only New York and Chicago.

The ratio between manufacturing employment and non-manufacturing has been changing steadily in favor of the latter.

As of 1958, 40 percent of employment in the Cleveland area was in the factory production of goods; in 1969, it was 37 percent; in 1977, it was down to 31 percent.

The growth in non-manufacturing enterprises, meanwhile, has been responsible for heavy downtown building construction to meet the increasing demand for office space. Among the factors, certainly, is the presence in Cleveland of the headquarters of 15 of *Fortune Magazine's* top 500 industrial corporations.

* * *

By fateful, happy coincidence, a strenuous attempt by the administration of Mayors Thomas A. Burke and Anthony J. Celebreeze to spur the lagging city through an urban renewal program in the postwar period appears now to have been a stroke of good timing. The result of their efforts was the Erieview program of redevelopment, which, in turn, stirred city developers into action over a wide area of downtown.

The Erieview plan was the modern counterpart of the Tom L. Johnson Group Plan and the Van Sweringen Union Terminal development. And, like those earlier programs, it had a profound effect on the design of the modern city.

Erieview, in effect, took up where the Group Plan left off, clearing off most of the area south of Lakeside Avenue from E. 6th Street to E. 12th Street, to Rockwell Avenue. Among the old city landmarks that fell in the redevelopment were the old Central Armory and the equally picturesque County Morgue, both on Lakeside Avenue.

An area bounded by E. 9th and E. 12th streets, grown ragged and mean through the years, felt the central force of the renewal effort.

A recognition that a permanent residential population was necessary in any born-again central city encouraged the planners to make provision for high-rise apartment buildings in the district to be rebuilt, especially in the rehabilitation of E. 12th Street.

The result has been the construction of four large apartment buildings and the conversion of two large hotels into buildings for permanent residents. The new apartments were The Chesterfield, The Park, the Ernest J. Bohn Tower and the St. Clair Apartments. The old Pick-Carter Hotel, a onetime Cleveland showplace on Prospect Avenue and the Manger Hotel, formerly known as The Allerton Hotel, were converted to residential apartments for the elderly and persons in low and middle income brackets. The Bohn Tower also is reserved for elderly tenants of moderate income.

Wintons on parade, September, 1901

Between Chester and Walnut Avenues, on the west side of E. 12th, the city created Chester Commons, a small masterpiece of urban planning; a mini-park complete with a waterfall. It immediately became a favorite lolling place for office workers, and especially popular as a place to eat a brown-bag lunch and listen to noontime concerts.

An extension of the beautification move resulted in the improvement of E. 12th that converted the narrow street into a four-lane parkway with a tree-lined median strip from Chester Avenue north to the street's end in the new Cardinal Mindszenty Plaza overlooking Lake Erie. Flanking the plaza are two new buildings, a high-rise Holiday Inn and the city's imposing Utilities Building, which is no more utilitarian-looking, say, than a Greek temple.

One of the factors that figured heavily in the city planning was the way Cleveland had slipped as a convention center after having been one of America's busiest convention cities for so many decades. Among the reasons for its popularity was the superiority of the Public Hall as a meeting and exposition site and the many fine hotels enjoyed by the city. But other American cities had countered with large new convention halls and hotels after World War II, while Cleveland's facilities suffered from age.

Cleveland's answer was to build an enormous new Convention Center that was, in reality, an underground extension of the existing Public Hall exposition space. It was built underneath the northern section of the 40-acre Mall, directly under the new Hanna Fountains — the gift of Leonard C. Hanna and certainly one of the most spectacular civic beauty spots to be found in any American metropolis.

The rejuvenation of Cleveland's hotel facilities began in earnest in 1962, when the oldest major hotel, the Hollenden, at E. 6th and Superior, was torn down to make way for a modern replacement called the Hollenden House.

The old Statler-Hilton Hotel at Euclid and E. 12th, already showing the patched look of neglect, next was taken in hand by new owners, and given a major remodeling that restored it to respectability. This restoration was especially important to the area of upper Euclid Avenue, which was suffering from the cruel developments of the postward period. The Statler-Hilton, renamed The Cleveland Plaza, is on the fringe of Playhouse Square — a grouping of some of the finest motion picture-vaudeville theaters in the United States.

The arrival of television and a different pattern of living spelled near-disaster for the big downtown theaters. One after another, the old marquees went dark: The RKO Palace, Loew's State, Loew's Ohio, Loew's Allen, Loew's Stillman, the Lake.

The Lake Theater, a tiny house that really didn't belong in such select company, was the first to go, dying before W.W. II. It, ironically enough, became the home of a television station; WXEL-TV, Channel 9, which later evolved into WJW-TV, then WJKW-TV, on Channel 8.

The Stillman was turned into a parking garage. The lobby of the Allen became a restaurant. All of the grand theaters in the Playhouse Square district might have crumbled under the wrecker's ball if it had not been for an heroic show of civic concern by a group called the Playhouse Square Association headed by Elaine G. Hadden and with Raymond Shepardson as its driving force. Shepardson, production director of the association, has brought the Palace stage back to life with the biggest names in American show business. Under the group's master plan, all three of the monumental movie houses, the Palace, the Ohio and the State, will continue to serve Cleveland as the nucleus of a revitalized Playhouse Square.

Only a few steps off Playhouse Square, south on E. 14th Street, the spendid Hanna Theater has managed to weather the postwar changes without loss of popularity as the city's leading legitimate theater. It has been one of the anchors that has kept the show business district from totally disintegrating under the force of the storm.

The famous Cleveland Play House, one of America's oldest and most distinguished repertory theaters, has been serving its audiences from the stages of three theaters in two separate locations: Euclid at E. 77th Street and E. 86th Street, between

ACTIVE
ISSUES TRADED %
QUOTRON SUMMARY
ADVANCE
DECLINE
UNCHANGED
UP VOLUME
DN VOLUME
FLASH
TIME

Left, Saint Theodosius Russian Orthodox Cathedral; here, scenes from the "The Deerhunter" were filmed. Insets, left to right, Stock Exchange, Cleveland Trust Lobby and Erieview Plaza. Above, "The Portal" in front of The Hall of Justice. Below, The Flats, renovated warehouse district.

Central Armory, circa 1905, razed for the Erieview complex

Euclid and Carnegie. But plans have been announced for the construction of a $10 million complex, including theaters and club restaurant, to be built in the near future on a large tract of land on E. 86th Street. The nationally-distinguished architect, Philip Johnson, a Cleveland native, has been commissioned to design the new Play House.

The most effective moves to correct the deteriorating hotel situation, meanwhile, have come in the recent construction of the beautiful Bond Court Hotel as a replacement for the old Auditorium Hotel at E. 6th and Superior, and the restoration of the classic old Hotel Cleveland at a cost of $10 million by the Stouffer Corporation, which has renamed it Stouffer's Inn on the Square.

The most conspicuous physical improvements in the downtown Cleveland scene are to be found in the new skyscrapers that have given historic E. 9th Street a wholly new look and a wholly new position of importance in the central city's commercial scheme of things. The street has become, within the last 10 years, the avenue of high finance and government.

Among the new buildings that have risen in that time on E. 9th are:

The Cleveland Trust Tower, a 27-story building overlooking the beautiful old Tiffany-domed institution at the southeast corner of 9th and Euclid. It is the first of two twin towers that will be joined, one facing E. 9th and the other facing Euclid Avenue.

The National City Center, a $60 million undertaking that is under construction at the northwest corner of the Euclid-9th intersection, opposite the Cleveland Trust bank.

Ohio Savings Plaza, a headquarters building for the savings and loan institution, on the east side of E. 9th, between Chester and Walnut avenues.

The Central National Bank, an outstanding architectural contribution, a red-brick skyscraper on the west side of E. 9th, covering the full block from Vincent to Superior avenues.

The Federal Building, a 30-story government skyscraper at the corner of Lakeside and E. 9th.

The Bond Court Building, at the corner of St. Clair.

The Erieview Plaza Tower, 40 stories high, on the east side of E. 9th, between St. Clair and Lakeside.

Plaza Nine, a new office building flanking the Erieview Tower.

Directly across St. Clair Avenue, opposite Erieview Plaza, is the large city block, from E. 9th to E. 12th, the site of a $50 million office building housing Medical Mutual's offices in Cleveland.

Other notable new buildings built in the recent surge of

Euclid Avenue, looking east from Public Square, 1912

downtown modernization are the Diamond Shamrock Building at E. 12th and Superior, and the new $20 million State Office Building. Named in honor of the former mayor, governor and senator, Frank J. Lausche, it has given a new touch of beauty to the neighborhood where the city had its beginnings on lower Superior Avenue, at the east end of the Detroit-Superior High Level Bridge.

The most historic area in Cleveland, the riverfront at the foot of Superior Hill — where Moses Cleaveland and his Connecticut Land Co. party first landed — also has felt the touch of renewal. The area, called "Settlers Landing," is the subject of a proposed $100 million project which would make it a center of tourism, entertainment, shops, boutiques and restaurants. Sponsor of the 10-year program, The Higbee Company department store, already has renovated the classic Western Reserve Building at the top of Superior Hill. Higbee has also converted an old trucking company warehouse on Old River Street, in the Flats below, into a popular restaurant called The Cleaveland Crate & Trucking Company.

Public Square itself, grown dowdy and dirty over the years, is one of the key targets in the Cleveland renaissance. A major face-lifting now underway at an estimated cost of $7.5 million, is calculated to make the old jewel in the city's center sparkle once again.

There were other developments in postwar Cleveland, meanwhile, which are sure to have long-range effects on the city's future, and which, in a few short years, have brought about significant results auguring well for the future.

The opening in 1959 of the St. Lawrence Seaway was such a development. It was the realization of an old dream, this construction of a navigable waterway connection between the Atlantic Ocean and the Great Lakes, and it turned Cleveland into a true world port.

An immediate result was a new use and a new face for the downtown lakefront, which had fallen into disuse after the demise of the passenger boat service to Buffalo and Detroit in the late 1930s.

Docks for the ocean-going vessels took over the lakefront from the Cleveland Stadium westward and the new warehouses and heavy crane equipment gave the area an exotic maritime look that it had not enjoyed since the halcyon days of the 19th century, when sailing ships and steamers of all descriptions plied the Cleveland waters.

Of more fundamental importance, of course, was the new wealth that the new overseas commerce added to the Cleveland economy.

An even more spectacular development in the downtown area was the addition of two large institutions of higher learning in the shadows of the skyscrapers: Cleveland State University and Cuyahoga County Community College.

Cleveland State University, a successor to Fenn College which occupied a 20-story tower at E. 22nd and Euclid Avenue, was launched in 1965 through the efforts of Gov. James A. Rhodes. By 1979 its 40-acre downtown campus boasted 20 buildings and extended from the Inner Belt Freeway west to E. 18th Street along Euclid Avenue and north all the way to Chester Avenue, converting what had been virtual wasteland into one of the city's most dynamic centers. The cost of the CSU campus has been estimated at $200 million, and the presence of the university, it has been predicted, will bring about another $100 million in private enterprise renewal of the adjacent neighborhoods.

Cuyahoga Community College, which opened its doors to classes in the old Brownell Junior High School on E. 14th Street in 1963, now has three campuses to serve the educational needs of the city. About 27,000 students attend classes at the Metropolitan Campus in the downtown area, near St. Vincent Charity Hospital, the Western Campus in Parma, and the Eastern Campus in Warrensville Township.

In less than 16 years, the institution had become the third largest college in Ohio, but its future prospects are even more remarkable. It is predicted that by 1985, CCC will have an enrollment between 40,000 and 50,000 students.

When the Eastern Campus, which has been using temporary buildings, is completed, the total investment in Cuyahoga Community College will be about $91 million.

31. Transition

Downtown Cleveland, 1930

There is no sure way to pinpoint accurately the day, or the month, or even the year, when a great athlete loses his forward drive and begins to lose ground. Sometimes it already has happened even as he is scoring his greatest victories.

Something of the same mystery prevents a clear view of the condition of a city, as it did in the case of Cleveland some 50 years ago.

At the time the city was amassing some of its most impressive statistics, there was at work it seems, invisibly, some basic chemistry that shortly would check the growth rate and bring about a period of change in the very nature of the metropolis.

The key period was the decade between 1920 and 1930.

Everything, on the surface, was going along in splendid style. The city never had seemed more powerful, more promising, or more prosperous. Its people swam in an air of confidence and moved in a euphoria that grew out of a history of constant, continuous growth.

Skyscrapers at the time were beginning to change the flat profile of the downtown, a great, bright theater district was coming into being on upper Euclid Avenue, and the central city generally was taking on a glamorous look, thanks to the changes wrought by the Group Plan and the impressive Union Terminal complex of buildings being erected by the Van Sweringen brothers.

The population index was robust. By 1920, Cleveland, with 797,000 people, stood out as the 5th largest city in the United States, trailing only New York City, Chicago, Philadelphia, and Detroit, in that order. Behind Cleveland were St. Louis, Boston, Baltimore, Pittsburgh, and upstart Los Angeles.

The Cleveland of 1920 was able to measure a land area of 57 square miles, or double the physical size of the city of 1890. Even with that land growth, the population density had reached 14,000 persons per square mile — a figure that still stands as the all-time peak of population density.

But when all the factors are brought together for closer examination, they suggest that 1920 actually was something of a turning point in Cleveland history.

This conclusion applies to the city's politics as well as its physical growth.

One of the most colorful political figures in city history, Fred Kohler, was elected mayor in 1920. His victory represented an amazing comeback. A scandal in 1913 had forced him out of his job as chief of police in which he had won national distinction.

Kohler struggled for years to get into the electoral swim and finally made it all the way to the top like a salmon that has triumphed over the rapids and cataracts of the spawning river.

As it turned out, he was the last mayor the city would have for quite a while. The voters approved the city manager plan of government and, at the expiration of Kohler's term, 1921-22, Cleveland became the largest city in the United States to adopt this idealistic system. A businessman, William R. Hopkins, was

Cleveland's Municipal Airport (above) in 1929, and now (left). Below, poster advertises the city's first National Air Race.

chosen to be city manager. The president of City Council — at the time, Clayton C. Townes — assumed the title of "mayor" in this form of government. It was purely a ceremonial position.

It was a time of exciting happenings: a radio station, WHK, went on the air in 1922, adding a new dimension to people's lives. It was Ohio's first commercial broadcasting station. The new Public Auditorium, finest facility of its kind in the nation, opened the same year and was put to the test in 1924 when it was the site of the Republican National Convention that nominated Calvin Coolidge for president.

Still another concession to the future was the dedication on July 1, 1925 of the new Municipal Airport off Rocky River Drive, signaling the move by aviation out of the daredevil era into the role of people transportation. Stout Air Lines inaugurated the first regular air service between Cleveland and Detroit in 1928. And the National Air Races, which had begun in 1920 at Mitchell Field, New York, transferred to Cleveland Airport in 1929, focusing world attention on the city every summer.

As the eventful decade neared its end, however, it became evident that there were two noble experiments that were not working out.

One of Prohibition. Cleveland, on the rim of Lake Erie directly across from Canada, had become a center of rum-running activities that introduced the problem of gangsterism into the city life.

MARKING DEVICES
ACE

National Historic Landmarks: far left, Euclid Arcade; above, The West Side Market.

Eliot H. Ness (left), Cleveland's director of public safety, in 1935, and unsuccessful mayoral candidate.

The other experiment was the city manager plan. It had not, as hoped, rid the city of political cronyism or inefficiency of government. If anything, it had eliminated the civic element of fun that political campaigns once had represented. Cleveland, disillusioned and torn asunder politically, returned to the mayor-council plan of city administration in 1932 — at the same time, by coincidence, that it, and the rest of the nation, gave up on Prohibition.

The city had to start all over again politically, flounder about in search of administrative leadership, with a depression settling in; it was a time when good, experienced leadership was most desperately needed.

Up to 1920, Cleveland had relief on immigration as its supply source of new citizens. There still were echoes of New Connecticut in the halls of management and in positions of civic prestige, among the elite, but the old dominance of New England in the streets had been long lost in the surge of new population from Europe.

The black presence in the city was minor. Despite an influx of Southern blacks during World War I, the non-white popula-

Cleveland State University

Case Western Medical School

Research at Cleveland Clinic

WPA workers at Forest Hill Park, 1938

tion of the city in 1920 still totaled only 35,000, or less than 5 percent of the city's population.

The most striking change after 1920 was the general overall slowdown in the city's rate of growth. Where the population had increased between 1910 and 1920 by a whopping 42.1 percent, the gain between 1920 and 1930 was only 13 percent. And while that increase gave the city its highest population total ever, a total of 900,500, Clevelanders had become used to quantum leaps; progress at a geometric rate of growth. This was a letdown.

A bigger shock was ahead in the census of 1940, which reported that Cleveland actually had recorded a loss in population; the first ever. In that result, the population count dropped to 878,336. With that also went a drop in the national ratings. Cleveland lost its coveted place as the nation's 5th largest city and became the 6th city. The only thing to cheer was that Cuyahoga County continued to demonstrate expansion strength and had risen to a population of 1,217,250.

The city rallied slightly in the 1940-50 period with a gain in population number of 4 percent, up to 915,000 total. Even so, it dropped in the national ratings to 7th city.

The city's downward slide in the growth rate was not about to be checked. The population dropped to 876,050 in 1960, making Cleveland the 8th city in size.

By that time the in-flow of immigrants from Europe had slowed down to a mere trickle in comparison with the numbers of foreign-born newcomers who had been making their way to Cleveland before World War I.

The two decades, approximately, between the wars were a period of lull in immigration, comparatively speaking, although some would prefer to call it the calm before the storm.

The most significant development in the postwar years was the decline in the white population of Cleveland and the tremendous increase in the black population.

In the 10-year period from 1940 to 1950, when the city's total population was increasing by a mere 4 percent, there was a concurrent decline of 4 percent in the white population and an increase of 76 percent in the number of blacks.

Similarly, in the period from 1950 to 1960, there was a decline of 19 percent in the white population and a gain of 69

Terminal Tower and the Moses Cleveland statue in Public Square

percent in the black population.

Where blacks had constituted less than 5 percent of the city's population in 1920, they represented 29 percent of the total number of people in Cleveland by 1960 — or a total of 253,000.

Another notable fact emerged in the census of 1960: for the first time, the population of the city was less than the combined population of the suburbs.

To illustrate the importance of this development, Cleveland, as recently as 1920, was able to claim 79 percent of the area's total population. By 1960, the city's share of the metropolitan total was only 46 percent.

Some sociologists found a relationship between these shifting percentages and the arrival in the city of the large black population from southern states, causing a "white flight" to the suburbs.

There could be no question that the change in the character of the city's population, especially on the East Side, had brought about new social problems and new racial tensions. The facts chagrined a lot of Clevelanders who had taken pride through the years in the city's reputation for liberality and its leadership in the promotion of good racial relations.

The pressures of the new social alignment finally culminated in race riots that roared through the Hough Area in 1966 and the Glenville Area in 1969. They were among the most violent of all the racial uprisings that tormented the United States in the crucial decade of the 1960s. The Glenville outbreak, for example, led to the deaths of 10 persons, three of them policemen who were shot by snipers. Some 23 persons were wounded in the fighting, among them 14 police officers.

Before peace was restored, some 3,000 National Guard troops were called in to patrol the streets and deal with the shooting and looting that turned Glenville into a war zone.

Ironically, the Glenville riot took place during the administration of Cleveland's first black mayor, Carl B. Stokes; the first black to be elected mayor of any major American city.

Stokes served two terms in the city's highest office before withdrawing from politics to become a television newsman in New York. His brother, Louis B. Stokes, however, kept the family name a powerful force in Cleveland by winning a congressional seat, representing the city's 21st district, in December, 1968.

City Council also reflected in its membership the changing population characteristics of Cleveland and the growing political influence of black citizens. As of 1979, the 33-member City Council numbered 20 whites and 13 blacks.

Following the departure of Carl Stokes from City Hall and the election as mayor of Ralph J. Perk, propelled into office by a heavy ethnic vote, the city's political scene settled down to a period of relative calm. But the lull ended with a bang in November, 1977, when the enfante terrible of Cleveland politics, 32-year-old Dennis J. Kucinich captured City Hall.

Kucinich, a former city councilman and clerk of courts, drew national attention by his unorthodox and controversial approach to city administration. He immediately aligned himself in opposition to the powerful banking interests, took up a

Race riots in the Hough Area, 1966, left burned buildings (above) and National Guardsmen patroling the streets (left).

Carl B. Stokes

Louis B. Stokes

fight against the Cleveland Electric Illuminating Co. by espousing the cause of the threatened Municipal Light Plant, disallowed tax abatements to developers as an inducement to build, appointed a youthful, inexperienced cabinet, named a controversial police chief and fired him shortly thereafter, and, in general, took a truculent position towards almost all of the people and institutions he considered to be part of "the establishment."

Kucinich's claim was that he was returning political power in Cleveland to the "people," and that his administration represented a victory for "urban populism."

* * *

Not too many people understood the meaning of urban populism, but the words had a nice moral ring to them and it pleased a lot of Clevelanders to think there was a people's champion in City Hall, even if one of the first acts of the Kucinich Administration was to banish the Little Sisters of the Poor from the lobby of City Hall.

The sisters went peacefully, but only to make way for political and philosophical tumult. Few mayors, if any, have had as uproarious a first year in office as did Mayor Kucinich. And much of the turbulence was provoked, deliberately it seemed, by the mayor and his aides.

Kucinich was, at 32, the youngest man ever to be elected mayor of Cleveland, but he looked like a senior citizen alongside some of his appointees. Among them were two sisters, Tonia Grdina, 21, assistant safety director, and Betty Grdina, 22, assistant director of community development.

MUSICIANS
UNION
LOCAL 4

Facing page, the many faces of Cleveland. Above, Beachwood Place, new shopping mall.

Joseph G. Tegreene, named city finance director, was 25. Mary Vodicka, appointed commissioner of Cleveland Hopkins International Airport and city ports director, was 30. The popular name for City Hall, overnight, became Kiddie Hall.

The most provocative personality in the new administration was that of Sherwood (Bob) Weissman, a former official of the United Automobile Workers Union, whose invaluable contribution to the Kucinich campaign had been lining up the support of organized labor.

Weissman was the angry man of the new administration, snarling at reporters and disconnecting a radio station news broadcaster while he was doing a broadcast from City Hall. Among the more tactful of the public statements by this aide to the mayor was his recommendation that businessmen should keep their hands off the city.

By way of contrast, the soft-spoken Tegreene was courting business executives and, according to a newspaper story, "soliciting their talents to help the city."

There was that kind of ambivalence in City Hall in those stormy first days. And they really were stormy in more ways than one. Perhaps the political turmoil was, at least in part, calculated for effect, but not even the wiliest of politicians could have anticipated the kind of turbulence that Mother Nature was about to bestow on Cleveland. The wintry weather that followed Mayor Kucinich's inauguration at the beginning of 1978 was, officially, the worst in history. Never before, in any year, had so much snow fallen on the city.

On January 20th, after weeks of unrelenting snow, Cuyahoga County and 26 other counties in Ohio were declared a disaster area. On the following day, a 36-inch water main burst at a downtown intersection, E. 30th and Payne Avenue, flooding hundreds of buildings and dangerously reducing water pressure. Then came the coup de grace. Even as hundreds of unhappy homeowners were complaining to City Hall about their uncleared, impassable streets, the worst blizzard in 100 years roared into Cleveland during the early hours of January 26th, with winds at times exceeding 100 miles an hour, lifting the snow off the ground and mixing it with another heavy fall to create, in effect, almost a total whiteout.

The blizzard and the heavy accumulation of snow diverted everybody's attention from the political scene for a while, but not for long. Mayor Kucinich's running feud with the Cleveland Electric Illuminating Company resumed, growing more bitter by the week.

Then, in March, there was the most violent political eruption of all when the mayor publicly suspended his police chief

Natural History Museum

Cleveland Museum of Art

University Circle

Music abounds: Cleveland Orchestra (top), Severance Hall (left), built for the city's orchestra, and Blossom Music Center (right), summer home of the orchestra.

Ralph J. Perk

Dennis J. Kucinich

of only four months, Richard D. Hongisto, and then fired him after heated exchanges between the two in front of the television cameras.

It was more than the Kucinich critics could stand. A concerted drive was begun to force the mayor out of office through a recall election. By late May, recall petitions bearing some 50,000 signatures were filed with the clerk of city council. The mayor challenged the validity of a lot of the signatures, but he was overruled and a recall election was set for August 13th.

That election, the first mayoral recall to be brought to a vote in the city's history, was one of the closest imaginable. Kucinich won, but only by the slimmest of margins — a mere 236 votes. Momentarily chastened, he thanked "God and the people of Cleveland for ignoring my imperfections and giving my administration another chance."

The remainder of that epochal first year of the Kucinich Administration was no less eventful. There was a running battle between the mayor and his arch-foe, George Forbes, president of City Council, every Monday night in the council chambers. That civic feature was interrupted by illness. The

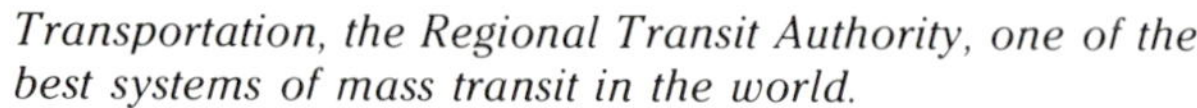

Transportation, the Regional Transit Authority, one of the best systems of mass transit in the world.

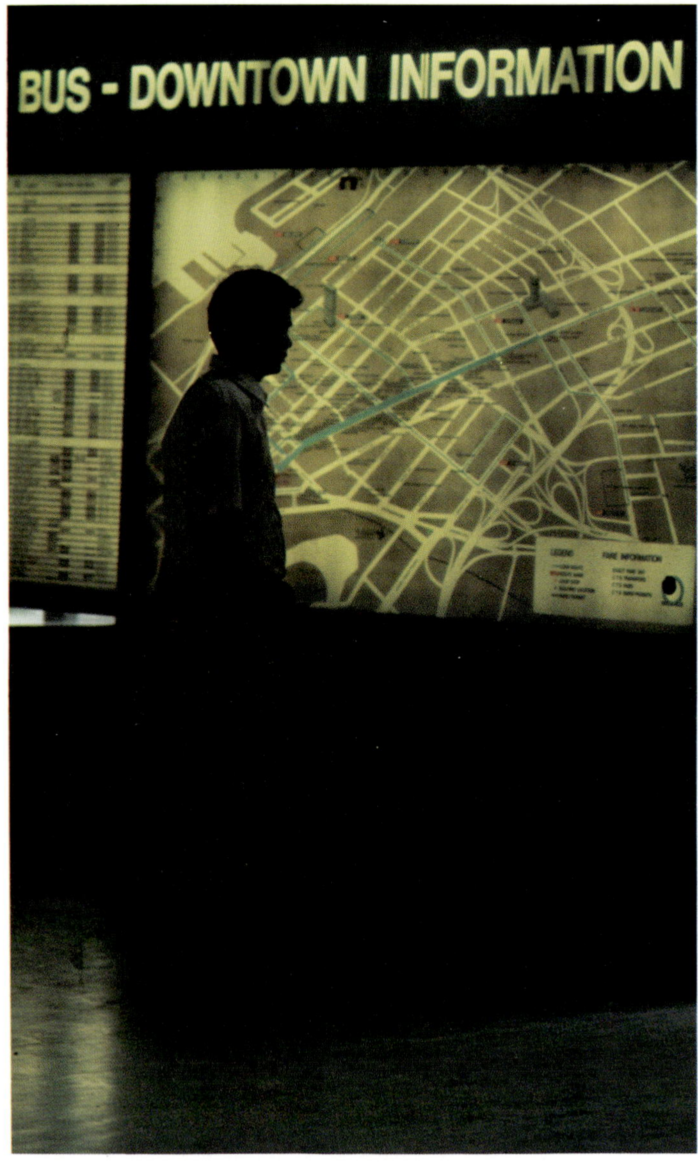

Renovation, Ohio City

Relaxation: The Goodtime II pleasure boat

Recreation, Hanna Mall

mayor suddenly was hospitalized in October for what was diagnosed as a stomach disorder.

Nine days after Kucinich returned to his desk in City Hall, however, confrontation politics resumed as if nothing had interfered. This time the mayor's chief opponent was the Illuminating Company. A federal judge had threatened to allow the company to seize city assets because Cleveland had failed to pay for power purchased from it. The judge, in addition, threatened to throw out the city's $330 million anti-trust suit against the electric utility unless the city paid the company $5 million by December 31st. Representatives of the power company, losing no time, began tagging city property in anticipation of seizure.

But it was December that brought the most ignominious moment to the Kucinich Administration — and, for that matter, to all the people of Cleveland. On the 15th of that month, the city went into default on $15 million in loans owed to six banks.

The mayor, enraged because the banks had not extended the city more time, spoke scornfully of the money-lenders, addressing his indignation in particular at the Cleveland Trust Company and its top officer, Brock Weir.

The mayor and the city council, still in disagreement, were arguing the pros and cons of the disaster even after the municipal ship had hit the financial iceberg. It was the sort of thing that sent editorial cartoonists rushing to their boards, pens dripping with imagery, to depict the Kucinich ship of state foundering in a sea of icy-faced bankers.

It was a serious situation, to be sure, but it stirred as much amusement as anger in the ranks of seasoned onlookers.

"When everything else fails, even television," quoth a man who had been around a long time, "there are always the politicians to make life interesting."

It has always been that way in Cleveland.

* * *

What visitors see, and what residents feel in Cleveland today, is the stirring of a city; one that went to sleep as an industrial caterpillar but which is emerging as a rather new kind of entity; no butterfly, certainly, but a brighter metropolis where the quality of life finally has asserted itself as the most important yardstick of all. The new profile tells the story.

The Cleveland of the 1980s surely will be a city different from the one that historians have known. Cities are inconstant creations, forever being reshaped by people and circumstances, by good fortune and bad.

It is not too much to conclude that the trials of the times probably have given this prodigy, this Cleveland, another mark of maturity that should prove helpful when the city comes to grips with future realities of survival and growth as it heads in new directions.

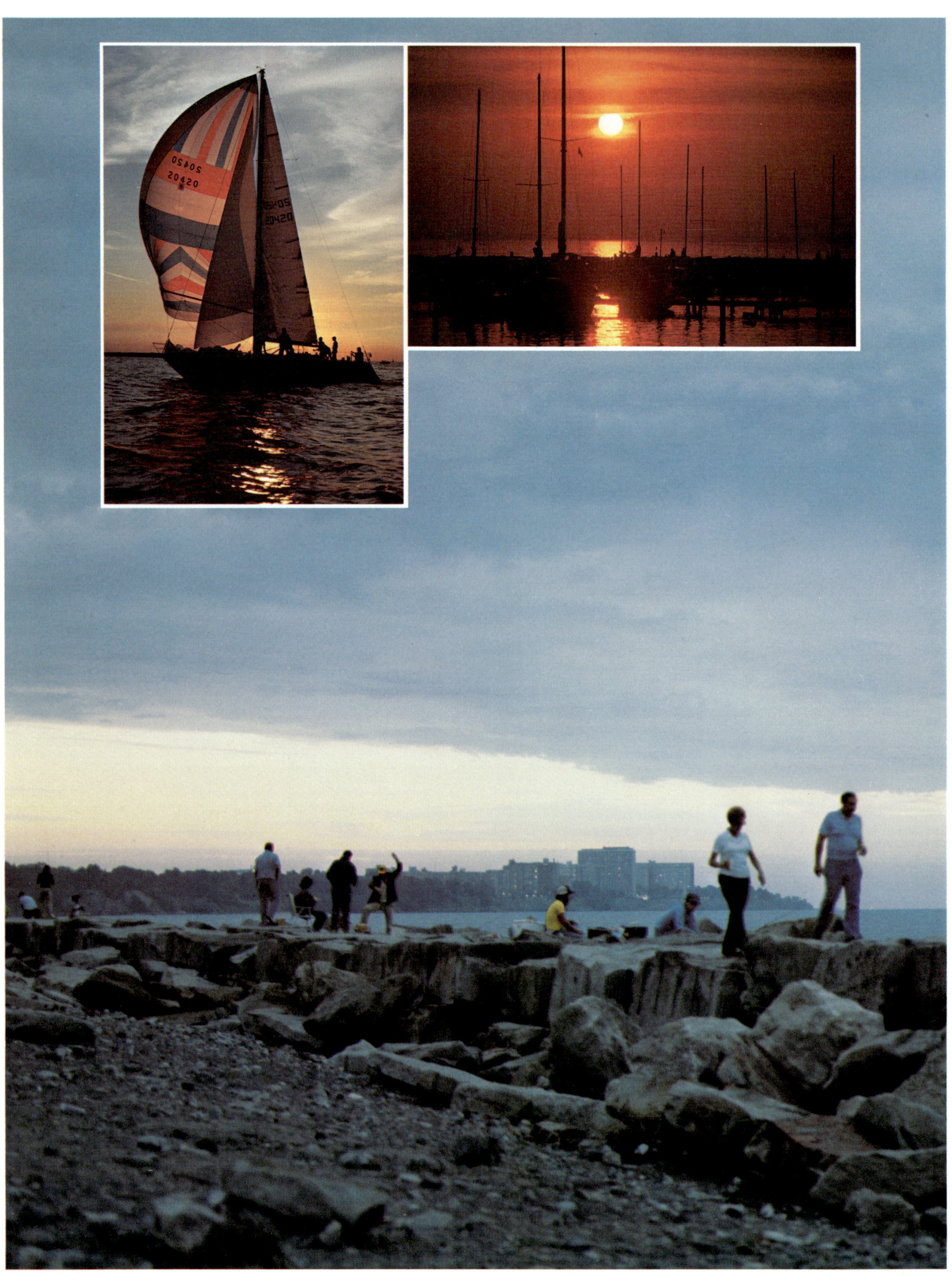
20420

Partners in Cleveland's economy

Red hot metal at Jones & Laughlin Steel Company

Free enterprise began Cleveland, and it was free enterprise which molded its existence. Today, the world of Cleveland business is making strides in the progress of the total community, and certain firms stand out as community leaders. The histories of many of those are told in this special chapter.

In early 1848 it was the emphasis on community progress and a need for organization that public notice was given for Cleveland merchants to assemble. According to Cleveland chronicler S. J. Kelly, writing in the Chamber of Commerce monthly, *The Clevelander,* in 1938, the collector of customs at the port had aroused key businessmen to the fast-growing importance of commerce. In 1847, more than $9 million in goods had been exported — all by water — flour, pork, wheat, corn and whiskey. Cleveland's "coast-wise" imports had totaled more than $6 million.

With such a volume, an association of merchants was imperative. In response to the call, a large number met at the Weddell House, at the northwest corner of Superior and Bank Street (West Sixth), Friday evening, July 7, 1848. Mr. Milford, a forwarding and commission merchant of Merwin Street, was made chairman.

Samuel S. Coe, also in the commission business on River Street, was appointed secretary. After a brief statement from the chair of the object of the meeting, on a motion of Mr. Joseph L. Weatherly, it was, "Resolved, that the merchants of the city now organize themselves into an association called the Board of Trade of the City of Cleveland, and that we now proceed to the election by ballot of the officers thereof."

Weatherly was elected president; Wm. F. Allen Jr., vice president; Charles W. Coe, an accountant, secretary; and Richard T. Lyon, treasurer; all were elected for one year. Weatherly, one of the old-type businessmen, long an agent for fire and marine insurance, had offices in The Commercial Exchange on the docks. He appointed Richard Hilliard, John B. Waring, Wm. Milford, Jona Gillett and L. M. Hubby a committee to prepare a constitution and by-laws for the board. They were to call a second meeting when ready to report.

Thus, the first organized body for the promotion of commerce and civic welfare in Cleveland was organized.

Before the famed Weddell House meeting on July 7, a group of men had been meeting during the spring of 1848 to exchange mercantile data. Many forces brought the leaders together. Gold had been discovered in California. The war with Mexico had ended. The potato famine and revolts in Ireland had brought Irish immigrants to America's Eastern and Midwestern cities.

The town's leaders were growing increasingly impressed with commerce churned up by vessels on the Great Lakes and the popularity of Cleveland's port facilities. There was a "big business" aura about the city, and its economic health required daily market reports to tie it to other centers of progress. The board supplied them.

What was Cleveland in 1848? It extended from the Cuyahoga to Perry Street (East 22nd) — that was the last graded street. From the lake shore it reached southward to Second Street, a block south of present Broadway. Its real southerly border line was the Ohio Canal that wound closely along this side of the river. Not a railroad ran into the city; not a locomotive whistle was heard. The population was 13,696. Thirty-one forwarding and commission houses and seven incorporated manufacturing companies were in Cleveland. The number of vessels that cleared the port was 1,515; and 1,486 entered. In 1848, canal boats landed 11,106 passengers in Cleveland.

The Peerless Motor Car Company, 1905.

The first regular meeting of the Board of Trade was held August 10, 1848, at Oviatt's Exchange, located at the corner of Superior Hill and old River Street.

Early records were destroyed by fire, but the purpose of the association adopted at its first gathering was: "To promote integrity and good faith; just and equitable principles of business; discover and correct abuses; establish and maintain conformity in commercial usages; acquire, preserve and disseminate valuable business statistical information; prevent or adjust controversies and misunderstandings which may arise between persons engaged in trade; and generally to foster, protect and advance the commercial, mercantile and manufacturing interests of the city."

A constitution and by-laws were adopted, and the board was to meet daily except Sun-

day, at 9 a.m. The Exchange was conveniently located near the heart of the shipping district, and for 30 years, until 1878, the Board of Trade remained there.

Coal was the principal item of trade, but the board reported all agricultural staples and daily prices, that were imported and exported from the city, and all manufactured and commercial articles shipped and received. Its books noted the arrival and departure of steamers and schooners — with their tonnage.

Railroads were built. The first through train over the Cleveland, Columbus and Cincinnati Railroad ran into Cleveland from the south February 21, 1851. A depot was erected on the lake front and piers built on the east side near the mouth of the river. The Toledo, Norwalk & Cleveland Railway, the last link in service from Boston to Chicago, was completed in 1853.

The railroads entered into a devastating competition with the canal, and soon with lake commerce, but the anticipation and advent of steam railways had added immensely to the population of the city. In 1851, 21,140 people were living in Cleveland and new residents were rushing in at a rate of 87 a week. The census for the year of 1852 showed 25,670. In the promotion of railroads and in securing bonded loans from the city, the Board of Trade had taken an active and energetic part.

On the evening of October 27, 1854, fire bells rang. The New England Hotel on the south side of Superior was in flames. Five hundred volunteer firemen from both sides of the river responded to the alarm. Companies came from east side engine houses as far out as Huntington Street (East 18th). They dragged the big Torrent engine from the west side over the Centre Street bridge with 70 firemen, but the hand pumping engines were of no avail. The fire roared and leaped across the street to the Oviatt Block, burned it to blackened walls, consuming the rooms of the Board of Trade. It was the largest conflagration that had occurred in Cleveland; the hotel and many blocks on Merwin Street which bordered the river bend and buildings southward were smoking ruins. Oviatt's Exchange was rebuilt and the Board of Trade occupied its old headquarters again.

The Board of Trade noted all commercial growth and gave daily reports of all imports and exports by water and rail, of ore, manufactured goods, grain, wool, hides, coal and merchandise, and it published itemized lists of prices on meats and produce. The early telegraph lines were drifting toward consolidation and during the winter of 1857-58, all lines became the Western Union Telegraph Company with general offices in the Washington Block on St. Clair Street, with J. H. Wade as general manager.

The Board of Trade received dispatches from connected cities and districts and published daily quotations on the markets, finance, the arrival of ships in eastern ports and the latest business news from Europe.

In 1860, Cleveland had a population of 43,417, and the city had water works with a fenced circular fountain at the center of the fence-enclosed Square. Perry's Monument was unveiled September 10th of that year and it was estimated that 100,000 people witnessed the ceremonies.

The year 1860 also was one in which many of the city's industries had their beginning. The old manufacturing of things for rural needs was taking a step back. That year, 29 firms with 232 establishments or plants engaged in manufacturing or production; they employed 2,795 men and 590 women and spent $995,370 in payroll. Total capital invested was approximately $1,800,000 and the total production was valued at $5,350,000.

With this increasing output, the activities of the Board of Trade greatly increased. Weatherly continued as president, and for several successive years beginning in 1854 and lasting through 1860, Arthur Hughes was vice-president. The latter year, John D. Rockefeller made his first investments in oil. The Board of Trade marched in procession with other civic bodies and crashing bands on President Lincoln's visit to Cleveland, February 15, 1861. In 1862, the most important commercial event was the organization of an oil refining company by Rockefeller, and his new corporation was to lead to the founding of Standard Oil.

On April 21, 1863, at its annual meeting, the board elected S. F. Lester president and M. B. Scott vice president. Weatherly had been presiding for 15 years, and had long been the president of the city's Board of Underwriters.

In 1865, Philo Chamberlain was elected president of the board, Richard T. Lyon was elevated to the vice-presidency and Jared H. Clark became secretary.

All commercial growth was itemized in the Board of Trade reports. The membership of the Board had increased from the original 36 members until in 1865, 230 firms and individual members were listed on its rolls.

Notwithstanding this growth, and although President Chamberlain had appointed committees of reference, appeals and inspection that were active, in 1866 they literally tore the Board of Trade to pieces. A group met January 13th and named Philo Chamberlain, George W. Gardner, J. F. Freeman and three others, as a committee to petition the legislature to legalize boards of trade. On April 3, 1866, the assembly passed "An Act to Authorize the Incorporation of Boards of Trade and Chambers of Commerce." On April 4th, 20 members appeared at the Atwater Block and signed articles of incorporation. On April 5, 1866, the Board surrendered its Articles of Association under which it had existed for 18 years and at once reorganized; its charter was signed the same day by William H. Smith, Secretary of State. A new set of 32 by-laws was adopted, and later many new rules and regulations; six vice-presidents were elected in place of directors.

J. D. Pickands, reporter for the Board of Trade, noted on April 13, 1868 in his annual report for 1867 that, "It is proper to state that the Association has been for the past year, and is now in as flourishing a condition, financially, as ever before. Eventually the Association will embrace within its membership most of those engaged in the commercial, mercantile and manufacturing interests of the city. That this would be the advantage of all, is too plain for discussion at this time. During the year, now brought to a close, several occasions have arisen for soliciting the expression of a full Board upon questions of general public interest." Such a report could be made today, more than 100 years later.

The same 1867 report notes that preliminary steps were taken to form a National Chamber of Commerce, and in 1870, Pickands reporting for 1869 stated, "The Board can congratulate itself in knowing that its action has had no little influence in carrying several of the more important measures through the

State and National Legislatures. The law makers of the land have come to attach more than common importance to the action of commercial associations, considering them to be composed of intelligent, active, business men, who take a comprehensive and practical view of all subjects that come under their observation, or are referred to them for consideration and action."

Once again, the efforts reported in the mid-19th century are still the charges of the successor organization in the late 20th century.

Until 1893, when it became the Cleveland Chamber of Commerce, the board kept pace in membership and scope of operations with the increasing growth of the city that culminated in a mighty swing upward in the last ten years of the organization.

In 1892, the board could claim a membership of nearly 1,000. An inside committee for the Promotion of Industry was appointed. Wilson M. Day was chairman, L. E. Holden vice-chairman, and Geo. T. McIntosh, secretary. They reported the Board of Trade needed a wider scope for its activities, that it could get involved in civic interests other than those of commerce.

The next year saw the first major reoganization of the Board of Trade. On February 6, 1893, the name of the Board was changed to the Cleveland Chamber of Commerce. In June of that year the new organization moved to rooms in the Old Arcade on Superior Avenue. Land had already been purchased facing the northeast corner of Public Square, where the Society for Savings once stood, for the erection of a Chamber of Commerce Building.

The new Chamber of Commerce embraced all matters of civic importance. Among the first efforts was the building of an armory on Bank Street, now W. 6th Street. It planned Cleveland's representation at the Chicago World's Fair, and induced the federal government to establish a hydrographic office here. It concerned itself with tax and insurance rates and raising funds for the poor who were caught in a depression.

In 1899, with a membership of 1,100 and $200,000, it built its home on Public Square, a building which eventually housed Cleveland College.

Then, as now, Cleveland was a committee-oriented community. The chamber's members and committees urged sanitation codes, meat and milk inspection laws, medical inspection of school children, elimination of grade crossings and dozens of other problems going hand-in-hand with industrial growth and growing population.

The Chamber in the 1920s and 1930s became active on national and state levels. It opposed wages and hours legislation and fought several state income tax bills in the '30s.

The Chamber, growing from the horse-and-buggy era to an automated-computer age, continued to be concerned with the business health of the communities. It came to grips with interracial and inner-city problems. Organized labor became a partner in programming. The Chamber prodded the city for a port authority, spearheaded traffic safety drives, sponsored job opportunity seminars to bring employers together with potential employees, and endorsed the renewal of Cleveland real estate taxes.

Cleveland's business, community and government leaders believed that the city's potential was unlimited, but there was also a strong awareness of the need to avoid "resting on one's laurels." Even then, astute business leaders expressed concern for tax laws that would make Ohio competitive for industrial development; for the need for river and harbor improvements and for effective use of the city's lakefront. A major project of the Chamber's Industrial Development Committee (working with the Cleveland Advertising Club), introduced in May, 1926, was a three-year campaign to sell Cleveland to the world.

By 1930, the stock market crash had obviously affected business. Nevertheless, in January of that year, the Union Trust Company ran an ad "What's the Outlook for 1930?" Union Trust felt, as did many others, that "the present recession is only temporary." Unfortunately, the economy worsened and the optimism diminished considerably.

The modern phase of the Chamber's history began in 1937 when A. C. Ernst was elected Chamber president and headed a Cleveland advancement program. His term was highlighted by a new sense of purpose and by a new business community determination to pull Cleveland from the depths of the Depression. As the economy slowly revived, the Chamber formulated the "Cleveland Plan" to boost the city's economic image damaged by national rumors that there was no money in Cleveland to spend.

"The Plan" was announced in July, 1938, with a goal of re-establishing Cleveland as a national market of immediate importance, worthy of first consideration by the nation's sales managers and space and time buyers. On December 6 of that year, the Chamber hosted New York and Chicago writers at "New Industry Day" activities, along with the representatives of the 57 companies that "chose Cleveland" that year.

The *Christian Science Monitor,* in a lengthy article on September 1, 1938, reported, "One of the first things the new leadership did was to move the Chamber of Commerce to new quarters. The Van Sweringens, who did startling things to the map of Cleveland, had moved the chamber to their Terminal Tower in 1928, but with their passing it languished there. It was brought down nearer the center of things on Euclid Avenue and given efficient new quarters and an entrance hall worthy of a Presidential office, (the Union Trust Building where the members also enjoyed the Mid-Day Club atop the building).

"The business men interested in the organization's renovation set out to get new members — both plain folks and higher-ups, who hadn't belonged before. They lifted the membership from 1,500 to 2,700, said Mr. Ernst. What was equally important, they hoisted the budget from $100,000 to $300,000."

During World War II, Cleveland's industrialists marshalled their forces for victory and cannily planned ahead, hoping to maintain the area's industrial growth when defense spending would slacken. Employment for returning veterans was also a matter of concern. A program was developed by the Chamber of Commerce and others to provide "Jobs for All After Victory."

Another look at postwar possibilities was taken in January 1944, by Frederick C. Crawford, president of Thompson Products and then chairman of the National Association of Manufacturers. Crawford challenged businessmen to exercise their influence to win the right kind of lasting peace through the development of international trade, taking advantage of new products and technologies developed during the war.

The 1950s saw resolution of problems whose existence were impeding the community's progress in the eyes of Chamber leaders. Such things as continued river and harbor improvements; stream pollution abatement and lessening of erosion along the lake were sought by the Chamber.

Air quality was in the news as well. Warner Seely, secretary of the Warner & Swasey Company and Chairman of the Citizens' Committee on Air Purification, reported in June 1952 that air pollution in Cleveland had been reduced by 31 percent over a six year period, largely achieved through the "conscious cooperative efforts of business and local government."

The Greater Cleveland Growth Board, headquartered adjacent to the Chamber of Commerce in the Union Commerce Building, was created in 1962 specifically to foster industrial and commercial growth of the Cleveland-Northeast Ohio area.

By 1967, community leaders felt the need for one organization — reflecting all aspects of the area, including business, government and labor. They structured a merger of the Growth Board and the Chamber of Commerce into a new organization, the Greater Cleveland Growth Association, chartered on January 1, 1968.

Since then, the expanding Growth Association has grown to more than 3,700 corporate members and more than 7,000 individual members with an annual budget exceeding $2 million, making it one of the nation's largest chamber organizations. Its programs have expanded to include support for small business' needs, minority business financing, manpower training programs, international trade and investment, leadership development and downtown and neighborhood renovation.

Since the first call to gather in 1848, concerned citizens have continued to address the needs of Greater Cleveland with commitment to solve its problems and to develop programs for continued progress.

The backbone of this organization has always been and continues to be its membership, those business firms which are dedicated to fair profit and a viable Cleveland economy.

The histories of some of those businesses are found here.

Acme-Cleveland Corporation

Always thinking productivity

Acme-Cleveland Corporation's roots reach deeply into Cleveland's history. In June, 1876, Jacob Dolson Cox, Sr., the founder of The Cleveland Twist Drill Company and then only 24 years of age, borrowed $2,000 from his father to purchase from Mr. C. C. Newton a half interest in a small twist drill company in Dunkirk, New York. Three months later they moved the business to Cleveland, Ohio, and four years later Mr. Cox bought Mr. Newton's interest.

Keeping the young business going was a struggle. Mr. Cox labored in his overalls every day and did the books, correspondence and machine design work evenings. In 1880, needing money and help with the sales side of the business, he sold a two-fifths interest to Francis F. Prentiss, a cousin of his wife. Mr. Prentiss, an optimist, proved to be an excellent partner for the more conservative Mr. Cox. He became thoroughly familiar with all phases of the business and had exceptional foresight in enlarging the manufacturing capacity that later made possible huge production increases during World War I.

From 1880 to the turn of the century, young Cox concentrated on designing and building machinery to make drills. But outside factors — the stormy economics of the period — continued to make survival difficult for the partners, so difficult that in 1886 they decided to sell the business, asking $75,000 for it. Fortunately, there were no takers so there was no alternative but to keep on struggling.

Mr. Cox, in a letter to his sons dated October 2, 1902, said in part, "Be sure a new machine will save something. If any changes that will improve it can be made, have them made, then put it to work as quickly as you can. Don't hesitate because it will cost $100 or $1,000. Don't say 'the old machine is doing pretty well, and we would have to throw it away.' Of course, you *must* throw it away. Things move lively in the manufacturing world, and the best machines are outclassed by new ones very fast."

Jacob Cox, Jr., joined the company in 1911 and succeeded his father as president in 1919. A student of economics and an author, his policies helped establish the company as a far-sighted and progressive employer. In 1915, an employee profit sharing plan was adopted — one of the earliest and most successful.

From its early years, Cleveland Twist Drill has been responsible for much of the metallurgical technology developed for cutting tools. Tungsten, molybdenum and other elements had key roles in the company's production of high speed steel products, particularly in World War II. Under the direction of Mr. Cox, Jr., and Mr. Arthur S. Armstrong, president from 1952 to 1968, the company's reputation as a manufacturer of quality high production cutting and threading tools spread worldwide. Today it is the leader in the cutting tool industry.

A custom-designed machining system for automotive engine blocks — LaSalle Machine Tool

Cutting and threading tools — The Cleveland Twist Drill Company

The struggles of Cleveland Twist Drill were paralleled by another manufacturer, destined to become a merger partner in 1968. This was The National Acme Manufacturing Company, begun in 1895 in Hartford, Connecticut by two young mechanics, Edward C. Henn and Reinhold Hakewessell. They built the first multiple spindle automatic lathe that worked, and its basic principles still stand today as the foundation for the economical, reliable, mass production of accurate interchangeable parts. A series of events brought the company to Cleveland, Ohio in 1901, where it prospered and in 1915 purchased the Windsor Machine Company, Windsor, Vermont, another manufacturer of multiple spindle automatic machines. These machines, named for their designer, George Gridley, had features that were incorporated into National Acme's machines. Since then, all multiple spindle machines made by National Acme have been Acme-Gridleys, a name known throughout the world.

In subsequent years, both of these Cleveland-based companies prospered, expanded, improved their lines and became leaders in their respective industries. In 1968, they merged to form Acme-Cleveland Corporation. Since then, other manufacturing divisions have been added: LaSalle Machine Tool, Inc., a leading manufacturer of total production systems; Namco Controls, electrical and electronic controls; Shalco Systems, foundry systems and equipment; Foundry Tooling, foundry tooling equipment; and two other divisions, one engaged in research and development, the other, in distribution and transportation.

Acme-Cleveland, headquartered in Cleveland and listed on the New York Stock Exchange, had sales of $289 million in fiscal 1978, employs more than 5,800, and has facilities in 11 states and several foreign countries.

The American Ship Building Company

Foresight and trendsetting led firm from wooden schooners to steel ships

Philip Minch might well have had mixed feelings as he watched his sizeable investment ONOKO — the Great Lakes' first compartmentalized iron-hulled freighter — splash into the choppy waters of Lake Erie at launching ceremonies in April 1882.

It was no small gamble he and several other prominent Clevelanders had undertaken as owners of a firm later to become The American Ship Building Company. Casting an ominous cloud over the gala launching festivities was the tragic sinking a few months earlier of the iron-hulled, but uncompartmentalized, steamer BRUNSWICK in a collision on the Lakes. The fate of the BRUNSWICK seriously placed in question the entire pioneering move from wood to iron hulls in the Great Lakes' shipbuilding industry in the closing years of the nineteenth century.

Cleveland Ship Building Company

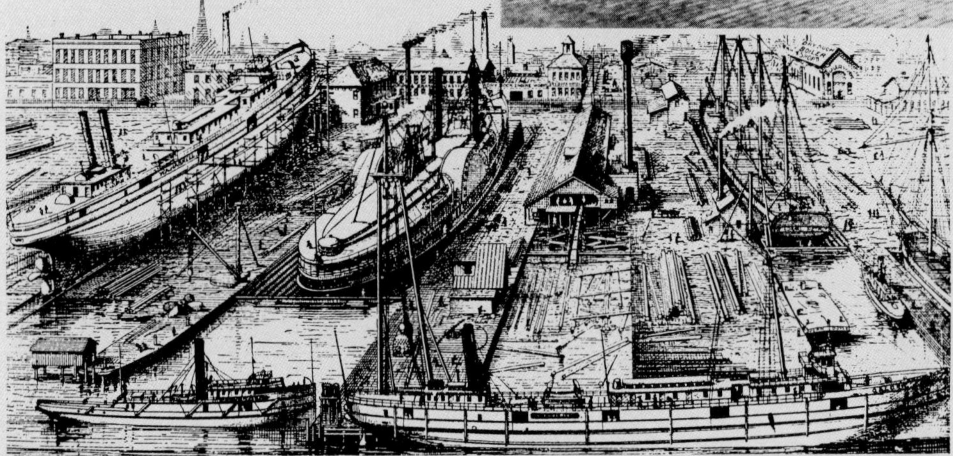

An 1884 view of one of six major dry dock companies that later formed The American Ship Building Company.

Philip Minch, however, lived to reap handsome dividends from his foresight and set a construction trend for the shipbuilding industry. The cost of the 287 feet of the rather ungainly looking, but most seaworthy, ONOKO had long been repaid as a result of the tonnage it had carried. By the time it was finally claimed by the erratically ferocious and mysterious Lake Superior on September 14, 1915. Unfortunately, Philip Minch could not know that his great great grandson, George M. Steinbrenner, III, would become chairman of the board of The American Ship Building Company almost a century later.

The American Ship Building Company emerged from a half dozen marine-related companies officially in 1899. Its early history is that of commerce and industry on the Great Lakes — the world's largest body of fresh water. The maritime history of wooden schooners, majestic sidewheelers, iron-hulls and, finally, steel ships is American Ship's heritage.

The company was molded in conservatism and reliability. It survived growing pains through the financial panic of 1907 and union squabbles while completing its expansion and the design and construction of the new, larger volume ships.

With the onset of World War I, the United States found itself totally unprepared and the subsequent demands on shipbuilding were substantial. In total American Ship delivered 250 vessels for the war effort. Mrs. Woodrow Wilson accepted the challenge of naming each of the ships for lakes in the United States. Most of these "Lakers" were laid-up or sold after the war as the country's merchant marine fell into a state of inadequacy.

Between the wars, however, the company was groomed into a smoothly run, capable business operation. The depression of the early '30s began to dissipate in 1936 with the company once again geared for production.

With the European war fully underway in 1940, American Ship set to work on construction of the so-called Liberty Ship — the most dependable and relied upon marine carrier. American Ship took an average of 51 days to mass produce a ship of this type. One ship, the GEORGE POINDEXTER, was built and launched in a record 31 days. The company had the honor of delivering the 1,000th vessel of the national Liberty program, in May, 1943.

The postwar activities of American Ship included expansion of its operation to encompass barge-building facilities in Nashville, Tennessee and the largest shipyard on Florida's West Coast.

The passage of the Maritime Act in 1970 sought to protect America's inland maritime industry. As the most economical means of transporting ore, grain, coal and other bulk cargoes, the Great Lakes and connecting waterways historically have proved vital to the country's economic growth.

The current energy crisis, with the added emphasis on low sulphur coal, has pointed up an ever-increasing need for Great Lakes shipping. This coal, large deposits of which are found in the Western states, can be transported most economically across the Great Lakes to meet the energy needs of industry and major power facilities.

The newest ships, designed and constructed by American Ship, are super cargo carriers, measuring 1,000 feet in length with a capacity to load and discharge 60,000 tons of cargo in a few hours.

Philip Minch would have had no mixed feelings about these giant super carriers, which transport thirty times the capacity of the ONOKO…his original gamble.

The Austin Company

Tradesman's visit to Cleveland led to building company international in scope

When, in 1866, Thomas Austin, a laborer in the English country village of Orton Waterville, apprenticed his 16-year old son, Samuel, to the village carpenter and builder whose shop was right next door, the forces that have shaped The Austin Company were set in motion.

Young Samuel took great pride in his trade, but, impatient with conditions in the family's bare, three-room stone cottage and the limited opportunities at home, he ultimately decided to go to America to help rebuild Chicago following its great fire.

After the 16-day ocean voyage, he set out for Chicago, stopping at Cleveland to carry greetings to some friends of the folks at home. The warmth of their welcome and the abundance of work that he discovered in Ohio made it hard to say no when these new acquaintances urged him to stay on. He lost no time in finding a job and was soon at work on a building at the corners of Case and Central Avenues.

In 1878, one of his friends, a physician, asked him to remodel his home. That first job went smoothly and Samuel's business began to flourish. Within two years he set up his own shop to supply sash, doors and other material for the houses on which he held the general contract. Residential work led to commercial building and in 1889, the Broadway Savings Bank decided to erect a new office. Austin got the job. Industrial and commercial work became his stock in trade.

His son, Wilbert J., graduated in engineering from Case Institute of Technology. They teamed up and after three years together, The Samuel Austin and Son Company was incorporated on May 7, 1904. Father and son gave impetus to the design-build concept. This was the first application of the undivided responsibility in America. Their first big break came in 1912 when the National Electric Lamp Association awarded them a $5 million contract to erect research facilities at what is now known as Nela Park in Cleveland. The Austin Method was born.

In 1916, the name of the firm was changed to The Austin Company. The company's operations spread, too — now to Chicago, New England, Canada, the Midwest and the West Coast. In 1918, the company established its first overseas office in Paris.

Year after year, Austin grew. It continually pioneered new construction techniques and tested materials. Construction innovations became a company hallmark as it developed welding methods, new structural designs, concrete use, wide span designs, controlled conditions buildings and a host of other forward-thinking concepts.

Austin's carpentry shop, circa 1880.

Looking ahead, Austin management prepared for the advent of entirely new industries as well. Opportunities in the field of electronics opened up in 1943, when the company was called in to assist the Navy in the development of training devices to increase the effectiveness of torpedo planes and submarines in combat. These activities and commercial projects which followed on the strength of this experience, led to the establishment of an electronics division, which today is deeply involved in aerospace, training and optical/electronic systems.

Samuel Austin, founder.

Austin's operations spread abroad — Latin America, Europe, Australia and the Far East. Like U.S. operations, each subsidiary is a completely integrated operating unit, fully staffed for administrative, sales and technical functions.

Each of the company's operating units and divisions is fully equipped to provide a full range of professional services from conceptual studies through facility design and development, start up and even facility maintenance.

The Austin Method has been responsible for the completion of thousands of facilities for general manufacturing, food production, chemical processing, banking and electronic data processing, warehousing and distribution, offices, research and development, communications, institutions, health care facilities, mining, metals processing, cement production and retail merchandising.

The Baker Material Handling Corporation

Meeting America's material handling needs since 1853

A 1915 Baker Electric lift truck in use at a Cleveland factory.

In 1853 on Columbus Road in Cleveland, a young German immigrant opened a horseshoeing and wagon repair shop.

Jacob Rauch's entry in the transportation market was the beginning of The Baker Material Handling Corporation, a multi-national organization in the material handling industry. Rauch wasn't thinking of global trade when he opened his shop, but he did establish a tradition which continues with Baker today — a quality product.

Rauch prospered from the start, due to hard work and his foresight in establishing his smithy on the Cincinnati stage route. By 1860, Rauch had a new shop on Pearl Road and was manufacturing custom coaches.

After the Civil War, the carriage and wagon industry grew rapidly. A new partner joined the business, and the Rauch and Lang Carriage Company began selling its product nationally. With an established reputation for quality, the company diversified in 1894 and began to manufacture small delivery vehicles.

During this same period, a young engineering graduate, Walter C. Baker, was helping to build an electric vehicle, the "Electrobat", for display at a Chicago exposition. Upon his return to Cleveland, Baker organized the American Ball Bearing Company which produced small bearings and axles. Baker's developments in this field, noted AUTOMOBILE magazine in 1903, paved the way for the rapid growth of the automobile industry.

This 1911 advertisement in Life magazine for Baker electric cars stressed their endurance and easy handling.

Despite his company's success, Baker was still intrigued with the "Electrobat" and returned to electrics in 1898 when he organized the Baker Motor Vehicle Company. In 1907, Baker added electric road trucks to his line and by 1912, more than 200 companies were using Baker fleets.

Baker Electrics were successful due to their quality and Walter Baker's innovations — including the first left-hand steering system, full-floating rear axles and streamlined styling, to name a few.

Rauch and Lang had also started manufacturing electric vehicles after the carriage and wagon industry peaked around 1900. Rauch & Lang electrics, superior in quality and design, were "the" car of the day.

However, the introduction of the self-starter in 1912 and the increasing popularity of the Ford Model T marked the electrics' decline. In 1915, the officials of Baker and Rauch & Lang announced their merger into the Baker R. & L. Company and began searching for new products to manufacture.

Baker R. & L. emerged with the Owen Magnetic — a gasoline powered automobile which featured magnetic ignition and spiral bevel gear drive (a Baker invention). Although the Owen Magnetic was successful, defense preparations interrupted production which was never fully resumed. World War I brought Baker into the production of its first industrial product, bomb-handling trucks, and determined a new direction.

This energy-conscious 1979 Baker Diesel Hydrostatic lift truck is representative of Baker's new generation of diesels with improved fuel economy, lower emission and reduced noise levels.

In years following, Baker added a line of platform trucks, began to manufacture truck bodies and added gasoline powered lift trucks in 1937.

World War II brought new needs: electric powered trucks for ordnance and munitions work and gasoline vehicles for loading. Baker was awarded an Army-Navy "E" award for excellence in production.

In 1952, Baker unveiled the Gas-O-Matic, the first gas powered electric motor-driven lift truck requiring no clutch or transmission and by acquisition, added gasoline and diesel side-loading vehicles to its line. The next year, Baker itself was acquired by the Otis Elevator Company.

Known as Baker Division, Otis Elevator Company, it improved its gasoline and electric powered trucks through the '60s. A major innovation in the material handling industry occurred in 1964 when the company introduced the first electric truck with SCR controls.

Two major acquisitions in 1967 further diversified the company's line and enforced its position in the market. First, the Moto-Truc Corporation brought the distinction of developing the industry's first powered pallet truck and a broad line of powered walkies and narrow-aisle trucks plus specialized design products. Then York Manufacturing was acquired, adding a series of high-capacity gas-pneumatic trucks.

Developments continued in the '70s and in 1977, a new path of growth was charted when the company was acquired by Linde Akiengesellschaft, the leading manufacturer of lift trucks in West Germany. The new company, Baker Material Handling Corporation, is the combination of Baker's more than 125-year tradition of quality manufacturing, and Linde's international marketing expertise and technology in engine powered trucks.

Linde also brings a long history of experience in diesel engines and hydrostatic drives, which, considering the nation's growing energy concern, is becoming an important consideration for manufacturers. These events have added an exciting new dimension to the material handling industry and once again re-positioned Baker for future growth.

Blue Cross of Northeast Ohio & Medical Mutual of Cleveland, Inc.

Pacesetters in health care insurance are Cleveland based

Friday, June 15, 1934. It was a warm hazy day in Cleveland. A veil of thin red dust moved lazily from the industrial valley toward Lake Erie. Though page one headlines heralded other events, perhaps the most significant story of the day unfolded quietly in a modest two-man office in the 1900 Euclid Building.

The Cleveland Hospital Service Association, later known as Blue Cross of Northeast Ohio, bravely opened its doors that day on the strength of a promised loan of up to $7500 from the Welfare Federation.

Today, nearly 1.8 million subscribers to one of the nation's first Blue Cross plans take it for granted that they can receive hospital care when needed. They are among the 112 million people who prepay their care through one of 115 Blue Cross and Blue Shield plans.

From the start, CHSA was different from most insurers — it was nonprofit and it offered hospital service rather than indemnity payments against the bill.

This startling idea grew locally out of the genius and dedication of a man named John R. Mannix, then chairman of the civic committee which created CHSA.

Family and hospital budgets alike were threatened by the Depression. Mannix's idea assured patients the care they needed while keeping hospitals afloat.

Years later, after service with Blue Cross plans in Detroit and Chicago, Mannix would head the organization he fostered. A determined leader even in the earlier years, Mannix bet a straw hat the fledgling plan would have 10,000 subscribers in five years. He won the hat only 10 months later.

Within a decade the subscriber count swelled to well over half a million in five Northeast Ohio counties, and CHSA again startled the conservative insurance industry by offering family and maternity coverage.

This department is typical of the legions of Blue Cross and Blue Shield employees who handled claims in the 1940s. The uniforms are gone now, of course, and many of today's employees work with the assistance of sophisticated computer technology.

The Rose Building, home of Blue Cross of Northeast Ohio much of its corporate life. Medical Mutual of Cleveland, Inc. also moved into this Cleveland landmark structure in 1947.

World War II ceilings on wages made health care benefits an attractive enticement in a tight employment market. So it was not surprising that another prepayment concept took hold in Cleveland. With the birth of Medical Mutual of Cleveland, Inc. in March, 1945, Greater Clevelanders could receive coverage for doctors' surgical-medical services as a natural companion to their Blue Cross hospital coverage.

MMC began with a membership of 150 and the backing of 16 leading Cleveland businesses, many of which are listed in these pages.

First architectural drawing of Medical Mutual's proposed new headquarters, to be occupied in the 1980s.

Now a certified Blue Shield plan, Medical Mutual protects 60 percent of the population in its service area.

BCNO and MMC work in tandem, sharing some benefit plans, operations and principles. Moreover, they share an impressive pioneer legacy in health care insurance.

Just as Medical Mutual's foundations were uniquely based in the business — not the medical — community, it has continued to diversify as a healthy, growing business. Under the direction of President and Chief Executive Officer Edward C. Lechner, the local Blue Shield Plan offers dental and vision care coverage, as well as individual and group life insurance (through its subsidiary, Medical Life Insurance Company).

For its part, BCNO, now headed by President Donald R. Riordan Sr., was the first plan in the nation to offer two full years of hospital benefits and was a leader in providing prescription drug service coverage, complete outpatient and ambulatory coverage.

Together, BCNO and MMC were among the first to offer catastrophic coverage to individuals not affiliated with groups. Today, they continue to cooperate on a wide range of cost-saving benefits designed to provide care in the most economical setting, including sponsorship of a health maintenance organization.

Yes, the focus has changed nationally, as it has changed in Cleveland. With combined annual benefit payments approaching a half billion dollars, the plans are hopeful the increase in health care costs will level off.

The very principle which marked the beginnings of Blue Cross of Northeast Ohio and Medical Mutual of Cleveland, Inc. — quality health care available to all at the lowest possible cost — now underscores their drive for cost effectiveness. Programs promoting healthy lifestyles and early care are just part of that effort.

The record of past and current accomplishments promises more new ideas from Cleveland's Blue Cross and Blue Shield plans in the years ahead.

The Broadview Savings and Loan Company

Ohio's largest savings and loan has grown with Cleveland.

On July 19, 1919, The Broadview Savings and Loan Company opened for business in a frame building at the corner of Broadview and Pearl Roads, with one kind of savings account, one kind of loan, and four employees.

(In 1919 a typical house cost $3400, with $200 down. A man's suit cost $18.50, a woman's dress $4. The first non-stop airline flight from Cleveland to Washington was made in 1919; total flying time was two hours, 58 minutes.)

From the very beginning, customers responded warmly and loyally to Broadview's services and the individuals providing them. The company quickly established itself as a useful and valuable addition to the Old Brooklyn area.

As a result of steady growth, Broadview moved across Pearl to 3344 Broadview, a newer stone building, in 1924. The company stayed in this location through the bleak days of the Great Depression, growing steadily. Broadview was one of the first local institutions to join the Federal Home Loan Bank System when it was created in 1933, and the Federal Savings and Loan Insurance Corporation (FSLIC), created by Congress in 1934 to insure savings accounts.

The company moved again in 1948, to a new building constructed to its specifications at 4221 Pearl, the site of the old Pearl Road School. The 4221 Pearl building established the architectural style now synonymous with Broadview branch offices, and included the first drive-in teller windows of any financial institution in the area.

Broadview Savings' original office at Broadview & Pearl Roads.

Broadview's new corporate headquarters at I-77 & Rockside Road.

The postwar years were prosperous ones for the Cleveland area and for Broadview. The single-family housing boom provided Broadview with the opportunity to help many thousands of families buy homes. Much of the residential lending in Parma, Parma Heights, Seven Hills, and Broadview Heights was done by Broadview during those years.

Further physical expansion began in 1954, with a merger with the County Savings and Loan Company and conversion of its office to the first Broadview branch office in Lakewood. Eleven additional branches followed in the next decade, including several by acquisition and merger. These included the former Liberty Savings and Loan Company, Northern Ohio Savings and Loan Association, and the Fairview Park Savings and Loan Company.

By year-end 1958, Broadview had grown to $136 million assets, surpassing all other savings and loan companies in Ohio. And, Broadview today is still Ohio's largest. Assets passed $200 million in 1963; $500 million in 1972; $1 billion in 1977; and $1.5 billion in 1979.

Over the years, Broadview has been a major factor in the growth and redevelopment of downtown Cleveland. Broadview provided the original financing for Park Centre (now The Park) in 1970 — at that time, the largest FHA-insured mortgage loan ever made by a savings and loan anywhere in the country (over $30 million). In 1973, Broadview provided construction financing for extensive remodeling and a major addition to Charity Hospital. Broadview, through a subsidiary corporation, completely restored the historic Cuyahoga Building, a Public Square landmark which is entered in the National Register of Historic Places. And, more recently, Broadview provided major financing for the renovation of Stouffer's Inn on the Square.

Broadview wasn't idle in the area of improved customer services, either. The advent of computers, and their application in financial services, provided a chance for a greater degree of personalized service than ever before, since routine transactions could be handled more quickly and accurately, and other services suited to each customer's needs could be offered more economically. Broadview took advantage of this technology quickly, installing an on-line teller terminal network.

In 1975, this capability enabled Broadview to offer a totally new customer convenience. The Money Service plastic card statement savings account, coupled with computer terminals, permitted expansion of Broadview's savings services to nearly 60 Pick-n-Pay supermarkets, providing customers with extended hours and one-stop convenience. In 1978, this convenience was enhanced further when a telephone bill paying capability was added, permitting customers to authorize payment of routine living expenses from an interest-earning savings account.

1977 saw the merger of St. Clair Savings, a long-established Euclid-area savings and loan, with Broadview, adding nine offices to an already-extensive branch network.

Over the years, Broadview has grown with Cleveland, expanding to a network of more than 35 offices in northeast Ohio. More than 300,000 account holders rely on Broadview for a generous interest return, and tens of thousands of Cleveland-area homes have been purchased by families with Broadview's professional assistance. A new headquarters building, near Interstate 77 and Rockside Road, is rapidly becoming a landmark familiar to residents and visitors alike.

Broadview Savings is, and will continue to be, an integral part of the Cleveland community.

The Catholic Diocese of Cleveland

Unity in diversity: the Catholic experience in Cleveland

The Catholic Church has been a major part of the development of Cleveland and the land known as the Western Reserve. From the first settlement, through the waves of immigrants, to the present, the Cleveland Diocese has been an amalgam of diverse peoples and cultures — a true reflection not only of the Church in America but also of the Church Universal.

The area of Cleveland and the surrounding Cuyahoga River region was especially attractive to the first settlers. Originally the Diocese of Cincinnati served the Catholics who lived in the Cleveland area — Irish Catholics who had fled starvation in their homeland and Germans who sought the elusive promise of religious freedom, and others.

The completion of the Ohio Canal and the building of the railroad insured Cleveland's role as an industrial and commercial center and its population increased rapidly. With the increase in population came increased needs and more demands on the church. Recognizing those needs, His Holiness Pope Pius IX established the Diocese of Cleveland on April 23, 1847.

Cut off from Cincinnati, the new diocese included all the territory from Pennsylvania to Indiana and from Lake Erie to the 41st parallel. As the first Bishop, the Pope chose Father Louis Amadeus Rappe, a French-born missionary, who was working among the canal workers in Toledo. Encompassing 33 counties, the Catholic population of the newly-formed diocese was about 10,000 people. There were 42 churches and 21 priests.

There was only one church, "Our Lady of the Lake," to serve the needs of the Catholics in Cleveland proper. It had been dedicated on June 7, 1840 and became popularly known as Saint Mary's of the Flats. It served as the pro-Cathedral of the diocese until the first Saint John's Cathedral was dedicated in November, 1852 at the present location.

Saint Mary of the Flats, the first church in Cleveland, was dedicated in 1840.

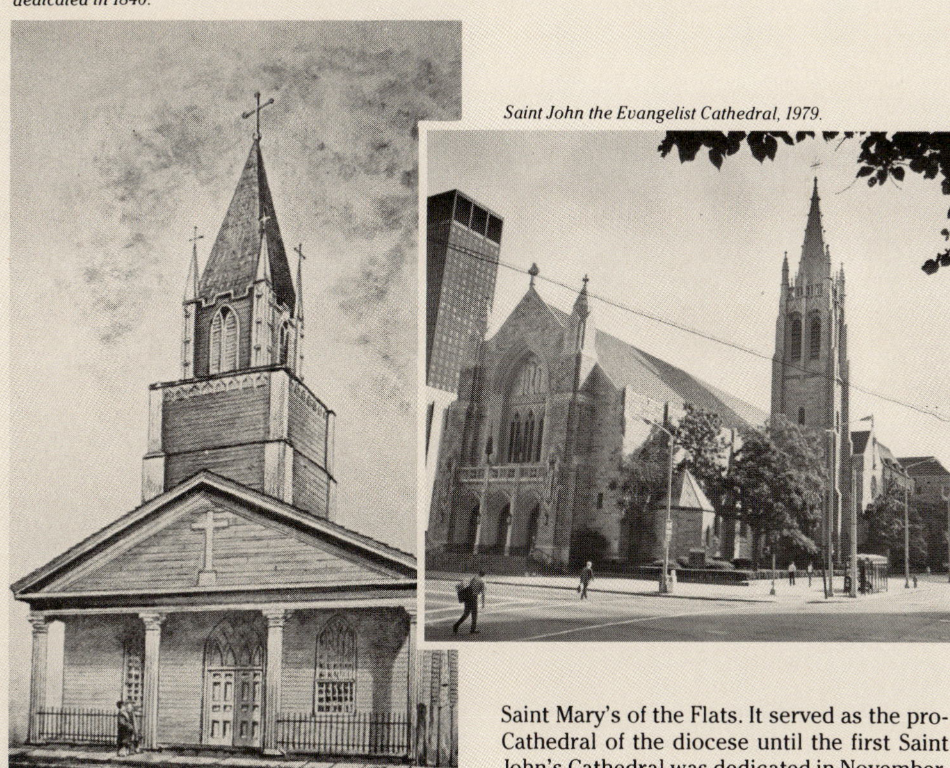

Saint John the Evangelist Cathedral, 1979.

What happened with Saint Mary's of the Flats is typical of Catholicism as it developed in the Cleveland Diocese. The rapid industrialization centering upon the steel mills in the Flats brought men from all over Europe, seeking jobs. Each ethnic group set up its community centered on the parish church. In a period of 20 years, Saint Mary's of the Flats served as the "mother church" for the following nationality groups: the Germans — who later formed Saint Peter's and Saint Mary of the Assumption, the Irish — who later established Saint Malachi's on the west bank of the Cuyahoga, the Bohemians — who later built Saint Wenceslas, the French — who later formed Annunciation, and the Polish — who founded Saint Stanislaus. Literally falling to pieces, Saint Mary's of the Flats was finally torn down in 1886.

The great strength of the Cleveland Catholic was drawn from the roots experienced in the preservation of ethnic traditions. Besides the Irish and the Germans, immigrants came from Poland, Czechoslovakia, Hungary, Yugoslavia, Italy and other European countries...seeking the American dream. Unfortunately, harsh realities awaited them in their new land. They survived these difficulties by working together with their unifying tradition of faith. This is the foundation of the deep faith of the people of the Cleveland Diocese that still endures today.

When Bishop Rappe resigned in 1870 his diocese embraced about 100,000 Catholics and 117 priests. During the years of his service, he had begun schools, a major hospital, an orphanage, and homes for the aged. He also established a seminary, Saint Mary (Our Lady of the Lake) which still flourishes.

In 1910 the Toledo Diocese was created from the western half of the Cleveland Diocese. In 1943 the Diocese of Youngstown was formed, leaving Cleveland with eight of its former 33 counties.

Today the Diocese of Cleveland includes not only the greater Cleveland area, but also Akron and Lorain, important industrial centers. Its diversity calls for ministry to urban, suburban, and rural areas, yet it continues to draw immigrants. There are more than 40 nationality parishes in the diocese, many of them vibrantly reflecting the unique religious heritage of their founders.

The Catholic population of the Diocese of Cleveland is presently nearly one million. There are 956 priests serving the Diocese. Bishop James A. Hickey, present bishop of Cleveland, is assisted by Auxiliary Bishop Gilbert I. Sheldon and retired Bishop Clarence G. Issenmann.

Central National Bank of Cleveland

Serving a growing community with innovative financial services

The Gay '90s were not so gay for banking institutions hard hit by the panic of 1893. But for three-year-old Central National Bank, they were the first in a long series of growth periods.

Formed by Colonel Jeremiah J. Sullivan, ex-Civil War soldier, state senator, bank examiner, and businessman, with $800,000 in capital stock, the bank opened for business on May 26, 1890, in the Perry Payne Building.

A staff of five people was ready to serve the public in the heart of Cleveland's business community.

As the city's commerce and industry grew, so, too, did the bank. By 1905 it had outgrown its original quarters. Next door, the city's first skyscraper — the 17-story Rockefeller Building — was being erected, and Central National took over the entire first floor. This action was the first of many the bank would take during its history to show its faith in downtown Cleveland.

Although the bank was growing steadily, national banks were prohibited from offering certain services, such as savings accounts and trust funds. In 1905 Colonel Sullivan organized the Superior Savings and Trust Co. to provide those services. First-day deposits alone totaled $2.6 million, indicating the demand was there.

Sixteen years later, when restrictions were lifted, the two banks merged and had combined capital of $4.5 million.

In the 1920s, Central became the first Ohio bank to establish an international banking department. Today, Central leads the state in international banking and is the only Ohio bank with an Edge Act subsidiary in New York City to facilitate foreign transactions.

Central National's concern for the future of

Rockefeller Building, where Central made its headquarters from 1905 to 1927 and where it still has a thriving branch office.

growing businesses was exemplified in 1925, when its corporate bankers assisted a fledgling publication whose "time almost ran out." TIME magazine, temporarily being published in Cleveland, was "technically busted" when Central advanced funds pending receipts from a Christmas gift-subscription campaign. The campaign was a success; and, although TIME returned to New York, Central still handles subscription checks for all Time, Inc. publications.

On November 18, 1929, less than a month after the infamous Black Thursday Wall Street plunge, Central National and United Banking and Trust merged. Central retained its national charter, and the new institution — Central United National Bank — became the largest national bank in Ohio, with total resources of more than $114 million.

During the Depression of the 1930s, 1,400 U.S. banks failed. But Central National ("United" was dropped in 1936 for brevity) continued to grow. At the end of the '30s, the bank had 12 suburban branches throughout Cuyahoga county.

During the decade following World War II, Central opened 18 new branches to serve an increasingly mobile population. Early in the 1950s, the bank installed the first auto-teller facility in Cleveland.

In 1965, 75 years after Colonel Sullivan greeted his first customer, Central's total assets reached $1 billion — then more than doubled in the next 14 years.

Present Central National Bank Building, completed in 1969, is headquarters for both the bank and its parent holding company, Centran Corporation.

Also in 1965, the bank reaffirmed its commitment to Cleveland when it announced plans for a 23-story main office building in the heart of downtown's thriving financial district.

The *Plain Dealer* of Cleveland said this decision "adds zest to the progressive spirit of the city. It is pace-setting."

The bank has continued its pace-setting efforts in other ways, pioneering in the first local all-purpose charge card for consumers in 1968. In 1979 Central National became the first Cleveland bank to introduce a "private label" Visa card, for a national clothing manufacturer and retailer.

In 1978 the bank opened the area's first free-standing automated banking machines, in non-branch locations, to provide customers convenient 24-hour banking service.

To ensure continued growth and achievements during the '70s and beyond, Central initiated in late 1971 the formation of Centran Corporation, a regional multibank holding company, of which Central is the principal affiliate.

Centran's affiliated banks and non-bank companies provide financial services through more than 100 offices in the United States and key international centers.

As Central National's second century of progress approaches, the bank is preparing to meet tomorrow's needs for innovative financial services.

Chase Brass & Copper Co.

Combining advanced brass mill technology with history and tradition

The over 100-year history of Chase Brass in the copper and brass industry had its beginning when most of America's brass mills were centered in Waterbury, Connecticut.

The first unit of what was destined to become Chase Brass & Copper was founded in January 1876, when the Waterbury Manufacturing Company was formed to manufacture brass goods, including such articles as umbrella furniture, upholstery trimmings, saddlery goods, patented novelties and brass castings.

Founder, Augustus Sabin Chase, was the initial president of the Waterbury Manufacturing Company, and members of the Chase family served as president until 1940.

It was in 1913 that the company, then a growing and major brass products industrial complex, combined the Waterbury Manufacturing Company, Chase Rolling Mill Company and the Chase Metal Works under the single

The Chase trademark

Cleveland Sheet Division today, including 20-story continuous vertical strip annealing tower, unique in the copper industry. The tower size is unusual, both as an industrial structure and as one of the tallest buildings on Cleveland's eastern suburban skyline.

name, The Chase Companies, Inc. Subsequently in 1936, the company adopted its present name, Chase Brass & Copper Co. Incorporated.

The Chase trademark was introduced in 1928, in a double page advertisement in the Saturday Evening Post. The centaur was chosen as an aggressive type of figure, well suited for the company's products and the industries served.

In 1929, the Kennecott Copper Corporation purchased Chase Brass. Shortly thereafter, Chase expanded its operations to the midwest and constructed the Babbitt Road brass tube mill in Cleveland. In 1946, Chase further expanded its Cleveland operations by acquiring the Cleveland Sheet Mill after its conversion from a war production plant.

Chase always believed that technological manufacturing innovation was essential in order to best participate in the brass mill products markets. The Cleveland mills illustrated this strategy, as shown by the unique 20-story continuous annealing tower at the Cleveland Sheet Mill.

In 1965, Chase Brass further expanded in the midwest with the construction, in western Ohio, of a highly automated brass rod mill. This mill, again, combined technology developed by Chase Brass with Chase's longstanding brass mill manufacturing experience to create what is now believed to be the most modern and efficient brass rod mill in the world.

Chase has also applied its metal fabricating technologies to other metals and processes. Chase Nuclear, a Canadian based division, has become the prime manufacturer of zirconium pressure tubes for heavy water nuclear reactors worldwide, as well as becoming a specialty manufacturer of titanium and other reactive metal products.

The Forged Parts unit, which remains in one of the original buildings in Waterbury, Connecticut, serves the custom engineered parts industry. A nationwide metals distribution organization, Chase Metals Service, is headquartered in Cleveland, and completes the Chase group of companies.

The Chase Brass group thus remains a leading fabricator of copper and brass, and continually strives to improve and utilize its metal fabricating technology in order to best serve today's industrial markets.

Chessie System, Inc.

Transportation company traces founding to George Washington

Chessie System, Inc., the parent for a diversified group of companies, traces its historical growth back to 1827 when Baltimore and Ohio, the first rail line in the nation, was chartered. And B&O, along with another of the Chessie companies, Chesapeake and Ohio, traces its corporate links to canal companies founded in the 18th century by George Washington.

The transportation company today includes three major railroads — the Chesapeake and Ohio, Baltimore and Ohio and Western Maryland — and some smaller subsidiary roads. Its other companies include several coal land development firms, an aviation company that sells, operates and maintains corporate aircraft, the world-famous Greenbrier Hotel at White Sulphur Springs, W. Va., and Chessie Resources, Inc., which is active in real estate and forest resource development and oil and gas exploration.

The railroads, largest segment of Chessie System, Inc., serve 12 states, the District of Columbia and Ontario, Canada with more than 11,200 miles of track. They make up the largest coal-hauling system in the country, and they are also a major carrier of merchandise freight.

One of the Chessie railroads, the B&O, has served northern Ohio since the mid-1880s. It reached Cleveland proper in 1894 with its lease of the Cleveland Terminal and Valley Railroad. By 1901, the B&O had acquired the Cleveland, Lorain and Wheeling Railroad.

A B&O passenger and freight depot, built in 1898, still stands at Canal Road and Columbus Street and is used as a freight office.

Cleveland became headquarters for the Chesapeake and Ohio on January 29, 1923, when O. P. and M. J. Van Sweringen, bought control of C&O from the widow and nephew of Collis P. Huntington. While C&O kept its main operating offices in Richmond, Va., in the early 1920s, its financial affairs were handled from Cleveland.

Chessie operations on the banks of the Cuyahoga River under the shadow of the Terminal Tower. The B&O agent's office (left, below new office building under construction) was built at the turn of the century.

Both C&O and B&O trace their corporate links to canal companies founded in 1785 by George Washington, C&O on the James River and B&O on the Potomac River. Over the years, both rail lines grew with the absorption of many smaller railroads, and by building their own tracks to serve the booming industrial area of America's heartland. Today they serve the rich Appalachian coal fields, the electric power companies, the steel mills, the automobile manufacturers, the chemical companies and the food and grain industry in Ohio, Kentucky, West Virginia, Virginia, Indiana, Illinois, Maryland, Pennsylvania, Delaware, New York, Michigan and Wisconsin, as well as southern Ontario.

"Chessie System," as the name for the combined C&O, B&O and Western Maryland, was formally unveiled in a civic ceremony on August 31, 1972, at Clark Avenue Yard, B&O's Cleveland terminal on 65 acres bordering the Cuyahoga two miles east of Terminal Tower. At that ceremony, Hays T. Watkins, Chessie's chairman, hailed Cleveland as the "father city" of many railroad companies.

Although C&O tracks never actually entered the city, the Vans maintained the railroad's headquarters in the Terminal Tower, as did five other railroads, off and on. Only Chessie is still there.

The Vans built the Tower (completed in 1930) and they also owned the Erie and Nickel Plate railroads, developed Shaker Heights and built the Rapid Transit Line linking that suburb and the city. The Terminal Tower, 708 feet and 52 stories high, was at that time the world's tallest building outside New York City. Until it was opened, the Vans had executive offices (1922-1929) in the Marshall Building, at the northwest corner of Public Square.

Chessie System locomotive in Clark Ave. Yard adjacent to Jones and Laughlin Steel mill.

In 1929, O. P. Van Sweringen became C&O chairman of the board and John J. Bernet became president. In 1935 the Vans moved their attention to other railroad properties, and the C&O presidency went to William J. Harahan. In 1937 Robert R. Young joined the C&O board and later became chairman.

Other prominent Clevelanders on the C&O board in that era included Alva Bradley, H. M. Hanna, Jr., Robert J. Bulkley and, perhaps most famous of all, Cyrus S. Eaton, whose tenure stretched into the 1970s.

Eaton, who died in 1979 at the age of 95, became C&O board chairman in 1954 when Young acquired the New York Central. Eaton had been a C&O director since 1943 and served C&O and Chessie for 35 years.

The company's corporate symbol is an outline of the famous sleeping kitten, Chessie, which has been "working on the railroad" since C&O started using her to advertise passenger trains in 1933. Today, she symbolizes "careful handling" of freight.

Cleveland Browns, Inc.

A classic sports tradition — winning, innovating, entertaining

A long list of credentials supports the statement that the Cleveland Browns are carrying on a winning tradition. Conference titles, division titles, four National Football League championships, and four All-America Conference championships are but a token example. The list goes on to include eight men in the Pro Football Hall of Fame in Canton, Ohio, enviable attendance records, stable ownership, innovative ideas, sports entertainment at its best and more victories than any other NFL team since joining the league in 1950.

Such are the hallmarks of the Cleveland Browns, an organization steeped in a winning tradition. Although recent seasons haven't been quite as glamorous as through the 1950s and 1960s, all signs point to a gathering of renewed strength for a fresh assault in the seasons ahead.

A continuation of the resurgence began last year through the efforts of Head Coach Sam Rutigliano, aided by an expanded scouting system that already is pumping highly regarded new talent into the team at an accelerated pace.

But back to the beginning.

Back to September 4, 1944, when formation of the All-America Conference was announced and included a Cleveland franchise owned by taxi cab magnate, Arthur B. McBride.

Back to February 8, 1945, when McBride hired Paul Brown, who then was still in service at Great Lakes Naval Training Station as head coach. Salary: $25,000, a record at the time.

Jim Brown, greatest ball carrier ever.

Back to September 6, 1946, when Cleveland's successor to the departed Rams played its first AAC game and demolished the Miami Seahawks, 44-0. In the intervening time, Paul Brown had rounded up outstanding talent such as Otto Graham, Bill Willis, Lou Groza, Marion Motley, Dante Lavelli and a seemingly endless stream of quality players.

So superior was the team that it was virtually untouchable in the fledgling AAC. Result: 47 regular season victories against four losses and three ties.

All of it was only a prelude to bigger things, however. Acceptance into the prestigious National Football League was a logical next step, but few other than the Browns themselves were prepared for the remarkably smooth transition accomplished by the 'upstart' outfit.

It began with a 35-10 stunner over the Philadelphia Eagles in September, 1950. It ended three months later with an 8-3 playoff decision over the rugged New York Giants defense, followed by a last-minute field goal by Groza for a 30-28 championship triumph over the Los Angeles Rams. The same Rams taken by the late Dan Reeves out of Cleveland after winning an NFL title in 1945.

The stage was set, the curtain was up, and

Cleveland Stadium, Cleveland, Ohio — one of 58 stadium events featuring 80,000 plus crowds.

the Browns were off and running...and passing ... and winning.

Six consecutive appearances in title games from 1950 through 1955. Others in 1957 and 1958, then the stunning 27-0 upset of the Baltimore Colts in the 1964 classic. There came other title game appearances in 1968 and 1969.

McBride had long since sold the club to a group headed by Dave Jones, Saul Silberman and Homer Marshman in the 1950s, and they in turn accepted an offer by Art Modell on March 21, 1961.

Paul Brown was the only head coach the Browns had until Blanton Collier assumed the role prior to the 1963 season. Nick Skorich succeeded Collier in 1971, followed by Forest Gregg in 1975, and Rutigliano in 1978.

The astounding success of the Browns from the outset made certain a parade of longtime Cleveland favorites would commence being enshrined into the Hall of Fame at an early date.

First to be honored was Graham in 1965. Then came Paul Brown in 1967 followed by Motley a year later, Jim Brown in 1971, Groza in 1974, Lavelli in 1975, Len Ford in 1976 and Willis in 1977. There will be others, too, more than a few.

Fifty-nine different Browns' players have appeared in the annual Pro Bowl game over the years, a strong indication of the caliber of athletes to represent Cleveland through more than three decades.

The fans have responded in kind, keeping the Cleveland Stadium turnstiles in a continuous whirl for 33 seasons. Regular season games alone in that period have brought in more than 13 million spectators.

Playoffs, championships, and pre-season games helped swell the home total considerably more. Modell's unique pre-season doubleheaders were a tremendous mid-summer attraction for many years.

There have been 58 crowds of 80,000 or more at Browns' home games, 56 of them during Modell's ownership. And counting road attendance, more than 31 million have seen the club in action since its inception in 1946.

A winning tradition.

It all comes together with the Cleveland Browns.

The Cleveland-Cliffs Iron Company

Pioneering spirit is a company tradition

Abundant reserves of high grade iron ore in Michigan's Upper Peninsula were a long way from Cleveland and a small group of young men who were most interested in them in the 1840s. Reaching these rich iron deposits was a rigorous journey requiring weeks of hard travel, but the pioneering spirit of these men was not to be denied.

Confirming reports of a mountain of magnetic ore along Lake Superior's southern shore, the Cleveland group, which included such entrepreneurs as Samuel L. Mather, promptly organized a company to mine and market the rich deposit. Under slightly differing names, Cliffs, the oldest of iron mining companies in the Lake Superior Region, has had a continuous life which spans the entire development of America's modern age of iron and steel.

Cleveland-Cliffs was organized as The Cleveland Iron Mining Company with Samuel L. Mather as its head in 1850. In 1891, it became The Cleveland-Cliffs Iron Company, a formidable competitor in the young industry, when it merged with The Iron Cliffs Company which Samuel J. Tilden, a lawyer and governor of New York had organized in 1864. Jeptha H.

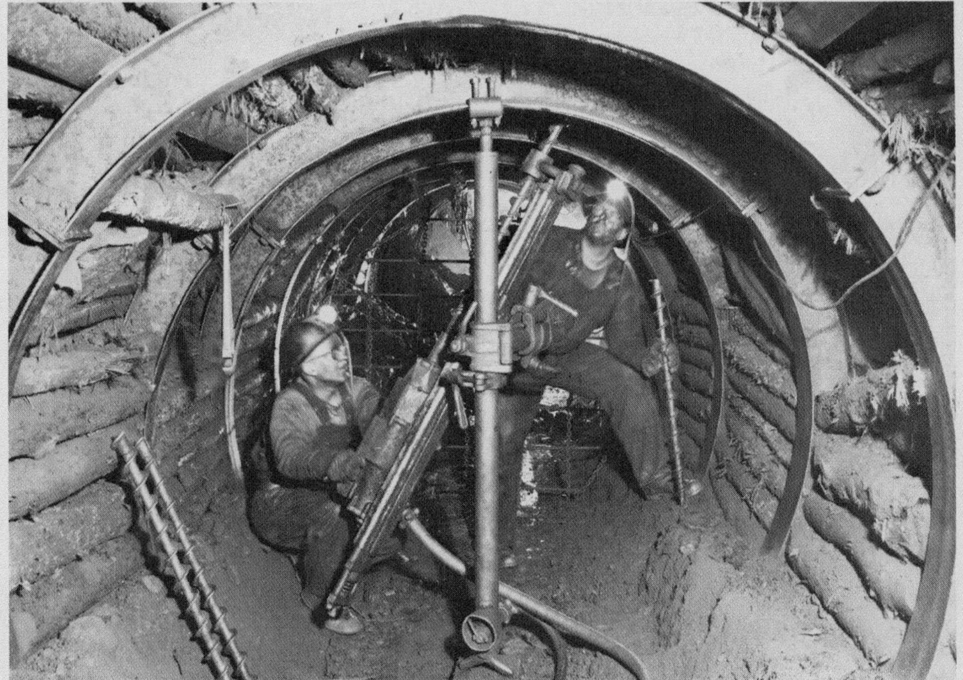

Underground drilling in the Mather Mine in 1952.

Wade, Sr. of Cleveland, a director of The Cleveland Iron Mining Company and founder of Western Union Telegraph Company, was the catalyst. By 1889, he owned more than 70 percent of Iron Cliffs' shares and had also become a director of that company. Both Wade and Mather died before the consolidation was complete. Wade's grandson, Jeptha Wade, Jr., and Mather's son, William G. Mather, completed it.

For nearly 130 years, the company's far reaching innovations in mining and processing technology, as well as employee relations, have served to strengthen Cleveland-Cliffs' reputation throughout the world's iron and steel industry. Noted for its willingness to accept new challenges, Cleveland-Cliffs' pioneering spirit was severely tested in the early 1950s. Believing the nation's reserves to be nearly exhausted after supporting nearly 175 years of vigorous economic growth, not to mention the heavy demands of two global wars, America's steel industry had started searching for new iron ore sources.

At the forefront of an intense research effort by industry to find ways for upgrading and handling the vast amounts of low-grade iron ore reserves remaining in Michigan and Minnesota, Cleveland-Cliffs led in the economic development of iron ore pellets. Cleveland-Cliffs accepted the tremendous risks inherent in using new and untried equipment to perfect the technology for concentrating and pelletizing low-grade iron ore, overcoming countless obstacles along the way to success.

With the successful developments of the low-grade ores reducing pressures for new foreign supplies, Cleveland-Cliffs expanded its operations to Canada and Australia in the 1960s. Acquiring substantial reserves in Australia, the company organized a major international joint venture consisting of American, Japanese and Australian interests and completed construction of a mine, pellet plant, railroad, port facility and two townsites in late 1972 at a cost of about $300 million.

The Tilden Mine, 1979.

Efforts in Canada in the late 1960s resulted in the development of a mining operation in Temagami, Ontario in conjunction with a major Canadian steel producer. Cleveland-Cliffs assumed management of a second mining operation owned by the same steel company at Kirkland Lake, Ontario in the early 1970s.

Cleveland-Cliffs' interest in Great Lakes shipping date back to 1869 when the company built the first vessel designed expressly for the iron ore trade. Today, the Cliffs' fleet of Great Lakes vessels numbers 14 with a combined single trip cargo capacity in excess of 250,000 tons.

Involvement in the forest products industry also dates back to the company's early mining days in Michigan when the timber was needed for mine supports and for charcoal to fuel the pig iron furnaces. Today the company harvests nearly 43 million board feet of hardwood saw logs, veneer logs, pulpwood and chemical wood annually from its 330,000 acres of Upper Peninsula timberland.

The company's diversification efforts of recent years include managing joint ventures engaged in the exploration and development of uranium in Wyoming and developing an economic process to extract oil from shale rock in the western United States. With the company's early background in coal, as well as in oil shale and uranium, an interest in other energy minerals was natural. In 1978, Cleveland-Cliffs formed a new subsidiary with the acquisition of a Texas-based contract drilling company to participate in the growing oil and gas drilling industry.

Today Cleveland-Cliffs stands as a tribute to the men and women who had the courage to pursue their convictions. This same pioneering spirit, demonstrated through inventiveness in countless ways over the last 130 years, certainly will be an integral part of Cleveland-Cliffs in future generations.

Cleveland Clinic Foundation

World-wide distinction in patient care, education and research

While serving in the U.S. Army medical corps during World War I, three noted Cleveland surgeons began formulating an idea that broke sharply with the way medicine had traditionally been practiced. So controversial was their concept, it would later be denounced locally as medical heresy.

The iconoclasts were Drs. George W. Crile, Frank E. Bunts and William E. Lower. Each had become impressed with the speed and efficiency of military medical teams in the war. Their idea: to form a clinic in which medical specialists, in a group practice setting, could deliver quality care.

The bold concept became reality in 1921 with the founding of the Cleveland Clinic Foundation, an institution that has since evolved into one of the largest privately-funded and renowned medical centers in the world.

Although Drs. Crile, Bunts and Lower were nationally known and respected in medicine (and each had enjoyed a large private practice before coming together as a team in 1895), their notion that medicine could be practiced efficiently by a group of physicians was not looked upon favorably by many Clevelanders in the 1920s. Many doctors feared group practice would give them unfair competition. Other persons feared it would destroy the basic fabric of medicine.

Despite opposition, the founders pursued their dream. They later incorporated Dr. John Phillips into their plan.

Patient care, medical research and medical education would be the Clinic's objectives, they decided.

With the help of associates, and personal friends such as Drs. Charles and William

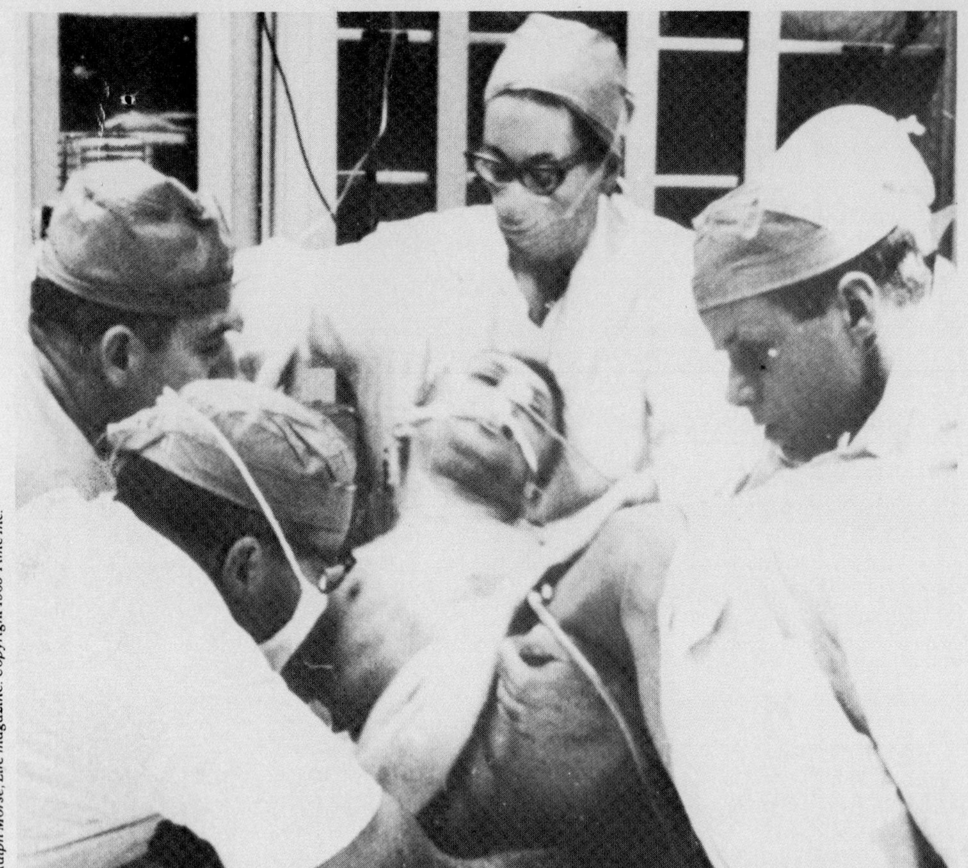

Ralph Morse, Life magazine. Copyright 1965 Time Inc.

One of the first kidney transplant patients is helped from operating table by Clinic physicians. Photo, taken in 1965, was used in Life magazine article on kidney transplants.

Mayo (founders of the Mayo Clinic), the four men opened the Clinic February 26, 1921 in a four-story building at E. 93rd and Euclid Avenue. This original structure still remains a part of the Clinic.

Crises and phenomenal growth highlighted the Clinic's early years. Soon after the Clinic opened, physicians in Cleveland, alarmed by the threat of salaried group practice, barred Clinic physicians from hospitals in which they had practiced. The Clinic countered by converting two neighborhood houses into a 53-bed hospital and later building a modern 184-bed hospital beside the Clinic.

A fire erupted at the Clinic May 15, 1929 in a room where x-ray film was stored. Toxic fumes spread throughout the building, killing 123 persons, including founder John Phillips. Despite the disaster and the 1929 stock market crash, the institution survived that infamous year.

Man Helping Man by Cleveland sculptor William M. McVey in courtyard.

It was also during these formative years that the Clinic's reputation was being built on Dr. Crile's surgical removal of goiters, endemic throughout the Midwest before the days of iodized salt. Dr. Crile averaged more than 20 such operations a day.

As its reputation grew, the Clinic recruited additional medical and surgical experts from around the world. Medical milestones ensued. Among them:

- Numerous advancements in neurological surgery and the treatment of colon and rectal disease.
- The perfection of one of the earliest practical heart-lung machines.
- Development of coronary cine angiography and cardiac catheterization, two procedures which make possible the visualization of coronary artery disease.
- Major inroads in the study and treatment of hypertension, the "silent killer".
- Development of the artificial kidney, now used by 40,000 Americans to cleanse their blood of lethal toxins after kidney failure.

Today, Clinic researchers are actively investigating such areas as artificial organs, heart disease, artificial joints, cancer and immunology.

The Clinic, quartered in 15 buildings on 50 acres and 11 square blocks, is comprised of a 1,008-bed hospital, extensive outpatient facilities, a division of research and an institute for postgraduate and continuing medical education that serves more than 5,000 physicians and allied health professionals annually. Employment at the institution totals nearly 6,000.

The Clinic's international reputation was emphasized in 1978 when King Khalid of Saudi Arabia underwent heart surgery at the institution.

Throughout its illustrious history, the Clinic has been guided by the founders' mission: "... Better care of the sick, further study of their problems, and more teaching of those who serve."

The Cleveland Electric Illuminating Company

Nearly a century of service in Cleveland-Northeast Ohio

Ninety-eight years cover the history of the Cleveland Electric Illuminating Company, a company proud of association with the great pioneers in electrical research and development.

Today, this investor-owned utility serves some 703,000 customers in a 1,700-square-mile service area in Cleveland-Northeast Ohio.

Charles Francis Brush, an Edison contemporary, was a founder. Brush demonstrated the first successful commercial street lighting in the world with arc lights on Cleveland's Public Square on April 29, 1879. By 1881 Brush founded the Brush Electric Light and Power Company, forerunner of The Illuminating Company.

Robert Lindsay, who joined the company in 1893 and was president from 1921 until 1933, worked in Edison's Menlo Park laboratories.

Incorporated in 1892, The Cleveland Gen-

The first of two 840-ton reactor pressure vessels was installed at the Perry Nuclear Power Plant in mid-August 1978. From a 250-foot-high vantage point the reactor pressure vessel can be seen being lowered into position inside the containment building at Perry. The vessel will contain the nuclear fuel, the source of heat to produce steam to run the turbogenerators. The first generating unit of the two-unit $2.3 billion Perry Plant is scheduled to be in operation in 1983, the second in 1985.

eral Electric Company acquired the properties and businesses of the two companies which had been producing and selling electric energy since 1881 and 1884. In 1894, the name was changed to The Cleveland Electric Illuminating Company. The original territory served was three-quarters of a square mile.

During subsequent years, the company expanded operations through acquisition of electric properties of other area utilities and by extending its own lines into rural areas.

The period 1894 to 1905 marked concentration of generating facilities under one roof. From 1906 to 1911 substantial load growth took place and decentralization of distribution centers began. From 1912 to 1924, further expansion of the CEI system covered the major portion of Cuyahoga County.

April 29, 1879 Cleveland became the first city in the world to light its streets extensively by electricity. While the arc light was not Charles Francis Brush's original invention, he combined it with a dynamo into a practical power station that was quickly adopted in New York City. In the years to follow, Cleveland plants were producing appliances, lamps, and diversified electrical products for home, industry and farm. Dr. Brush earned renown as one of the greatest pioneer scientists and inventors in the field of electricity and his inventions were important contributions to the founding of the General Electric Company.

The Illuminating Building at 75 Public Square in downtown Cleveland was built by CEI, serving as main office from March 1913 to February 1958 when the company moved into the new Illuminating Building, 55 Public Square, still its corporate headquarters today.

Expansion became the name of the game during 1925-1929, as neighboring counties came into the CEI fold — Lake, Geauga, Ashtabula, and the eastern part of Lorain. Hundreds of miles of transmission lines were constructed, and substations sprang up.

During the depression years — 1930-1939 — the number of customers steadily rose.

World War II made enormous demands for electrical energy on the company. By 1940, Cleveland was one of three pivotal cities of the nation in war production.

As early as 1940, CEI embarked on a program labeled "The Best Location in the Nation" to attract new industries into Cleveland-Northeast Ohio.

By 1948, total power output surpassed the 1944 wartime peak.

In 1953, a fourth power plant went on line, the Eastlake Plant, joining the Lake Shore, Ashtabula, and Avon Lake Plants.

"Better Service Cheaper" was the company's new motto in the '60s, and towards this goal, a highly sophisticated computer system was installed, and CEI helped form the five-company Central Area Power Coordination Group (CAPCO). Decentralization of service operations continued.

Throughout the '60s, the company continued to strengthen operation ties not only with CAPCO, but with ECAR, the East Central Area Reliability Coordination Agreement.

The '70s became serious years at CEI, as environmental pressures grew.

The company's 80 percent share of the Seneca Hydroelectric Plant's power came into the system in 1970. The Atomic Energy Commission, now the Nuclear Regulatory Commission, granted a construction permit for the Davis-Besse Nuclear Power Station in March 1971. Later that same year, CEI announced plans to construct, as part of CAPCO, the Perry Nuclear Power Plant.

To improve the economy of power generation and transmission, CEI opened a $7 million System Operation Center (SOC), one of the world's first master control centers.

In 1977, Toledo Edison Company put Ohio's first commercial nuclear power plant into operation, the Davis-Besse station, of which CEI owns 51 percent.

As the decade progressed, construction started on the Perry plant 35 miles from downtown Cleveland in Lake County. When it goes on line in 1983, it will be among the largest in the country.

As The Illuminating Company approaches the 1980s, it is still a company whose most abundant fuel source is coal. It remains strong financially with a high credit rating.

And...since electric generation will remain the key energy process of the future... CEI continually gears itself to meet its construction program so it can provide future power needs of a still-growing Cleveland-Northeast Ohio.

Cleveland Federal Savings and Loan Association

Rooted in Cleveland's past, S&L has interest in future

On a cold January evening in 1892, a handful of men — all of German ancestry — gathered in a small room on the near west side of Cleveland and organized what eventually became Cleveland Federal Savings and Loan Association.

They agreed to pool their savings and finance the purchase of a house until each member eventually owned his own home. The name they chose for their new venture was the South Side German Building and Loan Association, and its first quarters were located above the street car company's waiting room at Clark Avenue and West 25th Street. Use of the office space was made possible by Tom L. Johnson, one of Cleveland's outstanding mayors, and association meetings were held there weekly.

By 1910, the association had erected its own office building at 3115 West 25th Street, a building which still is in use as a branch of Cleveland Federal. With its new facilities, the association was now a permanent and viable entity. By 1917 resources exceeded $1,000,000. In 1920 the name was changed to the South Side Savings and Loan Association, and assets exceeded $1,500,000.

A big step was taken in 1938 when it became South Side Federal Savings and Loan Association. Along with the addition of the word "Federal" to its name came membership in the Federal Home Loan Bank System and the Federal Savings and Loan Insurance Corporation. Despite the Depression, during the 1930s the association grew and by 1940 topped the $4 million mark in assets.

During World War II South Side Federal found itself in a pioneering role when it hired women for teller positions and put the staff in uniforms. In 1942 Allen C. Knowles became the fifth president of the association, an event which heralded the arrival of the association's growth era. By 1945 assets were over $10 million, and the association directed its energies to financing the housing needs of returning veterans.

In 1951 South Side Federal took a giant, pioneering step which was to unalterably change the course of savings and loans in northern Ohio. At that time the association opened its first branch — and the first branch office of any association in the area — amid a furor of hurrahs and criticism in the local media. But the path had been laid, and two years later the second South Side Federal branch was opened.

Then in 1956, with the acquisition of the Heights Savings and Loan Company, assets grew to $75 million, and South Side Federal ranked among the 100 largest savings associations in the United States, a position it still enjoys.

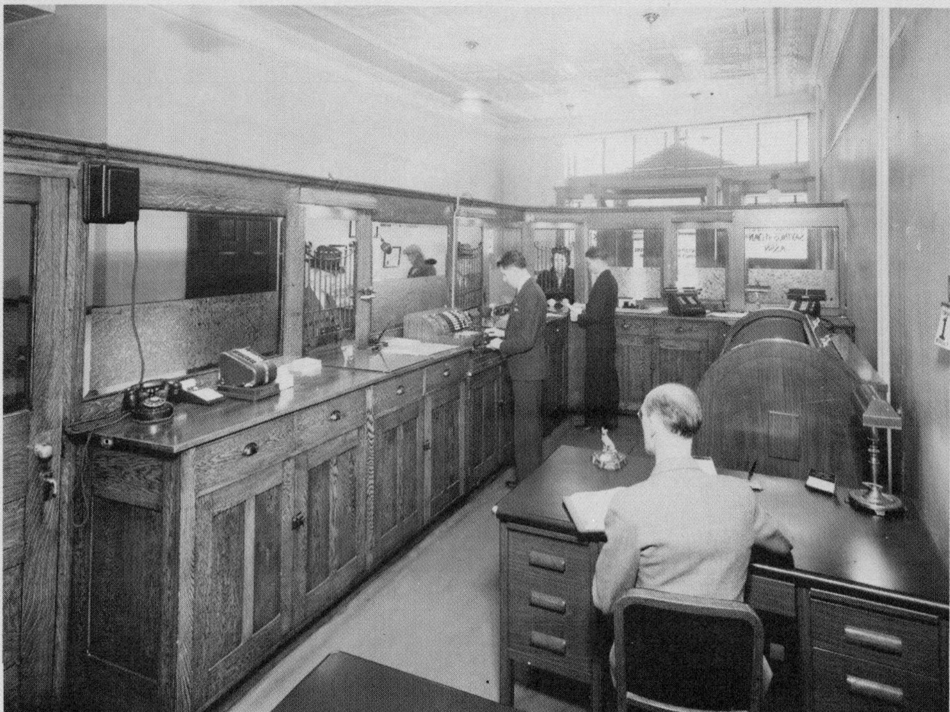

Back in the early 1930s, Cleveland Federal's only office at 3115 West 25th Street was considered both modern and secure.

Cleveland Federal Savings' Main Office at 614 Euclid Avenue serves as headquarters for $850,000,000 association with 35 locations in Northern and Central Ohio.

Branch expansion continued, and by 1960 it was obvious that "South Side" was no longer descriptive of the area served. Nor was the existing main office adequate for the needs of an association on the verge of greater growth and the computer age. These realizations brought about two events in 1961 and 1962: first, the name change to "Cleveland Federal Savings and Loan Association" and, second, the construction of a new five-story headquarters building, the first new office building constructed in downtown Cleveland in many years.

The opening of the new main office in September, 1962, ushered in a 17-year period of growth: in assets from $144 million to more than $850 million and office expansion from seven to 35 locations.

Significant among the 35 office locations are seven satellite facilities operating inside supermarkets — a means of making savings services available to more people.

Only two top management changes occurred during the 17-year period of greatest growth. Ovid Corsatea became president in 1968 as Knowles moved up to chairman of the board; William C. Buhrow was elected president in 1975 as Corsatea became chairman of the executive committee.

Also significant is that during the 1970s Cleveland Federal Savings extended its sphere of influence beyond Cuyahoga County into six additional counties — Lake, Portage, Lorain, Erie, and Medina in northern Ohio and Franklin County in central Ohio.

From humble beginnings above a street car company's waiting room to a position among the nation's largest savings associations in 87 years is the heritage of Cleveland Federal Savings and Loan Association.

Though deeply rooted in the past, at Cleveland Federal Savings "our interest is in your future."

Cleveland State University

A young institution with a long history

Cleveland State University's history spans only 15 years, but the lineage of its predecessor institutions reaches back at least to the 1870s.

The earliest forebears of CSU's 17,000 students were the handful of young men who showed up in the fall of 1870 for French and German classes at the local YMCA.

Those classes lasted only a few years, but it wasn't long before the YMCA renewed its educational efforts. By the time of the First World War 2,500 men were enrolled in 31 different courses.

With money donated by Clevelander Sereno Peck Fenn in 1928, the Y was able to erect a new building for educational purposes. The following year, the name of the school was changed to Fenn College of the Cleveland YMCA School of Technology. It was headquartered on Prospect Avenue, near the present CSU campus. During the 1930s the college acquired Fenn Tower, a 20-story structure which had been built as an elaborate private club in 1929. The club did not survive the market crash. After the building stood empty for several years, Fenn College took it over. The tower, and another Fenn acquisition, Stilwell Hall, are still in use by CSU's students.

In 1951 Fenn College became independent of the YMCA. Shortly thereafter G. Brooks Earnest became president, and served for the balance of Fenn's history.

On December 17, 1964, Ohio Gov. James A. Rhodes signed a bill creating a new state university in Cleveland. By September of the following year, Fenn officials had agreed to turn the assets of the college over to the new state university. That fall, CSU opened for business on the old Fenn campus with 4,500 students.

Planning began for expanded operations. Since 1969 CSU has erected one building after another in a construction project which has transformed the campus area, on the eastern boundary of downtown Cleveland along Euclid Avenue.

This $150 million construction program has produced CSU's Law Building, University Tower, University Center, Main Classroom Building, two science buildings, and a physical education complex, with plans for additional land and building projects.

The University is renovating the Samuel Mather mansion at the eastern end of campus. The mansion is one of the few vestiges of turn-of-the-century Euclid Avenue, when what is now the CSU campus was the fashionable address for wealthy Clevelanders, and when Samuel Mather was perhaps the wealthiest of them all.

In 1969, another long-lived Cleveland educational institution was merged into CSU. The Cleveland-Marshall College of Law can trace its history back to two separate institutions, the Cleveland Law School, which began in 1897, and the John Marshall Law School, which opened in 1916. They merged to form Cleveland-Marshall in 1946. For many years the law school was located on Ontario Street. In 1977, though, the college moved to its new $7.5 million headquarters. That building, at East 18th Street and Euclid Avenue, provides first-rate facilities for CSU's 1,100 law students.

Cleveland State University

Fenn Tower in the 1930s

Cleveland-Marshall College of Law

Since 1965 Cleveland State has developed into a leader among the nation's urban universities. By far the largest university in greater Cleveland, CSU does not measure its worth by size alone but can point to its academic accomplishments as well.

The University offers 58 baccalaureate programs, 25 master's programs, two postgraduate educational specialist programs, three law degrees, and three doctoral programs. Seven colleges comprise the University: Arts and Sciences, Business Administration, Education, Engineering, Graduate Studies, Law, and Urban Affairs, along with a Division of Continuing Education.

President Walter B. Waetjen has stressed excellence in every University activity. Cleveland State University first became known for the instructional skills of its faculty. In recent years it has built a solid reputation for its research findings. Its public service efforts have expanded to include a World Trade Education Center, a Speech and Hearing Clinic, an Educational Services Center, a Multicultural Education Center, a Labor Relations Institute, and many other units.

The University also has put together an outstanding Division I intercollegiate athletics program, featuring several nationally-ranked teams. The NCAA Swimming and Diving Championships are regularly held in the University's pool.

These accomplishments suggest that there is a lot of history yet to be written on the Cleveland State University campus.

Eaton Corporation

Moving people, materials and energy throughout the world

Trucks like these icewagons of 1920 were the basis for the founding of Eaton Corporation which began as a supplier of truck axles. Today the company is a worldwide supplier of transportation and industrial products.

At the dawning of the Automotive Age one of the industrial pioneers who envisioned a world of commerce on wheels was Joseph Oriel Eaton. In 1911, Eaton, a man of administrative and organizational genius, and Viggo Torbensen, a talented engineer, established a small company to build truck axles in a converted garage in Bloomfield, New Jersey. Although only seven axles were produced in the first year, the company quickly gained a reputation for quality and technological innovation. In order to be in the center of the burgeoning automotive industry the fledgling firm moved to Cleveland in 1915. After a few years of economic and financial growing pains, the company embarked on a growth path that has brought Eaton to the forefront of world industry in transportation and industrial products.

From the mid-'20s to World War II, internal growth and a series of key acquisitions established Eaton as a major supplier to the American automotive industry. Automobile springs and heaters were added to the now dominant truck axle line in Cleveland. Then came plants covering a four state area making engine valves, pumps, fan drives and a variety of precision engine components. A plant in Windsor, Ontario was opened in 1937 marking Eaton's first venture outside of the United States, the first step that would eventually lead Eaton around the world.

Eaton's plants and employees participated productively and vigorously in the nation's war effort. During the latter half of the '40s, Eaton expanded its growth pattern with the acquisition of companies in the fields of industrial power transmission and electronics.

More automotive products filled Eaton's catalogs. Forging operations and foundries were built and acquired to provide manufacturing strength. At the same time, the company's internal research and development capacity was growing fast, and, today, continues to be a major source of innovative products and techniques.

In 1958, the acquisition of the Fuller Manufacturing Company, the nation's leading manufacturer of heavy duty truck transmissions, put Eaton solidly in the top ranks of the world's automotive suppliers. Operations were underway in Europe and South America and Eaton was set for more dramatic growth beyond the automotive field.

The most significant move was the acquisition of the renowned Yale and Towne Company in 1963 and its worldwide leadership in materials handling systems and equipment. While the many acquisitions provided a more diverse product line there was also a close relationship in engineering and metals technology that produced a synergistic effect on the total picture. Among the acquisitions were a number of well known Cleveland companies: Airflex, Fawick, Tinnerman and Cleveland Worm and Gear.

With the expansion of its markets and greatly increased international activity, Eaton shot past the billion dollar sales mark in 1969 and reached two billion in 1977. In 1969, E. M. de Windt became chairman. Having spearheaded the international efforts of Eaton, Del de Windt was to become the driv-

The Eaton Axle Company ushered in the first year of the Roaring '20s by buying this 16-acre site on East 140th Street.

ing force in building a new, bigger and more balanced Eaton Corporation.

The new Eaton, operating at a $3.25 billion dollar sales rate, emerged in 1978 with the acquisition of Cutler-Hammer, a leader in electrical equipment and electronics; Kenway, a fast-growing pioneer in automated storage and retrieval systems and Samuel Moore of Aurora, Ohio, a maker of industrial tubing and controls.

Today, the vision of Joseph Eaton has more than been fulfilled. From his world headquarters in Cleveland, Del de Windt oversees operations of 65,000 employees on six continents. In addition to world headquarters, eight facilities are located in Cleveland, including manufacturing plants, a manufacturing services center and worldwide telecomputer center. Eaton and its employees have been recognized for outstanding civic involvement and corporate citizenship in Cleveland and are committed to a leadership role.

For Eaton, the road from those first seven truck axles to multinational eminence has been a fast track made possible by people of uncommon talent and dedication.

The H. K. Ferguson Company

A pacesetter since 1918 in engineering and construction

The H. K. Ferguson Company engineered and constructed the Globe-Wernicke Company building at 2044 Euclid Avenue in downtown Cleveland in 1920, two years after HKF's founding. The six-story structure and basement was erected at a cost of $343,965.50.

On August 5, 1918, Harold Kingsley Ferguson, a man of ambition and vision, founded The H. K. Ferguson Company in Cleveland.

Although he had limited capital, "H. K." and a handful of dedicated engineers quickly moved the fledgling company to a position of eminence in the field of engineering and construction throughout the world.

One secret for Ferguson's success was his willingness to accept challenges. While many established companies would try to avoid difficult projects, H. K. was willing to accept any challenge and under his guidance, The H. K. Ferguson Company became one of America's

The H. K. Ferguson Company did much of the engineering and construction of the U.S. Government's all-important nuclear complex at Oak Ridge, Tennessee, for the Atomic Energy Commission in the early 1950s. Even today, much of HKF's services are highly-confidential on this project.

first and foremost "total responsibility" engineers and builders.

The first of hundreds of total responsibility projects for Ferguson was a warehouse in Staten Island, NY, for Procter & Gamble. Work was completed in just 47 working days despite a major change in plans, and set the stage for more than 150 future contracts for P & G that have spanned six decades.

Another breakthrough idea H. K. had involved his Ferguson "Standard" building concept. This was a set of nine pre-engineered factory buildings that required substantially less time to complete because a standard set of drawings and prefabricated steel in stock could be utilized immediately for the type of factory desired.

The challenge of building industrial facilities quickly after World War I was met by H. K. and his "Standard" buildings. But, no sooner had he established his company as an innovative force in the engineering and construction industry, he accepted the company's most formidable challenge: help rebuild earthquake-stricken Japan.

The Japanese economy was near collapse. Earthquakes had devastated the country and engineering and construction companies in the U.S. didn't want any part in trying to rebuild the island nation. Ferguson welcomed the challenge and in 1922 the four-year-old firm was awarded a multi-million dollar contract to build a new heavy machine shop, a warehouse, a pattern shop and a forge shop for the Shibhaura Engineering Works.

Not only was the size of the contract astronomical at the time, but competitors, who initially were afraid of building in Japan, watched in amazement as Ferguson completed the work in two years. The Japanese were so impressed with the achievement that they awarded 17 more contracts to the company a short time later.

Within a few years of its founding, The H. K. Ferguson Company had completed an amazing 165 contracts. With a corporate motto of "A Good Job Done On Time," H. K. literally had turned the engineering and construction world on its ear.

Just as he had helped rebuild industry throughout the world following WWI, H.K.'s company was called on to help prepare for WW II. As war became imminent, the company engineered and built a series of defense plants and ammunition depots, nearly one-third of the country's chlorine facilities and also became the first company in the U.S. to build a synthetic rubber manufacturing plant.

Although at the height of the company's war effort death struck Harold Kingsley Ferguson at the age of 60, his work had to go on. The next year, the company he founded undertook the dramatic design and construction of the famous Manhattan Project in Oak Ridge, Tenn. At one point, the company had 25,000 employees, including 16,000 on a single project. The Oak Ridge facility was completed in record-breaking time, helping to bring an end to the war.

In post-war areas of construction, Ferguson was instrumental in bringing the basic oxygen steelmaking process to the Western Hemisphere, proceeding to construct one-quarter of all furnaces in the U.S.

In 1950, The H. K. Ferguson Company became the principal subsidiary of the Morrison-Knudsen Company of Boise, Idaho, and continued its aggressive program of accepting new challenges.

In the last six decades, The H. K. Ferguson Company has worked on over 3,000 projects throughout the world in such diverse industries as cement, chemicals, food, energy, petrochemicals, manufacturing, steel and metals, mining, pollution control, plastics and rubber.

Today, HKF is the world's largest engineer and builder to the beer brewing industry and a single project in Williamsburg, VA, for Anheuser-Busch, Inc. is the largest industrial expansion ever undertaken in the State of Virginia.

In the tradition of its founder, no challenge today is too great for The H. K. Ferguson Company to handle. It's doubtful there will ever be one in the future...

Ferro Corporation

International manufacturer of specialty materials and chemicals for industry

Cleveland is known worldwide, and one of the reasons is the international activities of Ferro Corporation. Founded in 1919 as Ferro Enameling Co., the company served industry by applying porcelain enamel coatings on cast iron and pressed steel parts for bathtubs, sinks and appliances.

A year or so later, it became apparent that what the enameling industry really needed was a standard set of material formulations to produce frit with consistent application and performance properties. Frit is the primary material used in porcelain enamel coatings, and this became the major product of the renamed Ferro Enamel Co. Frit is a special glass formulation that is smelted, cooled and processed into either a flake or granular form. It is then milled and mixed with other ingredients into an enamel material which is coated onto a metal part, dried and fired in a furnace to the point of fusion. The result is a lifetime, glass-like coating that is unequaled for scratch resistance, color retention and corrosion prevention.

Located on the near southeast side of Cleveland — just south of Harvard Avenue on East 56th Street — Ferro began to grow and serve the porcelain enamelers of the day with quality controlled materials and engineering services.

Ferro Enameling Co., 1929.

Ferro Corporation Cleveland Plant, 1976

Next came the production of specialty colors for porcelain enamels so sinks, bathtubs and stoves could be coordinated with the decor of a home.

When further engineering skills were acquired, Ferro expanded into the ceramic tile and brick market with glaze frits and colors for such familiar products as bathroom wall tiles, floor tiles and artware.

As early as 1927 Ferro entered the international market with a frit plant in Canada. In 1929 the company began operations overseas with plants in Holland and England. Today, with plants in 20 countries, Ferro markets its diversified products in more than 100 foreign countries.

In 1941, Ferro started its chemical operations in Walton Hills, Ohio, on the border of Bedford and southeast of Cleveland. Here, the company began the production of driers and specialty chemicals for the paint and plastics industries. Further expansions and acquisitions added refractory and ceramic operations plus other businesses such as composite materials, glass beads and industrial chemicals. At present, Ferro has 32 major manufacturing locations throughout the U.S. and 41 locations overseas.

With the constant diversification of products and markets, Ferro soon outgrew the offices in southeast Cleveland. To make room for production offices, the corporate headquarters was moved to Cleveland's Erieview area in 1969. Two years later, the Cleveland research and development laboratories were moved to a new Technical Center in Independence, Ohio, just south of Cleveland.

Since its founding in 1919, Ferro has grown in products, services, people and sales. In 1978, Ferro sales were $494,414,000 and of its 8,350 employees, worldwide, more than 3,000 are employed in the U.S. and 850 in greater Cleveland.

First National Supermarkets, Inc.

From dairy outlet to "super" chain

In 1928, Edward Silverberg opened a small dairy outlet in Cleveland called "Osborne Dairy Store." In the 1930s Silverberg's store gave birth to a chain of units which operated under the name "Farmview Creamery Stores."

Farmview's outlets prospered during the 1930s, and became the stepping stones to larger, more complete food stores. In 1938, Farmview opened a store on East 185th St. which afforded ample space for dairy products as well as a wide array of grocery items. The store was called "Pick-N-Pay."

A second Pick-N-Pay store was opened the following year, and by 1940, Farmview changed its corporate name to "Pick-N-Pay Supermarkets." By 1950, Pick-N-Pay was operating nine supermarkets in Cleveland. In that same year, the chain was sold to the Cook Coffee Company (now Cook United.)

In 1959, Cook added to its Pick-N-Pay Division by purchasing a food chain operating under the name "Foodtown." Foodtown, which operated as a division of ACF-Wrigley Stores (Detroit), was originally based in Cleveland.

The first Foodtown store was opened in 1941 by Clevelanders Julie and Milton Kravitz. In 1947, Julie Kravitz headed the formation of the Foodtown chain and served as its president.

With the acquisition of Foodtown came Pick-N-Pay's right to distribute "Edwards Brand" products, a brand which owes its

Pick-N-Pay Store, 1833 Coventry Rd., Cleveland, Heights, opened 1941.

name to Cleveland enterpreneur, Col. William Edwards, who had come to Cleveland in 1853 and opened a small wholesale grocery on River Street. The store marked the beginning of the "William Edwards Company," a massive wholesaling enterprise. Foodtown purchased the Edwards company in 1952.

Pick-N-Pay's growth brought prosperity.

The company became Greater Cleveland's top food chain in terms of market share, a distinction it held for a number of years.

During the mid-1960s, however, Pick-N-Pay began to experience financial and operational difficulties. Unable to reverse the chain's downward trend, the Cook Co. opted to sell Pick-N-Pay in 1972. Acquiring the chain was a group of investors headed by Foodtown founder, Julie Kravitz. Included in the group were Richard Bogomolny, William Prain, Glenn Willard, Raymond Korfant, and William Glazer (deceased), all of whom were well known in the Cleveland retail food industry.

Pick-N-Pay enjoyed an almost immediate turnaround under the new management. Product quality improved. Effective steps were taken to better serve customers, and particular attention was paid to upgrading the company's physical facilities. This newfound dedication to customer satisfaction enabled the company to regain its status as Greater Cleveland's number one supermarket chain.

One of First National's 12 Food Palace Stores, 1650 Snow Rd., Parma.

In 1975, Pick-N-Pay opened its first "Food Palace," acclaimed as one of the food industry's first true "super-stores." Twelve Food Palace stores are currently in operation. The Food Palace concept affords shoppers the ultimate in one-stop shopping convenience, and incorporates numerous specialty departments including a Fresh Fish counter, a Bake Shoppe, a Gourmet Meat counter, and a Flower Shop.

In 1976, Pick-N-Pay took another step to diversify by opening an "Edwards Food Warehouse" store in Toledo. The Edwards concept offers shoppers dramatic savings made possible by such innovations as palletized stocking, reduced product duplication, selling in large quantitites, and reduced overhead. Customers mark prices themselves and do their own bagging and carryout.

In May, 1978, Pick-N-Pay merged with "First National Stores" (Finast), a large New England-based food chain. Formed in 1925, Finast had long been the dominant food chain in New England, but increased competition, operating problems and an excess of small, inefficient units led to its rapid decline in the late '60s and early '70s.

Having successfully orchestrated turnarounds in the past, Pick-N-Pay's management team recognized Finast's underlying potential and assumed control of the merger's resulting entity, "First National Supermarkets, Inc." Sadly, slightly less than one year after the merger, Board Chairman Julie Kravitz died from gunshot wounds suffered at the hands of two ramson-seeking abductors.

Operating close to 300 units, First National today ranks among the top 15 food chains in the nation. Within a half-century, a handful of dairy outlets have evolved into a mammoth supermarket chain with annual sales exceeding $1 billion.

Certainly, Clevelanders can view First National as a "home-grown" company. Its origins are here, its "house brand" product line originated here, its corporate headquarters are here, and it is a company headed by Clevelanders who've played an integral role over the years in shaping Greater Cleveland's supermarket scene.

The Glidden Company

Early conglomerate now comprises four large units of SCM Corporation

Although it lineally dates back to the 1870s, Glidden's history really began in 1917, when a onetime school teacher, the late Adrian D. Joyce, and a few associates purchased the small but successful Glidden Varnish Company at a cost of $2.5 million.

The firm was incorporated as The Glidden Company and Mr. Joyce, aged 45, became its chief executive officer. Within two years, Glidden had acquired 11 additional paint concerns and was on its way to its present status of fourth largest U.S. coatings manufacturer.

Adrian Joyce had served Swift & Co. and the Sherwin-Williams Co. in managerial positions before beginning his career of more than 30 years with Glidden. In that period of time, Joyce built the company into a large conglomerate, utilizing three major operating precepts: control raw materials; fully utilize equipment, materials and personnel; and freely explore every avenue to develop new or related products.

An early step in the quest for control of raw materials was the purchase of a plant in St. Louis to produce linseed oil for paint manufacturing. Subsequently, because the linseed operations were idle part of the year, the plant was used to produce edible vegetable oils. This venture ultimately led to the purchase of E. R. Durkee & Co., a firm which originated in 1857 in Buffalo, New York, and which was a thriving producer of spices, condiments and salad dressing.

Under Joyce, Glidden became broadly diversified. Among its array of products were coatings, turpentine, rosin, pigments, resins, minerals, metal powders and an extensive range of food products: vegetable oils, spices, seasonings, condiments, sauces, salad dressing and many others.

One of the offspring of the Joyce era is the company's metal powders operation, which evolved from the need for red lead for protective metal coatings. The company is now number one in production of non-ferrous powders used by the automotive, appliance and other industries.

In 1947, Chairman and President Adrian Joyce relinquished the presidency to his son, Dwight, who had risen through the ranks to vice president of the paint division. Under his

The Dwight P. Joyce Research Center near Cleveland employs more than 400 men and women in the endless search for new and even better coatings and food products. This extensive SCM Corporation facility, in a 60-acre park-like setting, has recently undergone a 50 percent expansion.

leadership of that organization Glidden chemists had been developing a latex water reducible paint which was ready for the market in 1948. Called Spred Satin®, it was the first of its kind ever marketed. It was easily applied, fast drying and permitted tools to be cleaned with soap and water — it was a major factor in changing the emphasis of coatings research and pointed the way for waterborne industrial coatings.

Adrian Joyce died in 1954 at the age of 81, and Dwight P. Joyce became chairman and president. Under his leadership several new ventures were undertaken. One of these was the purchase of Pemco, an important manufacturer of porcelain enamel frits, a material essential in the making of glazes and coatings for appliances, wall tile, dinnerware and similar products.

Research in the company's turpentine and rosin operations, which were originally acquired by Adrian Joyce, led to the development of terpene chemicals. These products are used in vitamin intermediates, cleaners and disinfectants, pharmaceuticals, flavors, perfumes, and menthol for cigarettes. Today, the Organic Chemicals unit which processes turpentine derivatives is a world leader in the field.

In addition, Glidden is the second largest U.S. producer of titanium dioxide, the major white pigment used by the paint, paper, plastic and rubber products industries.

Dwight Joyce retired in 1967, and in that year Glidden merged with SCM Corporation. The former Glidden Company now constitutes four major SCM divisions: Glidden Coatings & Resins, Durkee Foods, Chemical/Metallurgical and Organic Chemicals. In fiscal 1978, these operations generated more than $900 million of SCM's $1.5 billion in sales. Paul W. Neidhardt, senior division president of SCM and a longtime Glidden veteran, directs the former Glidden operations.

In addition to the Glidden and Durkee products, SCM manufactures Proctor-Silex household appliances, Smith-Corona typewriters, Allied pulp and paper products and industrial and communications equipment. The corporation employs more than 27,000 men and women and has more than 70 manufacturing locations throughout the world. Principal SCM executive is Paul H. Elicker, who is president and chief executive officer.

The Hanna Mining Company

Company played a significant part in nation's iron ore development

Hanna's corporate antecedents date back to the mid-1840s when Daniel P. Rhodes, an ambitious young ex-Vermonter, began mining coal in the vicinity of Youngstown, Ohio, later expanding into pig iron production from local ores. This was when America was about to experience enormous growth in its iron production, in large part because of the rich iron ore deposits newly discovered in the upper peninsula of Michigan. The Lake Superior region soon became the prime source of the nation's iron ore, which could move inexpensively down the Great Lakes to the blast furnaces, and later the steel mills, of the lower lakes states. Dan Rhodes and his partners — who from the mid-1860s on included his son-in-law, Marcus Alonzo Hanna — participated fully in this geographical change, which was the foundation for the industrial development of the United States in

Iron ore pellets are heat-hardened at 2400°F in this rotary kiln, which is 22 feet in diameter and nearly half as long as a football field.

the post-Civil War period.

In 1885 the partnership of M. A. Hanna & Company was formed as a successor to Rhodes & Company and was engaging in iron ore and coal mining, shipping, coke production, and ironmaking. At about this time Mark Hanna became active in national politics, which led to his key role in the election of President McKinley in 1896. He later served as a U.S. Senator from Ohio.

With the 20th Century trend toward mine-to-mill integration in steel production, Hanna in the late 1920s put its blast furnaces, coke ovens, vessels, and most of its iron ore properties into National Steel Corporation, taking National Steel stock in return. Hanna continued to operate the iron ore mines and the vessels as agent for National Steel and it also developed new iron ore properties for its own account and in partnership with others. Today National is the third largest steel producer in the nation.

An essentially similar transaction took place in 1945 with the formation of Consolidation Coal Company, now a part of Continental Oil. Hanna put into Consol its bituminous coal properties, mostly located in southern Ohio, and took Consol stock in return.

In the early 1960s The Hanna Mining Company was set off as an independent corporation, to operate the mining properties, vessels, docks, and other related activities. In 1965, M. A. Hanna, which had become an investment company, was liquidated and its assets — exceeding $700 million — were distributed to its shareholders.

Today Hanna Mining has about 4,500 employees in the United States and engages in three principal areas of business: ferrous minerals, non-ferrous minerals and metals, and energy-related resources.

The company's basic business continues to be iron ore. As one of the world's largest independent producers, Hanna operates four iron ore pellet projects in the United States — one wholly owned, one jointly owned, and two in which it has minority interests. It is the largest stockholder of Iron Ore Company of Canada — with a capacity of some 30 million tons of iron ore annually — and serves as manager of the company. In Brazil, Hanna has an indirect one-third interest in a major iron ore company. The combined annual production capability of the iron ore properties in which Hanna has ownership interests approximates 53 million tons.

Hanna's largest single asset is its interest in Iron Ore Company of Canada, which was developed in the early 1950s under the leadership of George M. Humphrey, who went on to national prominence as Secretary of the Treasury in President Eisenhower's administration.

Three gigantic machines used in modern iron ore mining are a drill (top), shovel, and truck.

IOC, owned by leading Canadian and American mining and steel companies, was one of the most massive construction projects undertaken up to that time. A 360-mile railroad was pushed north from the Gulf of St. Lawrence through the wilderness to the huge iron ore deposits of the Quebec-Labrador field. Cities were built, power sources constructed, mines and treatment plants developed, all in an area that for many months of the year has temperatures in the sub-zero range.

In the non-ferrous area, for more than 20 years Hanna has operated a nickel mine and smelter in Oregon capable of producing some 26 million pounds of nickel annually. It produces silicon metal and ferrosilicon at a smelter in the state of Washington. In Guatemala it has a minority interest in a large nickel project and it is involved in a nickel development in Colombia. Hanna has a one-third interest in an integrated aluminum project in Brazil.

In energy-related activities, Hanna is a 50-percent owner of two low sulfur steam coal properties in northwestern Colorado, the larger of which has an initial production capability of 3 million tons a year. Hanna has interests in oil and gas production and has a half interest in one of the nation's large oil and gas well maintenance, work-over, and completion services companies.

Hanna operates bulk cargo vessels on the Great Lakes and in the St. Lawrence Seaway, an ocean shipping chartering agency, and coal and ore docks owned by others.

The company conducts geological exploration and metallurgical research, mostly concentrated in recent years on non-ferrous minerals and energy resources.

Hanna investments include minority holdings in National Steel, the two Canadian companies that hold the concessions on which Iron Ore Company of Canada operates, and a Brazilian petrochemical holding company.

The company's commitment to protecting the environment extends back many years and has involved millions of dollars of expenditures.

Hauserman Inc.

"... The pride of men in what they are doing."

When Parma born Earl Frederick Hauserman founded The E. F. Hauserman Company in March 1913, he was armed with little besides foresight and faith in an idea. An idea which was so essentially sound it has endured and is the basic philosophy today for Hauserman, Inc., a company with offices and manufacturing facilities in the U.S., Canada, and Europe. A company which not only measures sales of moveable walls and office systems in feet but in kilometers.

By undertaking to sell steel sash on what Earl Hauserman called a "delivered complete" basis (which meant that he took the responsibility for engineering, glazing, painting, and installation on himself) the Hauserman "single source" company was born.

The sale of steel sash boomed and in 1916

he built a warehouse and office at 1729 East 22 Street. A year later Hauserman bought the Metalcraft Company at 6800 Grant Avenue and began experiments using formed steel parts to make a partition. By 1927 his young company was producing moveable steel partitions exclusively.

According to Hauserman's son Ben, recently retired as vice president and secretary of the company, "Father was a one man show — an aggressive, progressive entrepeneur, demanding of himself and others. He had a good sense of humor, had many friends and enjoyed them." It is easy to believe that this man was undaunted by the fire that nearly leveled his plant in 1927 or war that necessitated the suspension of steel partition production. The company went to war in 1942 — a war Earl Hauserman was not destined to see end. But before his untimely death in 1943 he had converted the product knowledge, facilities, and organization of his company to joiner and deckhouse work, landing mats and aircraft parts.

At war's end, his eldest son Fred M. Hauserman, then president, returned to the manufacture of moveable metal walls. He built a network of direct sales offices and personnel, an installation and service organization which led to a customer list of most of American's major corporations and to a 1,000 percent growth in sales by 1972 when he was tragically killed in an automobile accident.

Fred Hauserman directed major company expansion here and abroad: Hauserman, Ltd., Canada (1955); Hauserman S.A., France (1962); and the acquisition of Educators Manufacturing Company and the Gotham Educational Equipment Company (1969). The decision to acquire these two companies changed the business direction of Hauserman as it began the development and manufacture of furniture and wall systems for the education and office markets. This new direction made it possible for the company to offer furniture and wall panels — individual work areas for open plan arrangements — as well as the accoustical privacy of completely enclosed spaces. With this significant change in potential, Hauserman moved into new markets.

To keep pace with this growth the company was reorganized as Hauserman, Inc. in 1972 with William F. Hauserman assuming the presidency on the death of his brother. All U.S. operations in the new markets became the province of The E. F. Hauserman Company (a wholly owned subsidiary of Hauserman, Inc.) — manufacturing and installing full height walls and open plan furniture systems for the space needs of business and industry. And in 1977 Hauserman introduced a new open office system with task/ambient lighting — the latter designed by Henry Dreyfuss Associates — adding another dimension to their full height wall capability.

Earl Frederick Hauserman, founder.

A year later, in 1978, Hauserman acquired Sunar, Canadian manufacturers of wood and metal office furniture and system designs by Douglas Ball. These award winning Sunar systems, with their superior reputation for fine design and quality manufacture, have enjoyed wide acceptance by architects and interior designers of corporate and industrial space in Canada, and more recently, in the U.S.

In a year's time Hauserman has expanded the scope of Sunar in the U.S. with showrooms designed by architect Michael Graves, added a complete textile collection, and begun a furniture design program which has seen the introduction of new seating and table designs at Sunar.

At the opening of the present company headquarters building at 5711 Grant Avenue, commissioned in 1958, Fred Hauserman said, "Imagination used creatively, materials used honestly, craftsmanship applied diligently, contribute an element that can make a building outstanding... the pride of men in what they are doing." What was said of the building could be said of the company.

The Higbee Company

A retail innovator for more than a century

There's been a Higbee's for almost as long as there's been a Cleveland. On September 10, 1860, only 64 years after Moses Cleaveland stepped ashore at the mouth of the Cuyahoga, Hower & Higbee opened for business at 237 Superior Street. The little shop was located on the north side of the avenue, one door east of what is now West Third Street.

The founders were John G. Hower and Edwin C. Higbee, enterprising young men from Lodi, Ohio, who (in the best American tradition) had come to the city to seek their fortunes.

The store, about 10 years after opening, needed expansion and it was moved to the south side of Superior Avenue to much enlarged space. In 1904, the store expanded by acquiring an annex located approximately

Downtown store, Public Square in 1969.

where Terminal Tower is today.

Higbee died in 1906 and was succeeded as president by his son, William T. In 1910, Higbee's built its own three-story building (later expanded to four-stories) on fashionable Euclid Avenue at 13th Street.

In 1913, Asa Shiverick, a retailer with vast experience in marketing quality merchandise, was elected president. In 1916, Shiverick purchased the common-share holding of the Higbee family. By 1929, Higbee's had built its annual sales volume to $11.8 million.

In the meantime, the legendary Van Sweringen brothers were exciting Clevelanders with dreams of a massive downtown development.

Mantis James Van Sweringen and Otis Paxton Van Sweringen had already demonstrated their enterprise by building Shaker Heights (the nation's first totally planned city) and Shaker Square (America's second shopping plaza). They were also connecting their suburb to the center city. Cleveland had already decided to abandon its railroad station because of an out-of-the-way location at the foot of West Ninth Street.

The Van Sweringen brothers were determined that their rapid transit line would be included in the new terminal, and that the only logical location was the southwest quadrant of Public Square. To gain public support for their position, the "Vans" had promised Clevelanders they would build: 1) a new rail-passenger terminal; 2) a group of office buildings; 3) a hotel and a large department store.

The Van Sweringens needed a prestigious department store for their new development. Terminal Tower, then as now the tallest office structure between New York and Chicago, was opened on June 28, 1930. On September 1, 1931, Higbee's opened for business in its present location, a million square-foot building erected at a cost of approximately $19.5 million.

In November, 1932, George E. Merrifield joined the company as vice president and treasurer. Messrs. Merrifield, Shiverick, and Charles Bradley (a partner of the Van Sweringens) guided Higbee's. Shiverick died in 1937, and was succeeded as president by Bradley. When Bradley died in 1943, he was succeeded a year later by John P. Murphy, his longtime friend and colleague from the Van Sweringen group and partner in 52 percent ownership of the Higbee Company.

The decade of the 1950s was a period in which America's leading department stores began to broaden their marketing perimeters by opening suburban branches. Higbee's, however, elected to invest heavily in modernization of its downtown facility as the first major step in creating a new and positive image. In 1958, the store began upgrading merchandise selections and expanding its organizational structure. In 1961, Higbee's acquired an existing store in Westgate Shopping Center. In nine months from the date of possession, the company had raised the roof to add a second floor, completely renovated the building inside and out, and opened for business. Higbee's had entered the era of modern suburban retailing. In the next nine years, the Westgate store was followed by stores in Severance Center, Midway Mall, Parmatown, Great Lakes Mall, and Belden Village.

Not all the company's growth has come by building new stores. In 1969, Higbee's acquired McKelvey's department store in Youngstown, Ohio. Since 1976 three additional suburban stores have been added — at Euclid Square, Randall Park Mall and Beachwood Place. Eleven proud Higbee stores now serve the residents of Northeastern Ohio. Herbert E. Strawbridge, chairman of the board says, "We always try to add that intangible extra that makes shopping at Higbee's a pleasurable and satisfying experience, which is why we say, 'Only Higbee's Does It Like Higbee's'."

The Albert M. Higley Co.

Helping to build a better city

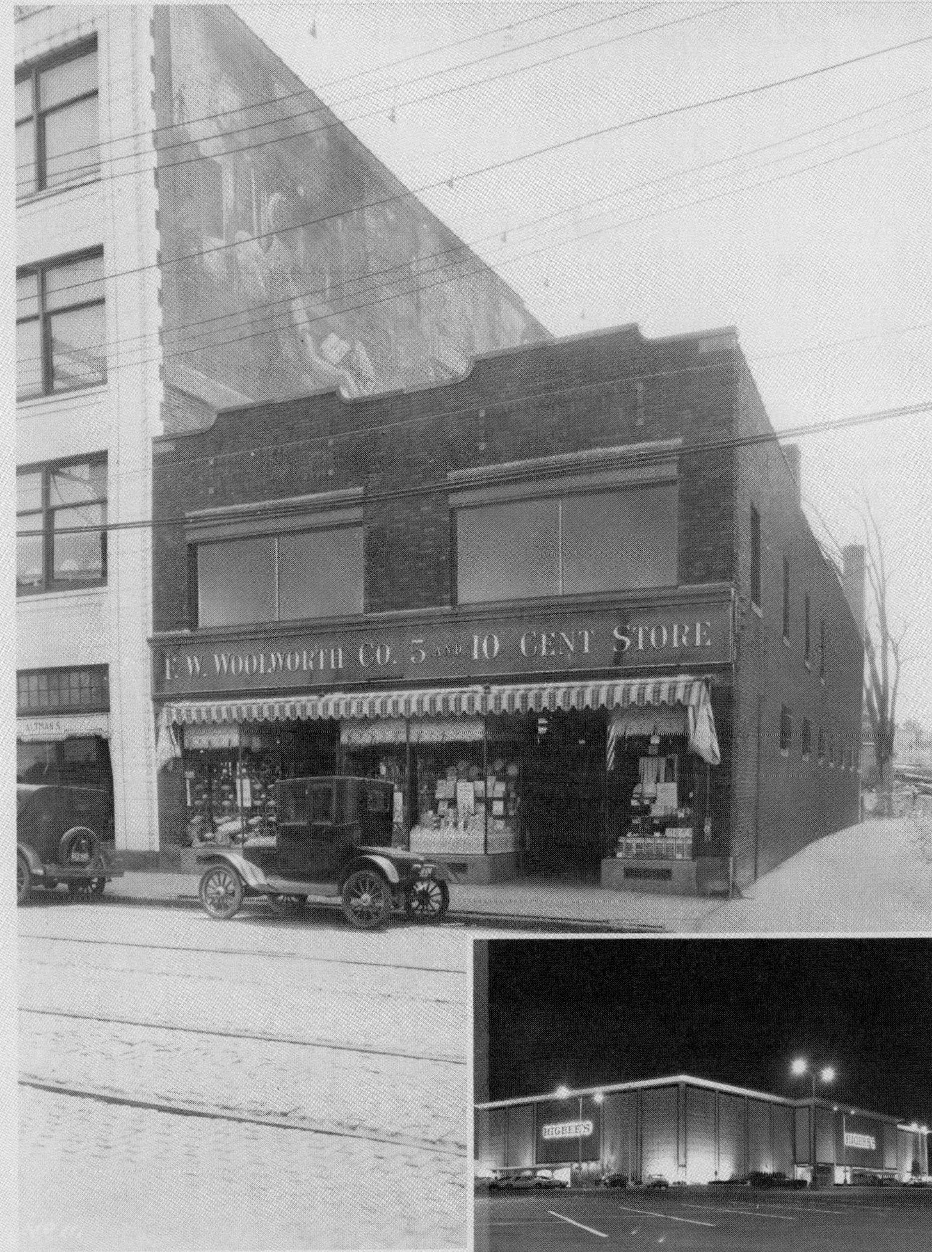

Higley Project No. 244

Higley Project No. 7,452

In the first month of its founding in 1925, the Albert M. Higley Company started on a small alteration job at the estate of William G. Mather in Bratenahl. Since that time, the Mather mansion, now known as Gwinn, has become one of the cultural institutions of Cleveland; and 51 years later the Higley Company was again there, this time doing major renovation of this stately mansion.

Since its founding, the company has been dedicated to excellence. Believing in an orderly growth, it has undertaken only those projects that it felt it was qualified to do and to do well. A look along Cleveland's skyline is proof that the company's original philosophy has been successful.

During the early days of its existence, the company was responsible for constructing such notable projects in the '30s as the Cleveland Skating Club, the Cleveland Coast Guard Station, many of the exhibits in the Great Lakes Exposition and the Cuyahoga County Airport on Richmond Road. By the end of the '30s, the company had 710 projects in this area under its belt.

The war days in the early '40s caused our nation to focus its energy toward a defense-related economy. During this period much of the company's work was directed toward building defense industries. One of the many industrial plants it built was Cleveland Pneumatic Aerol in Euclid, Ohio, which was one of the largest defense plants in this area. Since wartime restrictions hampered the availability of standard building materials, wood trusses and deck were used in place of steel in this project. Substantiating the company's dedication to quality construction, this huge complex is currently in use today, housing the Euclid Plant of the Fisher Body Division of General Motors.

With the war's end, Cleveland embarked on a period of commercial and industrial growth. Business responded to the changing economy. During this period, the Higley Company remodeled and altered the face of many commercial establishments which lined Euclid Avenue such as S. S. Kresge's, Bonwit Teller, and Sterling, Linder, Davis. Its new construction in the downtown area featured the sleek, modernized design of the Bond Store on the Northwest corner of East Ninth and Euclid Avenue, and the Greyhound Terminal on Chester Avenue.

With the rapid increase in population during the '50s and '60s, the Higley Company became actively involved in Cleveland's growing need for educational facilities. It was responsible for the construction of many new buildings for Case Institute of Technology and Western Reserve University including Case's Physics, Electrical and Chemical Engineering buildings and Reserve's Freiberger Library and Millis Science Center. At Fenn, it built a new Engineering Building. Business needs also changed due to the rapid increase in population. The need for parking in the downtown area saw the Higley Company involved in the construction of many parking garages including the May Company's Parkade. Business went "suburban" and the Higley Company followed, erecting Higbee stores in Elyria, Parmatown and Mentor, plus facilities for Sears, Roebuck and Company and May Company in Southgate.

In 1965 with the retirement of Albert M. Higley, Sr., Roy G. Harley, who joined the company in 1945, became president, and in 1970, Albert M. Higley, Jr. after 16 years with the company became chairman.

During the early part of the '70s, the Higley Company showed its flexibility by being involved in many widely diversified projects. These projects included, but were not limited to, a new Administration Building and Law School for Case Western Reserve University; a Physical Education Building and University Center Building for Cleveland State University (formerly Fenn College); Southwest General Health Care Center; additions to Deaconess, University St. Lukes and Huron Road Hospitals; a major portion of the Justice Center Complex; and Sea World in Aurora, Ohio.

As the decade of the '70s comes to a close, the company's work includes such energy and ecology related projects as Cleveland Electric Illuminating Company's Perry Nuclear Power Plant and Sewage Treatment Facilities for the Cleveland Regional Sewer District. The amount of work under contract has grown to approximately $125 million, and 9,912 projects have been completed since its founding 55 years ago.

The philosophy of the company has not changed. It prides itself in its flexiblity, and it continues to be dedicated to excellence, doing only that work which it can do well.

Jones & Laughlin Steel Corporation

A premiere steel mill that started with only a handful of employees

The Cleveland Works of Jones & Laughlin Steel goes back a long way in Cleveland — back to 1874, when Otis Steel was formed by Charles Otis.

Otis had acquired an iron furnace in Cleveland, which he expanded to include a forge shop and a rolling mill, for the manufacture of railroad axles and iron bars. He opened the Otis Steel Company to make open hearth steel, after obtaining a license to use this process in the United States.

In 1889, control of the plant passed to the English holding company which had owned Otis Steel for 30 years. In 1919, a group of Cleveland-based investors bought the Otis Steel Company.

Throughout all these financial wheelings and dealings Otis Steel prospered. It had acquired the Cleveland Furnace Company, with its coke-making ovens and blast furnaces, and had added rolling mills and a blooming mill.

More steel was needed to feed the nation's growing hunger for more cars, homes, and appliances — all made with steel. The growth opportunities were there, and Otis' management took advantage of them.

In the 1928 Otis Steel annual report, management reported that "Through rearrangement of our equipment and greater production efficiency, we have expanded our finished steel capacity by 55 percent."

The report noted that the 703,000 tons of steel shipped was a record, employment and payroll were at peace-time highs, and that large sums of money were spent on improvements.

But the boom days of the 1920s inevitably led to the Depression days of the 1930s. Business slumped as consumers snapped shut their pocketbooks. There was no great need for steel to build cars and appliances — no one was buying them anymore.

Things were bad, but not impossible. Otis Steel survived the Depression. As the war years of the 1940s approached, demand for steel began to grow. And Otis grew along with it.

In 1942, Otis Steel was acquired by the Jones & Laughlin Steel Corporation, the Pittsburgh-based steel company that is now the third-largest steelmaker in the country.

J&L poured millions of dollars into Cleveland over the next 20 years.

Two new blast furnaces rose up to replace the old Cleveland Furnace vessels. The open hearths were replaced with the more modern electric furnaces, which refine steel from scrap. Later, Basic Oxygen Furnaces (BOFs) were added, making steel from a combination of blast furnace iron and scrap metal.

A new blooming mill was installed. The finishing department was completely rebuilt with modern, state-of-the-art equipment.

This massive investment culminated in 1964 with the installation of a computerized

Top, this "skeetow," forerunner of the modern escalator, was featured in a 1946 Otis Sheet. *The device aided weary workers leaving the mines. Above, the docks along Cuyahoga River supply ore vital to Jones & Laughlin Steel.*

80″ Hot Strip Mill, which squeezes slabs of steel 6″ thick into coils of steel less than 1/2″ thick and a half-mile long.

Throughout the 1960s, the Cleveland Works prospered. Technological development, efficient management and innovation opened new opportunities for growth.

Today, the Cleveland Works of J&L stands poised to enter the 1980s as one of America's premiere steel mills.

The seven-ton furnaces of Otis have become a three-million ton per year facility — 370 acres of steelmaking muscle.

The original handful of employees has grown to more than 4,000, with an annual payroll of more than $75 million.

But all this is only part of the story of J&L in Cleveland. Long before pollution control became the law of the land, J&L was environmentally involved.

Its water pollution controls far exceed government standards. In 1975, the EPA gave the Cleveland Works water clarifiers an award of merit, calling it a "showcase". The Cuyahoga River, once known as "the river that burned" now supports a variety of fresh-water aquatic life.

More than 40 employees work daily to monitor and reduce air and water pollution emissions, helping to make the Cleveland Works one of the cleanest steel mills anywhere.

Management is deeply involved in the community by providing financial support and management time to help the many health and social service agencies that serve our community.

For more than 100 years, the Cleveland Works has been an intimate partner in this city's growth and prosperity. For more than a century, the Cleveland Works has been a good neighbor.

Lamson & Sessions

The Cleveland connection — how one company bridged the gap from horses to jets

In 1866, when Sam Sessions joined his cousins, Isaac and Thomas Lamson, to start The Lamson & Sessions Co. in Connecticut, the horse was the primary means of transportation. The young company's fastener business consisted mostly of carriage bolts used to assemble wagons, coaches and buggies, and tire bolts which held iron rims on wooden wheels.

Their entire product line, numbering only 30 items, produced sales of $70,000 in the first full year of operation. In 1869, after several exploratory trips by Sam Sessions, the company moved to Cleveland which he wisely identified as an area of expanding markets, raw material sources, transportation and plenty of coal for steam power.

Late in the century, transportation became big business for America and Cleveland was at the center of it all. The auto industry sprang up literally in Lamson & Sessions' backyard and the company had an exciting new customer and a unique new challenge — standardization of the size, shape and properties of products. Right from the start Lamson & Sessions was in the forefront of this activity and research and development increased in importance, an importance which continues to this day.

In the early 1900s Lamson & Sessions grew rapidly. During World War I military orders pushed sales into the $2 million range. Then, during the '20s and '30s, the Company added substantially to plants and equipment, developed major technological innovations and opened new distribution channels across the country.

World War II and the industrial expansion of the '50s and '60s produced additional growth for Lamson & Sessions as succeeding generations of management charted its path and strengthened it for a changing and challenging role in American industry.

Youngstown Steel Door Co. (a Lamson & Sessions subsidiary) is a major supplier of doors, sides, and other components for railroad freight cars of many types.

Lamson & Sessions entered the '70s known internationally as one of the world's largest independent quality fastener manufacturers, now serving most of the capital goods industries in this country. But of greater long-range importance to the company, its strength as a premier fastener manufacturer provided the springboard to move the company ahead dramatically and turn it into a far different and even more exciting company.

Lamson & Sessions' increasing number of specialized fastener systems are designed to satisfy unique industry needs.

While the fastener business was adapting to the needs of industry, Lamson was busy broadening its base of operations. In September 1976 the Company acquired The Youngstown Steel Door Company — one of the country's leading producers of railway freight car equipment. The timing of this move could not have been better. The railway industry had had a number of bad years and pent-up demand for new equipment was about to burst all bonds. In 1978, YSD contributed 40 percent of total sales with fasteners adding 51 percent and other industrial equipment accounting for nine percent. Indications are that this growth will continue into the next decade. But YSD was only the first move in a plan to broaden the company's horizons.

In the summer of 1979, Lamson & Sessions acquired Midsco, Inc. of Lakewood, Ohio, bringing together a number of old line Cleveland companies which had shared many of the growing pains of the early days of Cleveland's industrial history. Midsco was a holding company consisting of five operating units: Forest City Foundries — which began operations in 1890; Midland Steel Products — originally in 1894 The Parish & Bingham Company, manufacturer of bicycle parts and frames for the first Model T; Permold, Inc. of Medina, Ohio; Conneaut Die Casting Corp. of Conneaut, Ohio; and Slagle Manufacturing Corporation of Tulsa, Oklahoma.

The acquisition of Midsco increased Lamson & Sessions' role as a supplier to the capital goods market in the form of truck frames for the big three auto companies, heat exchangers for petroleum refineries and chemical processing plants and a wide range of iron, aluminum and zinc castings for original equipment manufacturers.

The growth of Lamson & Sessions is the classic evolution of a one product manufacturer, founded by Yankee entrepreneurs, into a leading manufacturer of a wide range of products for the capital goods industries which keep our country a vital force in the world economy. Lamson & Sessions has remained strong in Cleveland, still the center of America's capital goods market.

Sam Sessions and the Lamson brothers would be amazed that their little company has grown from $70,000 in 1866 to an annualized sales volume of more than $400 million in 1979 and has successfully made the transition from horses to jets. On the other hand, there's a good chance they would view all this as the natural result of American ingenuity and productivity.

The Lincoln Electric Company

World's largest manufacturer of arc welding products

The Lincoln Electric Company in 1907. From this humble beginning grew the world's largest manufacturer of arc welding products.

The Lincoln Electric Company is famous because of its unique incentive management system that has helped the company become the world's largest manufacturer of arc welding products.

Since 1895, when Lincoln was founded in Cleveland by John C. Lincoln, the company has enjoyed the reputation of being a high quality manufacturer. Lincoln, a noted inventor and an electrical engineering graduate of Ohio State University, started the company by designing, manufacturing and selling industrial motors. He soon found that his time could be better devoted to developing new products, so his younger brother, James F., was hired to act as sales manager. James Finney Lincoln brought with him the enthusiasm and confidence he had developed as a highly successful athlete at Ohio State University. His exuberance and refreshing approach to sales and later to management changed the organization materially at the same time that the company's efforts were being directed to the new process of arc welding.

The Lincoln Electric Company, under the management skills of James and the inventive genius of John, grew by leaps and bounds as the welding process became the universal tool for joining steel.

A major impetus to the industry came about because of the need for repairing naval vessels damaged in World War I. This need, coupled with the development of Lincoln's Fleetweld 5 covered electrode, helped launch the young company toward becoming one of Cleveland's most successful business enterprises.

From 1929 to the present, Lincoln's philosophy of producing a better product to sell at a lower cost to a greater number of customers has served to inspire employees to produce at phenomenal rates. The increased productivity and guaranteed quality have enabled the company to compensate employees in the form of a year-end incentive bonus each year since 1934.

The Lincoln Electric Company's world headquarters and main manufacturing facility in Cleveland, Ohio

The bonus is not guaranteed, nor is it a gift and it does not happen automatically. It is a sharing of the results of efficient operation on the basis of the contribution of each person to the success of the company for that year. The company follows the philosophy that individuals need and respond favorably to responsibility, security, recognition and reward.

Basic compensation for most employees is straight piecework, but hourly rate or salary may be paid as responsibilities dictate. Basic compensation, in general, approximates average Cleveland wage rates. Other features of the incentive program include:

1. Guaranteed Employment. No layoffs have occurred since the program began in 1958. Employees must accept job and schedule changes as required to make the system work. (Lincoln's last layoff was in 1949.)
2. Promotion from Within. Job openings are posted on all bulletin boards in accordance with the company policy of real and equal opportunity for all.
3. Retirement Annuity Plan. Started in 1936, and amended and augmented periodically.
4. Group Life Insurance Plan. Started in 1918.
5. Employees Stock Purchase Plan. Started in 1930. Approximately 50 percent of the employees own directly over 30 percent of the company stock.
6. Normal Fringe Benefits. Lincoln has been a leader in offering normal programs years ahead of other manufacturers.
7. Productivity is a function of employee effort and commitment combined with the proper tools to do the job. The Lincoln incentive program maximizes employee participation and provides the

optimum equipment needed for each operation.

Jim Lincoln's totally open, frank and honest management techniques have been carried on since his death in 1965 by William Irrgang who now serves as chairman and chief executive officer of the company. Irrgang has served the company in outstanding fashion as a production worker, inspector, engineer and executive for over 50 years. He is only the third chief executive in the history of the company. He and current President George E. Willis have been instrumental in encouraging many new manufacturing techniques that have lowered production costs and have improved efficiency. Most highly regarded is Lincoln's Innershield electrode for automated welding. As a matter of policy, the Lincoln sales staff thrives on a very real effort to lower customer welding costs.

The company is headquartered in Euclid and has a manufacturing facility in Mentor, Ohio. Nearly two million square feet of space is utilized by the company's 2,500 employees for manufacturing at these two locations. Wholly owned subsidiary companies are located in Toronto, Canada; Sydney, Australia and Rouen, France. These, coupled with joint ventures, licensing arrangements and dealers, supply Lincoln products world-wide.

Davy McKee Corporation

Engineering for today's needs and tomorrow's challenge.

The forerunner of Davy McKee Corporation, Arthur G. McKee & Company, began as a one-man iron and steel consulting firm in 1905. Since its founding, it has grown dramatically in size, variety of services offered and industries served, which today include petroleum, chemicals, petrochemicals, fertilizer, nonferrous metals, minerals, mining, iron, steel, food, pharmaceuticals, synthetic fuels, coal and natural gas.

Soon after Arthur G. McKee, a metallurgical engineer, opened his one-room office in downtown Cleveland's Rockefeller Building, he was joined by two associates. Robert Baker was an electrical engineer, and Donald Herr's background was construction engineering. In 1906, they formed a partnership and began offering complete engineering and construction services for iron and steel projects. Together they made a good combination, and soon gained a reputation for sound engineering and thorough, efficient execution of contracts. Before the year was out, the young firm had grown from one room to five floors of the building.

During their first ten years of business, McKee and his associates succeeded in supplying services in some form to about two-thirds of the iron and steel producers in the United States and Canada, and in 1915, the firm was incorporated under the name of Arthur G. McKee & Company.

In 1926, McKee merged with Widdell Engineering Company, a successful Oklahoma refinery engineering concern. This move greatly expanded McKee's sphere of operations — giving the firm the capability to provide design, engineering, purchasing and construction services to the world's two largest industries engaged in the recovery and processing of underground resources. This new combination, like the original partnership, was immediately successful with the addition of new business from the expanding petroleum industry.

During the war years in the 1940s, McKee played a major role in the design and construction of defense plants, and in the 1950s and '60s, under the leadership of H. E. Widdell and later Merrill Cox, the company substantially increased its international operations by establishing subsidiaries in Canada, Latin America, Australia and Europe.

Cleveland's historic Rockefeller Building, McKee's first home in 1905.

In 1961, a major expansion took place when McKee acquired San Francisco-based Western Knapp Engineering Company, specialists in designing and constructing plants for processing nonferrous metals and minerals. In addition to this capability, the acquisition gave McKee an operations office in Chicago, which now serves as the company's food and pharmaceutical technical center.

The years 1971 to 1978 stand as the period of the company's greatest accomplishment and growth. Under the stewardship of R. G. Widman, who in 1979 retired as president, chairman and chief executive officer of The McKee Corporation, earnings increased from a $2-million loss in 1971 to $8-million plus after tax in 1976, 1977 and 1978, and net worth increased 275 percent from $18 million to $50 million. During the same period the company's backlog passed $1 billion for the first time.

In 1977, McKee acquired Dresser Engineering Company of Tulsa, Oklahoma, designers and constructors of natural gas processing facilities. Another recent acquisition was Campbell, DeBoe & Associates of Toledo, Ohio, specializing in designing steam and electric power generating facilities for the municipal and industrial markets.

In 1978, McKee merged with Davy Corporation Ltd. of London, England, and in June 1979, a new U.S. holding company, Davy Inc. was formed and became the parent of Arthur G. McKee & Company, the name of which was then changed to Davy McKee Corporation.

Present Cleveland headquarters of Davy McKee Corp. and Davy Inc.

W. F. Richards, president of the Cleveland-based Davy Inc., is responsible for all of Davy's U.S. operations, which include, besides Davy McKee Corporation, DM International Inc., Davy McKee Latin America Inc. and Davy McKee Enterprises. In total, these companies regularly employ more than 5,400 persons in 26 offices around the world.

Davy Inc.'s headquarters building, a short nine miles south of downtown Cleveland on Oak Tree Boulevard off Rockside Road, is also the headquarters of Davy McKee Corporation and includes that company's technical centers for iron and steel and petroleum and chemicals. More than 1,400 greater Clevelanders from every section of the metropolitan area come to work here every day. The Cleveland office is also the hub of the company's pioneering efforts in the technical development of processes and plants to produce the synthetic fuels of the future from coal, oil shale and tar sands. McKee engineers are at work designing a $100 million pilot plant to make liquid fuel from coal and a demonstration plant to gasify coal. Crude shale oil from a plant in Colorado designed and constructed by McKee is now being refined in Toledo for testing by the U.S. Department of Defense. Davy McKee Corporation is truly engineering for today's needs and tomorrow's challenge.

The May Company — Cleveland

Ohio has been watching it grow for 80 years

When David May nailed the commanding slogan, "Watch Us Grow," above the entrance of his new Cleveland store in 1899, he was making no idle boast. The 73,000 square-foot store on Ontario Street, purchased from Hull & Dutton for $300,000, has grown to a 10 store operation.

The May Company-Public Square was the second store in the May Department Stores Company which today operates 170 department and discount stores and 18 shopping centers nationwide as well as the Eagle Stamp Trading Company.

Founder David May, an enterprising German immigrant, carried a stock of wares across the country to Leadville, Colorado, on a small burro in 1877. There, in a humble wooden framework covered with muslin, he established a successful retail business.

He chose Cleveland for the site of his second store, declaring it "the best location in the nation."

The standard of service set in that first little general store has enabled May to realize his precocious claim. His deep-felt sense of responsibility to his frontier friends developed into a maxim often repeated at the May Company — "Have the right merchandise at the right time with prices for every pocketbook."

In later years, Cleveland merchandise manager Sam Rosenberg reinforced the May Company's dedication to satisfying customers' needs, "We don't figure merchandise, we finger it."

In 1899, David May nailed the sign, "Watch Us Grow," above the entrance of the former Hull & Dutton Company on Ontario Avenue.

Commodore Louis D. Beaumont, David May's brother-in-law, introduced May's principles to Cleveland as the store's first general manager. Within a few years, the May Company established an unblemished record of integrity and dependability.

Nathan L. Dauby, a "merchant with flair" who leased the store's first shoe department, became manager in 1904. Under Dauby's nearly six decades of guidance, the May Company enjoyed great growth and strengthened its reputation as a retail leader.

Outgrowing the six-story Ontario store and its Euclid Shoe Annex, the May Company made plans to grow upward and outward. The annex was enlarged twice — to three stories in 1900 and to six in 1903. In 1907, acquisitions of Taylor's Cushing Building, the Fulton Market and several small properties extended the store east on the northern Euclid front and south to Prospect Avenue. The Ontario tower clock, an old Cleveland landmark, was raised with roof when two floors were added in 1910.

Dauby was fond of saying, "I'd rather be right than first." He was often both. In 1914, he convinced David May to construct a $2.5 million structure replacing the labyrinth of additions and ramps covering the city block between Euclid and Prospect Avenues. May, wondering if "a city as small as Cleveland" could support a department store as large as the one proposed, trusted Dauby's sincere belief that Cleveland would "grow up to it."

The six-story building, with two floors added in 1931, still stands today.

Dauby's predictions proved true and in 1932 the May Company celebrated its first million dollar day.

The Cushing Building adjoining the Euclid Shoe Annex was purchased in 1907.

The "moving stairway" in the modernized building was just one of the Cleveland firsts instituted by Dauby. The stubby-nosed brown bus which made the mile round trip between the store and the first 1925 patron's garage became Public Square tradition. Complete air-conditioning facilities and a unique playground, visited by 250 children daily, were notable Dauby innovations.

As the enlarging population reached outlying areas, the May Company reacted with customary vigor. Familiar with painted barn sides proclaiming, "The May Company — Watch Us Grow," suburban residents now watched the May Company grow in their own communities. May's-on-the-Heights opened in 1957 followed by: Parmatown, 1960; Southgate, 1961; Mentor, 1964; Great Northern, 1965; Sheffield Center, 1967; Randall Park, 1976; and Euclid Square, 1977.

In 1965, a multi-level parking garage was built making the flagship store one of the largest department stores in the country.

Current management, under the direction of H. Gene Nau, president and chief executive officer, J. Warren Harris, chairman, and Matt Kallman, vice chairman, continues to foster May Company growth and maintain high standards of quality and service.

The year 1978 saw a total renovation of the downtown store. In March 1979, the opening of the Sandusky Mall store, sixty miles west of the original Public Square location, signified a new phase in the May Company — Cleveland's growth — its debut as a major regional department store company.

National City Bank

From era of financial turmoil arose a stalwart banker's bank

National City Bank, organized in 1845 under the name City Bank of Cleveland, is the city's oldest bank. It was created during a period of financial turmoil following President Andrew Jackson's veto of the bill extending the Bank of the United States. Many banks issued their own currency in those days, but their values fluctuated so constantly that the period was called the era of wildcat currency. By the early 1840s, every bank in Cleveland had closed. Only exchange brokers and insurance companies performed a few banking functions.

Cleveland's unfortunate situation came to an end through the genius of Alfred Kelley. Kelley was the builder of the Ohio Central Railroad, which gave Cleveland a pre-eminent position in trade and commerce. In 1845, Kelley sponsored the Ohio Banking Act, making possible an effective banking program. Under its provisions the Fireman's Insurance Company, which had been organized in Cleveland to establish pensions for disabled volunteer firemen, reorganized as a bank. This bank became the City Bank of Cleveland with capital stock of $25,000 and a charter to run for 20 years.

During the Civil War crisis, the United States Congress passed the National Banking Act, enabling the federal government to establish control over banking and currency. In 1865, as the war ended and the charter for the City Bank expired, the bank reorganized, becoming the National City Bank of Cleveland.

National City Bank is still housed in the Old New England Building at 623 Euclid Avenue.

The bank grew in strength and prestige and by the beginning of the 20th century its assets reached $2 million. Two decades later, as World War I ended, the bank began an era of great expansion. This growth synchronized with the growth of Cleveland which, in 1920, was the fifth largest city in America. The bank purchased the Garfield Building on Euclid Avenue at East 6th Street. Constructed in 1895 and called the first skyscraper on Euclid Avenue, it represented a sharp contrast to the old headquarters in the Leader-News Building. Heretofore, the bank's activities had been limited almost entirely to commercial bank-

National City Bank's East 6th Street building in 1930s.

ing. Many of its accounts grew dramatically, a number of the companies gaining national and international recognition. An important ingredient of expansion was the establishment of both a savings department and a trust department.

The period of expansion was drastically altered by the stock market crash of 1929. To Cleveland, this was a period of great financial stringency. During the next four years, the bank's assets were decreased about 25 percent. Yet the only time the bank closed was briefly during the country-wide Bank Holiday of 1933. While the other Cleveland banks limited withdrawals to five percent of deposits or less, this bank placed no restrictions on withdrawals. The bank's successful weathering of the Depression was attributed to its slow and steady growth and to the fact that it was never involved in heavy real estate or railroad loans. When two of Cleveland's largest banks failed, National City obtained for its own staff some of the best banking talent in the community.

Following great activity during World War II, the bank embarked upon another period of expansion. It purchased the adjoining Guardian Building which it had in part rented since 1933. At the same time, it initiated an extensive branch banking program. In the 1950s, the bank was described as the "banker's bank" with other banks keeping more funds on deposit with it than any other bank in Ohio. During the 1960s, it experienced phenomenal growth, developing as well a reputation for excellent performance. The total assets of the bank (in 1962) exceeded the one billion mark. Two years later, the bank's International Banking Division won the coveted President's "E" award for excellence in developing export markets.

In 1973, its name was changed from The National City Bank of Cleveland to National City Bank and plans were completed to make it a wholly owned subsidiary of the National City Corporation. This holding company has affiliated banks in other areas of the state and non-banking subsidiaries that relate chiefly to such activities as automobile financing. Today the Corporation has total assets of over $4 billion with a staff of more than 2,800. This represents a dramatic increase over $35 million, the total assets of the bank in 1932.

Currently National City Bank is on the threshold of an extensive development program significant by its plans to occupy a substantial new building on the northwest corner of East 9th Street and Euclid Avenue. It continues to provide a complete range of banking services, with 51 offices in Cuyahoga County, of which 16 are in Cleveland.

Oglebay Norton Company

Serving the raw materials needs of our nation for 125 years

Oglebay Norton Company traces its origin to the bustling Cleveland waterfront of 1854 and two men of enterprise in the commission house on Merwin Street.

The Cuyahoga was a forest of ships' masts and spars. Streets were muddy, sidewalks wooden, buildings unpainted frame, but the riverfront teemed with horses, men and ships. There was frustration, too. Business leaders had sent a scientist to Michigan's Upper Peninsula in search of silver, gold or even copper. What he returned with was red rock — handfuls of iron ore.

Isaac Hewitt and Henry Tuttle were not dismayed. They had staked a claim in America's Iron Age. The first cargo of this red gold had come to Cleveland in 1852. Dug by hand,

The first shipment of Mesabi iron ore was dug from the Mountain Iron Mine and moved by rail to the docks of Duluth, Minnesota. Whaleback barge No. 102 loaded the 2,073-gross-ton cargo on November 11, 1892, and began her journey in tow of the Steamer Alexander McDougall.

six barrels were wheelbarrowed onto a wooden ship, portaged around the St. Mary's Falls and carried, an enduring legend says, to the firm of Hewitt & Tuttle.

In 1855, the Soo Canal opened for passage of its first cargo — 132 tons of iron ore aboard the brig Columbia. A new waterway now linked billions of tons of Lake Superior iron ore to cities of the East.

Iron fever gripped the Great Lakes. Some 7,000 tons of ore came down the lakes in 1855. By 1869, ore movement had increased to a torrent of 650,000 tons. In those years, three men pursued separate courses unknown to each other, but all had their eyes on iron ore. Henry Tuttle's son, Horace, joined the firm, absorbing his father's zeal for ore. David Z. Norton worked as head cashier in the Commercial National Bank. Earl W. Oglebay, banker and merchant of Wheeling, West Virginia, tramped the ore country of northern Michigan and Wisconsin. He would soon come to Cleveland, meet Henry Tuttle and found Tuttle, Oglebay and Company, agents and mine managers for iron range companies.

The pieces came together in 1890 when Earl Oglebay joined forces with David Norton, responsible for mining and delivering iron ore from the Lake Superior Consolidated Iron Mines. Within two years, Oglebay Norton sold and supervised the first shipment from the Mesabi Range in Minnesota.

In 1920, Oglebay Norton assembled its own fleet of 11 vessels, the Columbia Steamship Company, later to become the Columbia Transportation Division. Four years later, Earl Oglebay and David Norton retired.

Oglebay entered the coal business in 1928, establishing a department that would lead to management and ownership of coal mines in Ohio and West Virginia, developed the Ferro Engineering Division for the manufacture of insulating products for steel ingot pouring, and later undertook management of several docks on the Great Lakes.

Testing and development of low-grade taconite minerals under Oglebay Norton management would open a three-billion-ton reserve of iron ore once considered useless.

The same foresight which perceived the coming need for iron ore in 1854 saw the depletion of high-grade ores possibly as early as the 1950s. That insight led Oglebay Norton to play a major role in the development of Minnesota taconite, including the early development of Reserve Mining Company and the Eveleth Mines project. In the largest venture in its history, the company in 1965 became manager and part owner of iron ore mining and pelletizing operations of Eveleth Taconite Company and in 1975 initiated operation of the Eveleth Expansion Company.

Oglebay Norton mining operations today also include the Saginaw Mining Company, producing bituminous coal in southeastern Ohio; the Central Silica Company, producing glass and foundry sand; and Texas Mining Company at Brady, Texas, mining fracture sand for the petroleum industry.

The company operates 19 vessels, moving iron ore, coal, limestone and other bulk cargoes on the Great Lakes and operates rail-to-barge coal-loading terminals on the Ohio River at Ceredo, West Virginia, and at Wilder, Kentucky. T & B Foundry Company pours gray and ductile iron castings in Cleveland.

The Ohio Bell Telephone Company

Cleveland — 100 years on the telephone

Nineteen seventy-nine is a milestone year for Ohio Bell and Cleveland as the telephone company and the community mark 100 years of continuous telephone exchange service.

Alexander Graham Bell received his first telephone patent on March 7, 1876, and about a year later the first telephone line in Ohio was placed in service. That line linked the offices of a Cleveland coal company with the firm's retail yard.

It was not until three years after Bell's invention, however — on September 15, 1879 — that the city's first exchange opened for business. And it has been a flourishing business ever since.

For the first few months of its existence, the Cleveland exchange was owned and operated by the Western Union Telegraph Company. Rates for telephone service were steep in those early years. A private line cost $72 a year within a one mile zone of the exchange and was payable quarterly in advance.

Early advertisements for telephone service in Cleveland are amusing — if not confusing — by today's standards. One such ad claimed: "The outfit and the service, within limitations, are first class."

On the other hand, customer dialing instructions in early Cleveland telephone directories were direct and to the point. "When the bell rings three times, you are wanted. Take the telephone from the hook and answer. Pay no attention to irregular ringing of the bell."

Telephone exchange service in Ohio — both Bell and independent — grew fast and furiously in the late 1870s. Columbus, Zanesville and Toledo also opened exchanges in 1879; Piqua, Findlay and Middletown in 1880.

Back in Cleveland a Bell-licensed group

This early telephone "vehicle" is a forerunner to the nearly 900 telephone installation and repair vans that Ohio Bell now dispatches daily to serve customers in Greater Cleveland.

purchased the exchange from Western Union for $16,000 at a time when the company with the "new fangled" phone had assets valued at only $3,700.

By 1882 the configuration of what is now known as Ohio Bell was beginning to take shape. Construction of lines linking Clevelanders with the rest of the state was financed through the sale of coupons, redeemable for long distance calls at a later date.

With the expiration of Bell's patents in 1894, competing independent telephone companies sprang up in most Ohio cities, Cleveland included. Canvassers went door-to-door to entice customers with offers of introductory free service.

In 1920 the Bell-affiliated Cleveland Telephone Company changed its name to Ohio Bell and shortly after purchased the Central Union Company, which furnished Bell service in many other parts of the state. In 1921 the Public Utility Commission of Ohio approved a merger with the Ohio State Company, an independent. Ohio Bell, as we now know it, became a corporate reality.

From that official beginning Ohio Bell has grown to a company providing communications to nearly five million telephones in Ohio.

Of these about 30 percent are located in the

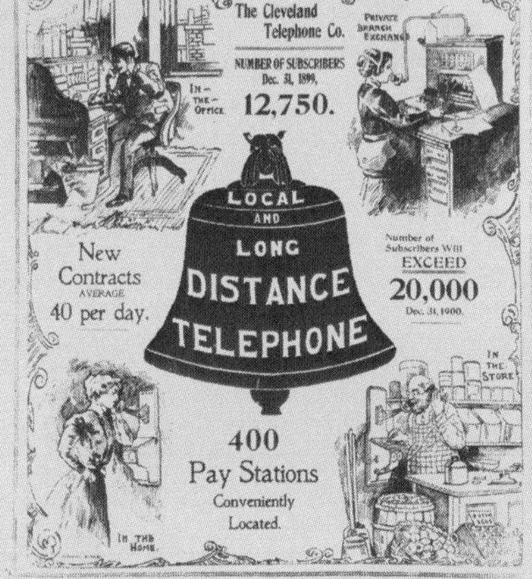

A turn-of-the-century telephone ad boasts of 400 convenient pay stations. Ohio Bell now has more than 14,700 "pay stations" throughout the Greater Cleveland area.

Cleveland metropolitan area, one of the largest local calling areas in the country, covering more than 500 square miles.

Since 1964 Ohio Bell headquarters have been located in one of Cleveland's most famous urban renewal complexes, Erieview Plaza.

There also has been a steady stream of service improvements over the years.

In 1927 new switching equipment in downtown Cleveland gave customers in the old MAin-CHerry exchanges the ability to dial their own local telephone calls. And in 1954 Clevelanders were among the first Ohioans to be able to dial long distance calls.

In 1967 Ohio Bell's first electronic switching system (ESS) also went into operation at 750 Huron Road for downtown customers. Since then, more than one-third of the business and residence customers of Ohio Bell have been converted to similar systems.

ESS provides significant improvements in call-switching capabilities. Its "memory" features also make possible Custom Calling options such as Call Waiting, Call Transfer and Three-Way Calling.

Recent years also have seen widespread use of Touch-Tone® (pushbutton) service, computerized handling of long distance calls and the introduction of international direct dialing.

Today, work is underway in Cleveland on the installation of a new computer-based long distance switching machine which will handle up to 550,000 calls an hour.

To keep pace with the communications needs of its customers, Ohio Bell employs approximately 24,500 people throughout the state. The company's total annual payroll in 1978 amounted to more than $470 million, and construction spending was nearly $400 million.

Ostendorf-Morris Company

Real estate innovators with a sense of perspective

In 1939, a couple of seasoned realtors joined forces to establish a new company in Cleveland. Edgar L. Ostendorf and Warren L. Morris founded the real estate company that bears their names in the belief that they could bring a new perspective to the real estate business in Cleveland and surrounding areas.

They brought together several specialized real estate services into one company for the first time. By combining brokerage, property management, financial and appraisal services they not only expanded their capabilities to serve clients, they also enabled their new company to minimize the effects of cyclical swings in the real estate industry. This stabilization also permitted them to implement another innovation involving the method of compensating their people. Rather than a commission basis, they employed sales and other professionals on a salaried arrangement. This method enabled the professional realtor to offer long-range guidance to clients and to assist their associates in solving their clients' problems. This proved to be an attractive approach — so much so that in the first year, Ostendorf-Morris retained the services of 20 professionals.

Realizing the need for a continuing new perspective, the partners became active in the national real estate scene through professional organizations. Ostendorf served as national president of the American Institute of Real Estate Appraisers and the National Association of Real Estate Boards. Morris was national president of the American Institute of Real Estate Appraisers, the Urban Land Institute and the American Society of Real Estate Counselors.

As the new company began to grow, its perspective shifted as the nation contemplated, then entered, World War II. O-M was heavily involved in assisting government and industry in building production capacity. For example, O-M assembled a 105 acre site on which the Defense Plant Corporation built a one million square foot plant for Thompson Aircraft Products' war production. After the war, O-M negotiated the purchase of the plant from the government by Thompson, the forerunner of TRW Inc. In White Sulphur Springs, West Va., the renowned Greenbrier Inn became an Army General Hospital. O-M appraised the property to determine a fair acquisition price, and after the war, reappraised it for resale by the government to its former owner.

Following the war, the perspective again changed and Cleveland, with its ample labor supply, became an area of strong industrial growth. O-M again was involved in that progress through appraisal, mortgage financing and negotiation of sales and leases of land and properties for companies like Warner & Swasey, General Motors, Van Dorn, Westinghouse, U.S. Steel, White Consolidated and numerous others.

The old Whitney "Power" Block, above, housed a number of important Cleveland industries in earlier years. Today, a modern office complex, housing major international corporations, stands on the same site. Ostendorf-Morris has served as exclusive leasing and managing agent for both properties.

In the early '50s, O-M recognized a need for more prime office space in downtown Cleveland. Providing the impetus, O-M brought several interests together which ultimately led to the construction of the 55 Public Square Building. This kicked off a 20 year period of building which markedly changed Cleveland's skyline, with the construction of the East Ohio, Erieview, Investment Plaza, Central National, Bond Court and Diamond Shamrock Buildings. In all, ten major new office buildings were constructed and O-M was involved in each one with services ranging from leasing and management to financial, appraisal and brokerage.

By 1957, O-M had become the leading full service real estate firm in Ohio. Management of the company was transferred to a trio of employees: Donald P. Cloak, William B. West and Stephen C. Morris. Under their leadership, O-M continued to provide a new and changing perspective to its clients.

Another new perspective arose from the long-term relationship O-M has with many of its clients. As these companies began to grow and expand nationally, they called upon O-M to find and acquire plant sites, warehouses, retail space and office facilities in cities across the nation. With companies such as Harris Corp., O-M functions as their real estate department in lieu of an internal staff.

In the '70s, management of O-M is in the hands of a larger group with Steve Morris as chairman of the board. The company is still growing and expanding its perspectives and services. In 1978, O-M took a major step into commercial estate when the people of Priemer, Barnes & Associates, the largest commercial brokerage firm in the Mid west, joined O-M.

Today, with 82 people handling over $300 million of real estate annually, O-M is the largest commercial-industrial real estate company in Ohio and is expanding rapidly into the national market.

As Steve Morris puts it, "We've built our business on the ability to bring new and creative services to clients' real estate needs. O-M has been doing this in Cleveland since 1939 and enjoying every minute of it."

Parker Hannifin Corporation

Yesterday only a vision, today a global supplier

Cleveland-based Parker Hannifin Corporation — one of the biggest unfamous companies you'll find anywhere — is a leading worldwide supplier of fluid power systems components for industrial, automotive and aviation/space/marine equipment with more than 90,000 products for 300-plus markets. Parker employs about 20,000 people in Parker facilities in 20 countries — including over 3,000 in the Greater Cleveland area.

Obviously, Parker wasn't always a giant. It all began with only two employees in a two-story brick building on Cleveland's commercial near West Side. From this, Parker has grown to a substantial member of Cleveland's industrial community with annual sales approaching $1 billion.

But the times were not always so kind.

Parker was founded in 1918 by Arthur L. Parker — an engineer by training, an inventor by design, and an entrepreneur by character.

With two employees and one primary product, Parker Appliance Company — as it was known then — was successful in a small way. Mr. Parker designed a new type of pneumatic braking system which used compressed air to stop heavy trucks and buses in difficult situations. In 1921, to promote his new idea and product, he decided to build and outfit a truck and make a demonstration run over hilly, dangerous roads from Akron, Ohio to Boston.

But the Parker truck never made it to Massachusetts, and as a result his entire company went downhill. Literally. Somewhere in north-central Pennsylvania, the vehicle, through no fault of the braking system, went over a hill along with the entire capital of the fledgling company.

This two-story building on Cleveland's near West Side was the beginning of Parker Hannifin Corporation.

An aerial view of the corporate headquarters of Parker Hannifin Corporation today at 17325 Euclid Avenue.

To re-capitalize his enterprise, Parker went to work for Nickel Plate Railroad as an engineer. In 1924, he and Carl Klamm, his original employee, again started the Parker Appliance Company.

In the interim, new uses had been found for compressed air and new technologies evolved. Parker Appliance Company found more markets than originally anticipated for its line of flared pneumatic fitting products, and the business prospered.

One of those markets was the embryonic aircraft industry. Parker worked closely with the industry since both were located in Cleveland.

Parker helped aircraft builders — such as Glenn L. Martin and the men who went on to found Lockheed Aircraft Co., North American Aviation, and Douglas Aircraft Co. — solve a major problem of excessive weight by developing hydraulics to move control surfaces and other critical components in the air. As the aircraft industry continued at a modest rate during the Great Depression, so did Parker.

During World War II, Parker became the largest producer of hydraulic connecting and metering devices in the world. At one point in World War II, the company employed more than 5,000 in the Greater Cleveland area.

Then unexpectedly, Arthur L. Parker died of a heart attack on January 1, 1945.

The complete shift to wartime production nearly proved fatal also, for Parker Appliance Company. At War's end, the need for the company and its products abruptly ceased to exist. With no revenue from its products, the company was again virtually bankrupt...and also without a leader.

At this point, Parker's widow, Helen Parker, came forward. Helen Parker had been the second of two original employees of the company. Following the death of her husband Arthur, she strongly resisted the liquidation of the company, and recruited two proven executives to rebuild the company in the critical post-war years.

Both from Cleveland-based Reliance Electric Company, S. Blackwell Taylor came to Parker as president and Robert W. Cornell as comptroller.

By the late '40s, the idea of industrial automation — using machines to do what had previously been done by human hands and arms — began to make sense.

The new Parker management saw the opportunity to adjust its ability to make precision devices to a growing demand in industry for using fluid controls and components to do heavy work.

By 1950, the company's volume had recovered to approximately its pre-war level, employment had stabilized and a small profit realized on its operation.

In 1957, the company made what at that time was a major acquisition. Management merged the company with the Hannifin Manufacturing Company of Des Plaines, Illinois, a leading manufacturer in the world of hydraulic and pneumatic power cylinders. It also changed the name from Parker Appliance Company to Parker-Hannifin Corporation and marked a shift point in Parker's history.

Since that time, Parker has acquired almost 30 other industrial companies around the world. Companies whose technology and talent serve to complement Parker's position as a balanced company serving three prime sectors of the world economy — industrial, automotive and aviation/space/marine.

The corporation which Arthur L. Parker began, and Blackwell Taylor and Robert Cornell helped guide, is today a growing, worldwide enterprise headed by Patrick S. Parker, son of the founder, as chairman and chief executive officer.

Pickands Mather & Co.

Since 1883 a tradition of trust

Animals and machinery worked side by side stripping the overburden from the Mahoning Mine in 1895. The mine yielded iron ore for 80 years, 50 of which were under Pickands Mather's managership.

In the spring of 1883 three Ohioans left the security of their well-established careers and joined together to form a small dealership in iron ore and pig iron. Although Samuel Mather, James Pickands and Jay Morse were starting with just one ship, two small mines in Michigan and 1,800 tons of ore on a dock in Michigan, they saw a future in supplying the steel industry with its vast requirements for raw materials.

From that inauspicious beginning, Pickands Mather & Co. has grown into a major supplier of raw materials to the steel industry. The company manages iron ore mines in the United States, Canada and Australia, coal mines in West Virginia and Kentucky, limestone and coke operations and operates a fleet of modern Great Lakes vessels.

The company's near 100-year history provides solid testimony to its slogan "A tradition of trust." The steel industry has chosen the company to manage over 60 iron ore mines since 1883. Among those are some of the most famous, including the Mahoning Mine in Minnesota which operated for 80 years and yielded 129,760,000 tons of ore.

The company was one of the early pioneers in researching low-grade ores called taconite.

Reserves of natural ores were not unlimited and in the '30s Pickands Mather, along with several steel companies, began experiments in extracting iron from taconite. After years of research, a process was proven economically feasible and the five iron ore operations managed today by the company owe their existence to these pioneering efforts. (In a change from its traditional role of managing only, the company now takes partial ownership interests in the new mines.)

Pickands Mather has perhaps been best known for its iron ore activities (sales as well as mining) but it has also played a major role in other areas of business.

Lakes shipping was one of the company's first endeavors. Starting with a single ship, the company soon had several fleets under its management. Since 1913 Interlake Steamship Company has been the Pickands Mather-managed fleet.

The fleet has a long list of accomplishments to its credit. In the '20s and '30s the Steamship HARRY COULBY was known as the "Queen of the Great Lakes," setting numerous tonnage records. Ships like the JOHN SHERWIN (built in the '50s) maintained the fleet's predominant position into the '70s.

With the '70s came the supercarriers. The company was one of the first to recognize the economic advantages of these 1,000-foot giants and built two, the M/V JAMES R. BARKER and the MESABI MINER.

Pickands Mather's involvement with coal mining started in 1919. The first mine ran for 45 years and produced 33 million tons of coal. In recent years, responding to the country's growing energy needs, PM has greatly expanded its coal mining divisions. Today the company manages, and in some cases has partial ownership in, eight coal mines capable of producing nearly nine million tons annually.

Coal sales occupied an important position from the start. Taking ownership coal and agency and non-agency accounts, PM routinely moves over 10 million tons a year.

The Steamer PEGASUS shown upbound near Sault Ste. Marie, Michigan. Built in 1902, this 436-footer sailed under the PM houseflag until 1946.

For almost 100 years Pickands Mather has been a major supplier of merchant pig iron. The company also has important dealings in ferroalloys and coke, including its Milwaukee Solvay Coke Division.

Rounding out Pickands Mather is The Carbon Limestone Company. Carbon has been supplying high-quality flux stone to the blast furnaces of eastern Ohio and western

Pennsylvania since the late 1800s. It became a division in 1962.

Pickands Mather was a partnership until being incorporated in 1960. A significant development came in 1973 when PM was bought by Moore McCormack Resources, Inc. The new parent corporation backed the company in a $230 million expansion program that included the two new supercarriers, a new iron ore facility in Minnesota and coal mines.

Downtown Cleveland has always been the home of PM's corporate offices. Originally located in the Western Reserve Building, the company moved to the Union Commerce Building in 1924 and then to its present offices in the Diamond Shamrock Building in 1973.

Today Pickands Mather is still expanding. Another 1,000-footer is under construction and a new coal mine is about one year from start-up. Studies of iron ore deposits continue on a world-wide basis, and as the steel industry's need expands, new iron ore mines will come. The young men and women joining the company can look back to a proud past and look forward to many opportunities to preserve the tradition of trust that is Pickands Mather & Co.

Picker Corporation

Ongoing dedication to innovation, customers, and those who are ill

On November 8, 1895, Professor Wilhelm Conrad Röntgen, a physicist at the University of Wurzburg, Germany, discovered a "new kind of ray". He called the radiation "x-rays", and reported on the phenomenon a month later to the learned Wurzburg Society, in a modest paper destined to win him the Nobel Prize. In describing this historic event in 1897, Sylvanus P. Thompson, physicist and founder of the British Roentgen Society, noted: "The invisible rays — for they were invisible save when they fell upon the chemically painted screen — were found to have a penetrative power hitherto unimagined. They penetrated cardboard, wood and cloth with ease. The discoverer, interposing his hands between the source of his rays and his bit of luminescent cardboard, *saw* the bones of his living hand projected in silhouette upon the screen. The great discovery was made."

Later, the potential medical applications of the new discovery accelerated when Röntgen found photographic plates to be sensitive to the rays, and the resultant images of consistently-acceptable quality. He reported: "We are therefore in a condition to determine more definitely many phenomena...to avoid certain deceptions...to see inside...to gain *insight.*" That insight, that inward search, became a turning point for humanity.

Utilizing the x-ray's ever-increasing capability to search, to reach inward, created a hunger for a matching parade of more perceptive equipment. It began with the need for film and protective clothing and, even more, for someone who would make support of the new modality a consuming mission. James Picker.

He was not a doctor nor an engineer but a druggist, a young man of vision, courage and administrative ability who came to America in 1901 from Russia seeking the opportunities found in the United States.

James Picker was 19 when he landed in New York. Nearly penniless, he found a job at $5 a week in a drugstore located at 101st St. and Madison Avenue. He worked 12 hours a day, seven days a week. Having had pharmaceutical training in Russia, he went on to become a registered pharmacist and in 1910, encouraged by his new wife, he bought the store from his boss.

Picker's famous U.S. Army Mobile Field X-Ray Unit and ancillary equipment in "E-Award" display, circa 1941.

James Picker, founder.

Immediately, Picker's vision and ingenuity were evidenced. A drugstore should provide more than drugs. He put in Kodak film and opened a soda fountain that quickly became popular with staff members of nearby Mt. Sinai Hospital.

From his hospital patrons, Picker learned of the need by the hospital for x-ray film and ancillary radiological supplies. Because of his contacts with Kodak he was able to obtain x-ray film in sufficient quantity to become a convenient supplier to Mt. Sinai. His prices and conscientious service brought new business which before long reached such a level that in 1914 he sold the drugstore and went into "business to serve doctors," supplying them with x-ray film, chemicals and other products important to the field.

In 1916, the James Picker Company was established and in 1921, with the goal of manufacturing x-ray units themselves, the Picker X-Ray Corporation became a reality. Until 1929 operations were confined to the New York area at which time Mr. Picker, looking to the production of a broader line of diagnostic machines, bought Cleveland's Waite and Bartlett Co. located at East 30th and Superior Avenue. This became the Waite-Picker Mfg. Division which in 1931 produced the first vertical enclosed, shock-proof fluoroscope. Picker was now a name of importance in the field.

During World War II, Picker was the sole producer of portable military field x-ray units for the U.S. and its Allies. At war's end, Mr. Picker returned $4,000,000 to the U.S. government — extra profits he felt should not be made from the tragedy of the war. He died in May of 1963 at age 81.

In 1958, five years before James Picker's death, the company was acquired by C.I.T. Financial Corporation, and continued to grow upon the firm foundation established by its founder. Since that time, new ventures have been made into the innovative diagnostic modalities of nuclear medicine, ultrasound, and clinical laboratory techniques and, most recently, into the fast-growing area of sophisticated computed tomography. To reflect the broad scope of its expanded activities, the company was re-designated Picker Corporation in 1967.

Presently, from its World Headquarters in the Cleveland suburb of Highland Heights, Ohio, Picker Corporation is solidifying its position as a leading manufacturer of high-quality diagnostic products, and as a major supplier of x-ray film and processing systems, radiographic accessories and supplies.

Today Picker Corporation and its 6,000 employees worldwide, have an ongoing commitment to explore all avenues of diagnostic technology. Echoing a credo of James Picker, "We are determined to extend our participation in the future, with emphasis on product development, quality and service to our customers and those who are ill."

Republic Steel Corporation

Productive relationship with Cleveland spans nearly half a century

Republic Steel Corporation, headquartered in Cleveland, is one of Ohio's largest home based industries, with sales exceeding $3.5 billion. Republic operates three steelmaking districts in the state, largest of which is its Cleveland District steel plant and strip mill. The company is the industry leader in production of high grade alloy steels and one of the nation's leading producers of carbon sheet steel for appliances and automobiles and hot rolled and cold finished bars for the automotive, farm equipment and machinery industries. Its employment statewide approximates 25,000 men and women, with about 10,000 employed in Greater Cleveland.

The Cleveland roots of Republic Steel extend well back into the 19th century although the corporate name did not become familiar in Cleveland until the 1930s. At three locations, each a part of a separate corporate enterprise, facilities which were later to become a part of Republic were operating busily in Cleveland before Republic came into being in its present corporate form in 1930. The three predecessor companies were Corrigan-McKinney Steel Company, Steel and Tubes Incorporated and the Bourne-Fuller Company.

Earliest to establish operations in Cleveland was Bourne-Fuller and its predecessor company, the Union Nut Company. Originally a Connecticut enterprise founded in the 1850s to produce carriage bolts, the company was headed by Andrew Upson, a pioneer of the bolt and nut industry.

The business prospered and in 1901 Upson acquired adjacent property on the banks of the Cuyahoga of the Cleveland Iron Company, which included the old River Furnace, an iron making blast furnace originally built in 1879. Around this operation Mr. Upson built a com-

Prior to 1930 most steel was rolled laboriously on hand mills, right. Modern continuous hot strip mills can produce in a few minutes the quantity of sheets which would have been produced on a hand sheet mill in a year's time, with much superior quality.

Republic Steel's 84-inch continuous hot strip mill in Cleveland, lower right, one of the largest, fastest and most modern such rolling mills in the nation. Much of the steel rolled on this mill ultimately is shipped to automobile producers for the fabrication of passenger car bodies.

plete steel plant. About a year later the stock of the company was acquired by Bourne-Fuller Company, but the business was carried on under the Upson name. In 1928-30 a series of mergers was implemented around the Republic Iron & Steel Company of Youngstown which resulted in the corporate form of Republic Steel as it is today. Bourne-Fuller Company along with its properties, Upson Nut Company and Union Rolling Mill were included in that merger.

Corrigan-McKinney had its origins as an iron ore and lake shipping business in the 1880s. But after a time, many of Corrigan-McKinney's customers had acquired mines or lake iron ore carriers of their own. The company decided to move into the merchant iron business so it leased four blast furnaces to use its own ore. Two of these furnaces were in New York State, the third was in Pennsylvania and the fourth was the aforementioned River Furnace.

By 1934 it was obvious that Corrigan-McKinney would have to raise a large sum of money to build additional finishing mills to use its steel output or would have to join with some other company that had finishing capacity but was short on raw steel. Various factors pointed toward the latter choice. Major stockholders approved a proposition worked out between their company and Republic for Republic to acquire Corrigan-McKinney's plants and facilities.

In the ensuing decades, tremendous expenditures were made at Cleveland by Republic and the plant today bears little resemblance to that which was there in 1935.

The third company that entered the Republic fold after a successful period as an independent company was Steel and Tubes Incorporated. It was the creation of the Wick family of Youngstown. The company, incorporated as Elyria Iron and Steel Company, produced no steel but processed purchased steel into tubular products of a wide variety. Its first plant was in Elyria, Ohio; in 1915 the firm decided to build an additional plant in Cleveland near E. 131st Street. Steel and Tubes was acquired by Republic Iron & Steel in 1928 and merged into Republic Steel Corporation in 1930.

Since the mergers of the '30s, a fourth facility has been added to Republic's complex in Greater Cleveland, the Republic Research Center in Independence, Ohio.

Cleveland and Republic have had a productive relationship now spanning almost half a century. With headquarters of the company here since 1935 and a brightening future for the steel industry after a decade of severe problems, the outlook for the next several decades for Republic in Cleveland is brighter than ever.

The Sherwin-Williams Company

More than 100 years of beautifying homes, buildings and products.

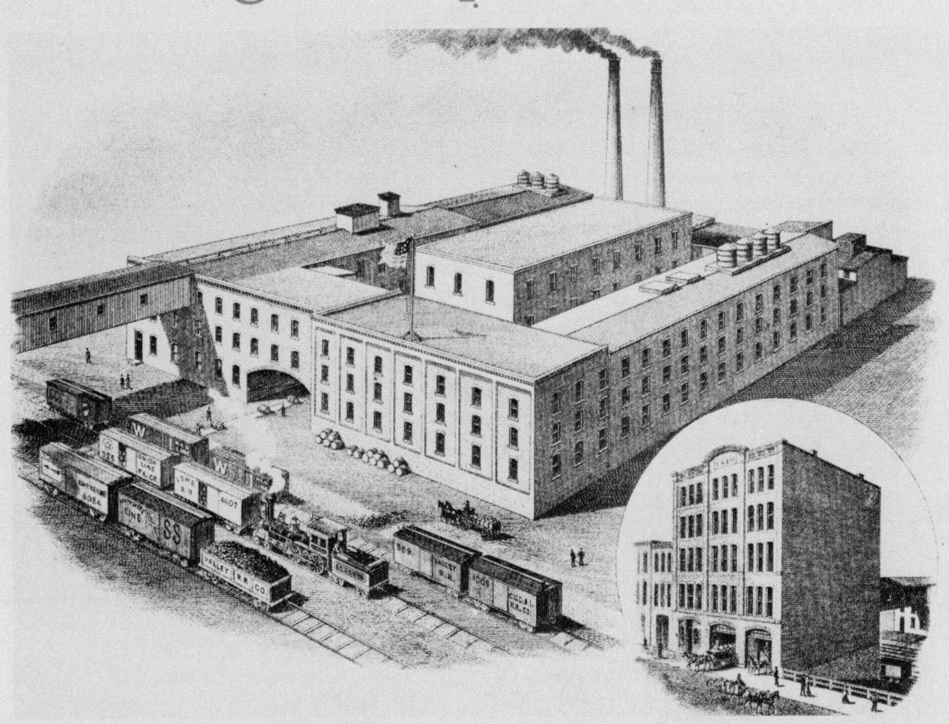

The Sherwin-Williams plant in Cleveland's "Flats", circa 1884. The original plant (in the center) was purchased in 1873. By the mid '20s, Sherwin-Williams had become the largest paint and varnish manufacturer in the world.

Sherwin-Williams' home decorating centers from coast to coast supply painting contractors and the general public with paint and wallcovering. Some stores also carry floorcovering and draperies.

Like most business enterprises born in the nineteenth century, Sherwin-Williams was the creation of hard-working, purposeful men with vision. Henry Sherwin came to Cleveland in 1859 at age 17 and found work in a dry goods store. Next he became a bookkeeper in a wholesale grocery operation. And at 24, he invested his life savings, some $2,000, to gain a partnership in a paint company.

The partnership lasted only three more years until Sherwin's associates decided they wanted to concentrate on the linseed oil part of the business. Sherwin emerged from the dissolution with the paint interests.

In 1870, he was joined by Edward P. Williams, a willing new partner, and The Sherwin-Williams Company was officially launched. Williams was a born salesman — congenial, a good mixer and knowledgeable about his product. In this formative period, Sereno Peck Fenn was an early employee and later became a partner and vice president-treasurer, a position he held for many years. Fenn became a wealthy man, and endowments from his estate helped establish Fenn College, now Cleveland State University.

By 1873, Sherwin-Williams had grown to the point where it was able to buy a building in Cleveland's industrial "Flats" from the Standard Oil Company, and from this first factory emerged the world's leading manufacturer and marketer of coatings.

In those days, paint manufacturers sold ingredients, which the purchaser had to mix to make his own paints. Early ready-mixed paints were of poor quality, weathered fast and turned customers against them. Sherwin vowed he would develop a ready-mixed paint he would be proud to put his name on.

In 1880, he succeeded. SWP ready-mixed paint was so superior that Sherwin patented the mill that made it, a move that gave Sherwin-Williams a strong manufacturing advantage for many years. Moreover, to overcome buyer resistance, Sherwin-Williams offered an ironclad, money-back guarantee. SWP was an immediate success, literally revolutionizing the paint industry and the company itself. SWP gave new impetus to product development and made possible an ambitious expansion program.

By 1888, Sherwin-Williams paints were in wide use by the railroad industry, and the company focused its attention on Chicago, which was not only a rail transport hub but was also becoming an important center for manufacturers of farm implements, buggies and wagons, all important users of paint. Sherwin-Williams bought the small Calumet Paint Co. near the great Pullman Co., an important railway car customer. The Chicago plant eventually became the largest paint manufacturing complex in the world.

Sherwin-Williams made its first venture outside of the U.S. in 1895 when it established paint and varnish making facilities in Canada. Today, Sherwin-Williams has interests throughout the free world.

From 1917 through 1930, Sherwin-Williams grew rapidly through a series of major acquisitions, most notably: Martin-Senour Co., Acme Quality Paints, Lowe Brothers, and John Lucas & Co. This was also a period of further product development, highlighted by new automobile lacquers which reduced painting and drying time from 21 days to a few hours.

It was during World War II, when most basic paint ingredients were restricted as strategic commodities, that Sherwin-Williams introduced its most innovative new product to date — Kem-Tone®, the first water-based, fast drying paint that was to change forever the nation's interior decorating habits, especially when used with Roller-Koater®, a paint applicator as simple as the wheel. A water-reducible paint, coupled with easy roll-on application, ideally met the desires of America's homemakers.

There followed a number of Kem® products: Kem-Glo®, which soon became the country's most widely used enamel, and Super Kem-Tone®, a latex interior paint for the do-it-yourselfer. In 1960, A-100®, a latex exterior house paint, set quality standards so high they have yet to be surpassed. And, in 1959, Sherwin-Williams' research achieved a major advance in automotive finishes with the introduction of acrylic enamel.

Today, the name Sherwin-Williams is virtually synonymous with "paint," and the company's products are readily available to painting contractors and the general public through Sherwin-Williams stores across the nation. Moreover, the company has also won a leadership role in coatings for manufactured products and automotive refinishing. And as it has grown, it has developed major allied businesses, such as cans for paints, aerosols and other products; brushes, rollers and other paint applicators; and chemicals for a wide range of industries.

Sherwin-Williams today is very much what Henry Sherwin wanted it to be — a company devoted to protecting and beautifying homes, buildings and products.

Society National Bank

Bank is a dynamic force in Cleveland's history

Morse's electric telegraph was in use, but Sutter had not yet discovered gold in California, when the idea for Society for Savings, predecessor to Society National Bank, was being born.

The year was 1849 and the population of Cleveland, Ohio numbered only 16,000. Gas illumination was still under consideration, and the advisability of a waterworks system and railroad was up for grabs.

Prominent Cleveland residents and businessmen, however, were pursuing the idea of a bank which would provide "a secure investment to persons of either sex, who receive money in small sums and are desirous of saving it…to assist and encourage the industrious and frugal to lay by such part of their earnings as they may be able to spare…to aid them in putting their money out to advantage…to provide for the safekeeping of money lodged in it…"

Discussions continued until the fledgling Society unceremoniously opened its doors for business on the warm afternoon of August 2, 1849. Mrs. D. E. Bond became the bank's first customer with her deposit of $25.

Historic records show that expenses for the first year totaled $172.45 — $3 of which paid for the bank's first sign. There were 130 depositors who had saved $9,537.99.

By 1857, when a nationwide panic paralyzed industry, caused suspension of specie payments and forced many businesses to bankruptcy, the Society was flourishing. Business was so good that the bank moved to its second home in larger quarters.

This snappy group of workmen are the stonecutters employed in the late 1880s in the construction of Society National Bank's main office building, now a designated landmark on Cleveland's public square. The building represents one of the first uses of structural steel. Its base is Missouri granite, while the upper floors are red sandstone.

Cleveland was steadily growing. It had built its own waterworks sytem, and had become the junction of four railway lines. In its first decade, Society had also grown and deposits now were $403,370.93.

The Civil War had little effect on Cleveland's development, and for the Society it was a period of unparalleled growth. From 1860 to 1865, in just five years, records show twice the number of depositors and a quadrupling of deposits.

By 1866, Society was already in its third home described as "the most modern office building on Public Square," the first thoroughly fireproofed structure in the city.

Society's fourth home is today a designated Cleveland landmark. The building has a commanding position on the Public Square. Its rough-hewn stone walls and deep window openings are familiar to all Clevelanders. The style is a combination of various periods of the Gothic, but there are also Romanesque and Renaissance details, with unusually rich and well-executed stone work and associated metal ornament. A marvelous lamp in the form of a glass basket hanging from a wrought-iron vine adorns the southwest corner of the building. It was Cleveland's first outdoor incandescent light and has remained lighted everyday throughout the decades.

Today, the building is the main office of Society National Bank and the headquarters location for Society Corporation, parent organization of a statewide network of Ohio banks affiliated with the multi-bank holding company.

Society National Bank with branches around the state is the lead bank in Society Corporation.

The stock market crash of 1929 and the Great Depression of the 1930s had little effect on Society. In fact, the bank's records show increases in deposits during the last years of the Depression as depositors realized the solidarity of the bank and felt secure putting money away for future needs.

At the time of Society's Centennial celebrations in 1949, there were just under 204,000 depositors in every state of the Union and in many foreign countries. Begun as a mutual savings bank, it is today a leader among national banks offering highly innovative banking services.

As a matter of record, banking history was written on December 31, 1958, when Society for Savings was unified with Society National Bank of Cleveland.

This photo was taken in 1890 at the completion of Society National Bank's main office building(center). A section of Cleveland's then public square area is also shown, as well as the famous Old Stone Church (left) which still stands opposite the historic bank building.

In 1970, Society National Bank became the first commercial bank in the United States to use the on-line universal teller terminal. Online handles all teller transactions quickly and efficiently, while simultaneously updating records by linking individual tellers directly to a central computer. With a single stop at a teller window, Society customers can quickly complete a wide variety of financial transactions.

In 1978, Society invented SuperBanking which links the bank to Fazio's supermarkets throughout the state. Through the use of point-of-sale terminals and SuperBanking "branch offices" inside the food stores, Society National Bank makes it possible for people to combine grocery shopping with banking needs, thus accommodating many current lifestyles well, while leading naturally into the lifestyles of the 1980s.

Society's International department has more than 1,200 correspondent banks around the free world. The commercial banking department offers highly sophisticated cash management services to business and industry and is generally recognized as a leader in cash mobilization.

Great care has been taken and will continue in developing Society's multiple banking services, including trust and charge cards. Just as Society was a pioneer in the early days of banking, the challenge is to continue.

One of the bank's most important commitments has always been its dedication to ongoing community involvement. Change... a history of firsts... community betterment... Society expertise set into practice in 1849 will continue to be a relevant force in the future as it has in the past.

Society National Bank stands ready to serve the needs of the twenty-first century and beyond.

The Standard Oil Company

Sohio starts its second century in Cleveland

John D. Rockefeller formed The Standard Oil Company in Cleveland in 1870.

The business and marketing genius of Rockefeller and his associates led the firm through phenomenal growth. Standard Oil grew into the largest oil company in the United States. Its operations became worldwide.

In 1882 the Standard Oil trust was created to manage the business of The Standard Oil Company and its affiliated corporations. The original Standard Oil Company lost its dominant position and became merely one of a number of companies in the trust.

The trust agreement provided that other

companies with the "Standard Oil" name be established in various states, with the state name as part of the corporate title. Thus, we have today's Standard of California and Standard of Indiana. Although the word "Ohio" is not in Sohio's official corporate name, it commonly is used to distinguish Sohio from the others.

In 1899 all assets controlled by the trustees were transferred to Standard Oil Company (New Jersey) as a holding company. Twelve years later the United States Supreme Court ordered Standard Oil Company (New Jersey) to divest itself of its holdings in 33 companies.

The decision resulted in the formation of 34 independent companies, eight bearing the name "Standard Oil." Sohio emerged as one of the smaller companies. It owned one refinery (in Cleveland), a string of bulk stations, a fleet of tank wagons, and marketing operations in an area confined to Ohio.

The advent of the internal combustion engine made gasoline, previously the unwanted by-product in the refining of kerosine, the most important product of the industry. Sohio grew and became the leading retail petroleum marketer in Ohio, with major refineries at Toledo and Lima, Ohio. The name Sohio was introduced in 1928.

Sohio gradually acquired oil properties and conducted oil exploration and development in the United States. It joined in constructing pipelines to bring oil to Ohio; and it established a pipeline system for distributing petroleum products from its refineries throughout the state that was the most efficient in the nation. In 1956 Sohio expanded its marketing outside Ohio under the Boron Oil Company brand name. However, the company's own production of crude oil continued to be far short of its refining requirements.

In 1954 the company entered the chemicals business with a plant at Lima to produce agricultural chemicals. Discovery in Sohio's research laboratories of a revolutionary process to produce acrylonitrile, a basic chemical used in textiles and plastics, expanded the chemicals operations. Most of the world's acrylonitrile now is produced using Sohio's process.

In 1964 Sohio joined in experimental ventures to develop oil shale. The company entered the coal business in 1968 with the acquisition of Old Ben Coal Company of Chicago and leased uranium lands in New Mexico the same year.

Just 100 years after its founding, Sohio began its second century by signing an agreement with The British Petroleum Company Limited of London, England. Under its terms, Sohio acquired valuable oil leases on the North Slope of Alaska and marketing and refining properties on the East Coast of the United States. British Petroleum received stock in Sohio that since has grown to approximately 52-percent common stock interest.

Sohio owns approximately 53 percent of the oil in Alaska's Prudhoe Bay Field, which is estimated to hold nearly 30 percent of U.S. total proven reserves. The company joined in building the transAlaska pipeline to bring this oil to U.S. markets and owns approximately 33 percent of that pipeline.

In its first 100 years, Sohio grew to a company with roughly $1 billion in assets. Since then, it has grown to $8.3 billion in assets — the 17th largest industrial corporation in the nation in terms of assets.

Sohio is proud to be part of the Cleveland story for more than 100 years and looks forward to contributing to and sharing in Cleveland's development in the years ahead.

Cleveland's Public Square during the 1890s. Sohio's first offices were located in the building bearing the "Hull & Dutton" sign.

In 1929 Sohio introduced distinctive Tudor-style "servicenters" — like this one at East 89th Street and Carnegie Avenue in Cleveland.

SIFCO Industries, Inc.

Growing internationally with the grain of the steel

A new facade and much larger plant mark the site SIFCO chose for its first major expansion in the 1920s.

SIFCO calls its forgings "the muscles and sinews" of an aircraft, an oil rig or a big piece of mining machinery. The fiber in those muscles is the grain of the metal and its other qualities as changed and improved by heat and pressure. Expert knowledge of these qualities started SIFCO in business and account for its growth, in Cleveland and well beyond, over almost 70 years.

The Steel Improvement Company was organized in Cleveland in 1913 for the heat treating of metals, primarily steels. Shortly, drop forging was added through merger. The expanded company's name, The Steel Improvement & Forge Company, served until 1969 when it was broadened to SIFCO Industries and listed on the American Stock Exchange. The years between saw some serious problems solved, some notable technical feats, and the emergence of the diversity within the sphere of metalworking on which the company has continued to expand.

A drop in volume after World War I had brought Charles H. Smith into the company. His job as an engineer and manager was to solve the combination of sales and production problems. Smith's plans stressed two points: avoid mass-produced, low priced automotive forgings, and gain a competitive advantage by forging materials not normally considered forgeable.

An early success was with Monel metal, a tough corrosion-resistant alloy that had never been forged. Quantities of Monel forgings, such as "still plugs" for oil refineries, bulked large in the company's sales recovery.

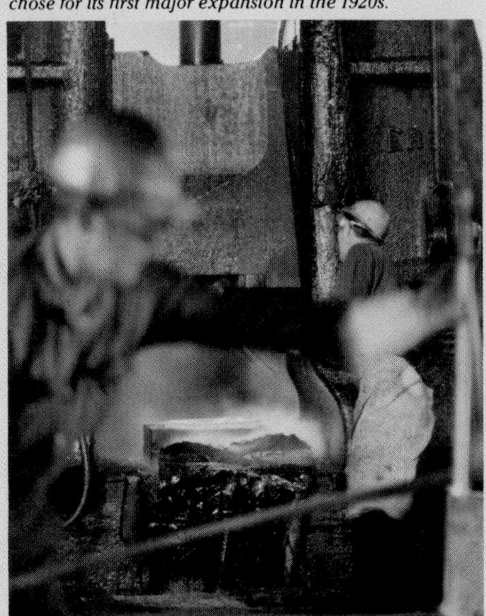

While forging technology has advanced many fold since SIFCO's early years, the skill of the hammermen is still an essential quality.

Other successes followed — with difficult parts for new types of aircraft engines, titanium, beryllium copper, and other parts, metals and alloys that appeared with nuclear and aerospace requirements.

During World War II SIFCO supplied high volumes of forgings for both British and U.S. aircraft. Shipments to England reached a railroad car a day, seven days a week. For the U.S., SIFCO also produced torpedo parts, including a complicated four-bladed torpedo propeller. The strength added by forging instead of casting the propeller helped perfect an aerial torpedo that would retain its accuracy after impact with the water. SIFCO won Ohio's first Navy "E" for its effort.

When Charles Smith died suddenly in 1942, Charles Smith, Jr., a few months out of Massachusetts Institute of Technology, stepped into his father's job as president. A critical project at that time was producing the first turbine wheels for military aircraft engine superchargers. Then came the forging of turbine wheels and blades for the first U.S. jet engines. This work demanded forging to very close tolerances since precision machining in high-temperature alloys was then almost non-existent. SIFCO's capability in close tolerance forging led to many additional contracts for new aircraft projects and then programs in aerospace. It was also the seed for growth beyond the U.S.

The company's first international project was building and operating a forging plant for Canadian fighter plane engines during the Korean War. A forging plant in Argentina followed, and a joint venture in Brazil. Organized in 1958, Sifco do Brasil is now the largest forging operation in the Southern Hemisphere. SIFCO's technical assistance also helped form and guide an enterprise in India that has grown into the largest forging operation in Asia beyond Japan. In all, SIFCO's transfer of its forging technology to developing countries has helped create enough new employment abroad to equal the industrial job base for a city of 80,000.

Under Charles Smith, Jr., SIFCO had also been expanding and diversifying domestically. Acquisitions of a precision machining business led into jet engine component repair. Other specialty products and services acquired and developed include selective electroplating for industrial repair and the design and production of large-diameter bearings. Key figures working on these projects with Smith, chairman since 1970, were A. H. Milnes and Kevin O'Donnell, who succeeded Milnes as president in 1976.

SIFCO's latest project is a press forging operation producing high-volume commercial forgings, as opposed to short-run specialized hammer forgings. This enterprise gives entry to a number of new markets, including automotive. The early decision to avoid this field was tactical, not strategic. SIFCO's growth strategy has changed little in the 50 years between — to combine the technical resources available with the production resources needed to capture the opportunities with the best potential.

The Stouffer Corporation

From a buttermilk stand to hotels, restaurants, frozen foods...

In 1922, a small, standup buttermilk stand was opened by A. E. Stouffer in Cleveland's "Old Arcade," now a national historical site. In addition to dairy products from the Stouffer farm, Mrs. Mahala Stouffer began making her Dutch Apple Pies for the lunch counter. They were an immediate success and her other recipes became the backbone of the first Stouffer menus.

Vernon and Gordon Stouffer watched their father's venture with interest while completing their educations and both sons entered the restaurant business with him — Vernon in 1924, and Gordon in 1929. They made a great team!

Stouffer's first restaurant opened in downtown Cleveland in 1924, called the "Stouffer Lunch." Total investment for the new facility was $12,000. It offered two sandwiches — toasted cheese, and bacon, lettuce and tomato, and apple and lemon meringue pie.

Within a year, additional Stouffer restaurants opened in Detroit and in the Citizen's Building in Cleveland. The menus were expanded to include charcoaled steaks, baked ham and broiled lamb chops. Other restaurants were added in Pittsburgh.

During this early growth period, a management staff was formed and a workable formula for multiple operations was conceived.

When the Depression came, Stouffer's tightened its belt, rechecked value to guests and its quality standards and service. Expansion into larger restaurants emerged with the opening of Cleveland's Playhouse Square in 1936, and New York City's Fifth Avenue and Pershing Square restaurants.

World War II temporarily interrupted expansion, but Stouffer's resumed in 1946 with its first suburban store — Shaker Square.

At the urging of customers, Wally Blankinship, Shaker Square manager, began freezing some menu items that were then sold in a take-home pantry, adjacent to the restaurant, called the "227 Club." From the start, Stouffer's pioneered in quality frozen prepared foods offering entrees, side dishes and desserts. By 1954, volume of business had grown so much, a processing plant was opened on Woodland Avenue in Cleveland and later expanded in 1956.

The Woodland plant could not keep up with growing sales volume, however, and Stouffer's opened a modern, highly automated frozen food operation in Solon in 1968.

With record sales annually, Stouffer's became the nation's leading producer of quality frozen prepared foods including entrees, side dishes, French bread pizza, baked goods and crepes. The company has grown since its beginning in 1954, with 25 production employees, to approximately 2,100 employees today in its Foods Division and markets its products throughout the 50 states.

The small, standup buttermilk stand, which was opened by A. E. Stouffer in 1922 in Cleveland's "Old Arcade," featured dairy products from the Stouffer farm and Mrs. Mahala Stouffer's Dutch Apple Pies.

Stouffer's Inn on the Square in downtown Cleveland, which has recently undergone an extensive renovation, features 520 guest rooms, excellent meeting and banquet facilities, three fine restaurants and a 10-story atrium in the center of the hotel.

Because of its reputation for quality, Stouffer's participated with NASA in the quarantine feeding of the Apollo 11, 12 and 14 astronauts returning from the moon as well as the scientist-aquanauts on Tektite II, an underwater research project.

Another expansion growing out of Stouffer's restaurant experience was the founding of Stouffer's Management Food Service Division in Philadelphia in 1956. MFS, with nine operating districts and more than 130 accounts, provides food service to commercial industrial operations, health care centers, schools, nursing homes and leisure-recreation areas including Blossom Music Center and Severance Hall.

In 1960, Stouffer's entered the hotel business with its purchase of the Anacapri Inn in Ft. Lauderdale, Florida. Other hotels followed in Michigan, Illinois, Missouri, Ohio, Texas, Kentucky, Indiana, Pennsylvania, Georgia, Virginia, Colorado, New York and Iowa. Stouffer's first resort venture was the beautiful PineIsle Resort Hotel in Lanier Islands, Georgia.

Today, Stouffer's national hotel chain includes Cleveland's Inn on the Square featuring 520 guest rooms, three fine restaurants and a unique 10-story atrium in the center of the hotel with a pool, swim-up bar, waterfall and live trees and plantings.

The 1970s saw Stouffer's undergo the greatest expansion in its history with additional hotels, restaurants and dynamic growth in its frozen foods. In 1976, Stouffer's acquired the Borel Restaurant Corporation, known nationally for its popular "Rusty Scupper" Restaurants, and Top Services, which handles route vending operations in Northeastern Ohio.

From its historic beginning as a buttermilk counter in the Old Arcade, Stouffer's has grown to include many restaurants around Greater Cleveland including Westgate, Pier W, The Whole Grain, John Q's, Top of the Town, Rusty Scupper, James Tavern, The Cheese Cellar and the Stouffer's at Summit Mall.

And Stouffer's is proud to call Cleveland its national headquarters for all of its operations with more than 3,300 Stouffer employees earning their livelihoods in Greater Cleveland providing products and services for fellow Clevelanders as well as the rest of the nation...

TRW Inc.

More than 75 years of growth through high-technology

Just after the turn of the century, five men put together $2,500 in capital and began a business based on technological innovation. The first products of that company, then called the Cleveland Cap Screw Company, were bicycle bolts and cap screws.

Soon after the company opened its doors in 1901, it applied its technology to the production of valves for the fledgling automotive industry. The company quickly became the recognized leader in the manufacture of auto valves and is still the world's largest independent producer.

From auto valves it was a natural, yet technically demanding, step to making airplane valves. The company took that step in time to meet the needs of Allied forces in World War I. TRW valves were in the engine that powered the French Spad fighter plane. A company innovation, the hollow, chemically-cooled valve, helped Lindbergh fly across the Atlantic. Other historic flights which relied on TRW valves included the first air crossing of the Pacific by Sir Charles Kingsford-Smith and the trans-polar journeys of Commander Byrd.

In 1929, the company, renamed Thompson Products Inc., initiated the world famous Thompson Trophy races. These not only served as practical proving grounds for new technical ideas that brought faster air speeds and safer transportation, but also exhibitions of skill and daring for pilots like Jimmy Doolittle and Roscoe Turner.

During World War II, the company applied its aircraft technology to fuel booster pumps which enabled the first high altitude flights.

As the company reorganized for the peacetime economy, management recognized that much of its future success would hinge on meeting the needs of emerging worldwide markets. So TRW began investing in related overseas companies. Today, TRW has become a major supplier of automotive products virtually everywhere vehicles are produced.

Since its earliest years, TRW has been recognized as a leading supplier of automotive valves.

During the 1950s, with its extensive experience in military markets, the company decided to enter the growing fields of electronics and ballistic missile development. In 1953, it provided financial support for a new electronics system company in Los Angeles, The Ramo-Wooldridge Corporation, which was named for the two engineers who created it. Their firm soon became a leader in electronics and systems engineering and served as technical director for the Air Force ballistic missile programs.

In 1958, Thompson Products merged with Ramo-Wooldridge to form TRW. Following the merger, company sales reached an annual rate of about $400 million.

During the 1960s and early '70s, TRW grew both internally and through selected acquisitions. The company entered new markets — including bearings, with the Marlin-Rockwell company; fasteners, with United-Carr; tools, with United-Greenfield; oilfield equipment with Mission Manufacturing and Reda Pump; and electronic components, with IRC, Cinch,

During both World Wars, TRW supplied the Allied forces needs for aircraft parts.

and Globe Industries. Overseas affiliates and subsidiaries flourished, giving TRW a truly multinational character.

TRW was a pioneer in the design and manufacture of unmanned spacecraft, and today has a prominent role in the nation's space programs. The company has built over 100 spacecraft to date. Its space work ranges from the Apollo lunar module descent engine to the Pioneer series, including Pioneer 11 which is on its way to Saturn, and the Viking Biology Instrument, which searched for life on Mars.

TRW now employs more than 93,000 people in more than 300 worldwide locations. Sales exceed $3.5 billion. The company continues to use its technological expertise and its innovative spirit to explore new areas from better ways to communicate data electronically to unique alternate energy sources.

But besides its success as an economic unit, TRW also must serve its employees and the communities in which it operates. The company firmly believes in promoting the quality of work life for its employees and encouraging their volunteerism within the community. Through the TRW Foundation, the company also supports education, health, civic and cultural activities, youth and United Funds within its plant communities. About one third of Foundation funds are awarded within the Cleveland area. In addition to its international headquarters, TRW has facilities in Cleveland that produce automotive valves, pistons and aircraft components and distribute automotive replacement parts'.

Union Commerce Bank

Helping to build a great American city

The roots of Union Commerce Bank go deep in the history of Cleveland, Ohio, spanning some 125 years and including 36 different financial institutions on the company's family tree. It all began with the formation of The Bank of Commerce in 1853, just 40 years after Cleveland was little more than a mosquito-ridden pioneer settlement with less than a dozen inhabitants on the edge of the western frontier. But by 1853, it had become a significant mercantile town whose city directory proudly counted "30,000 souls", and a place civilized enough to host The National Woman Rights Convention in that year.

The bank served the business community exclusively, growing and playing an important part in the rapid development of Cleveland as a major industrial center and port city. By 1920, the city's population had swelled to 796,841, making it the fifth largest in the United States, and The Bank of Commerce was merged with several other major Cleveland banking groups to form The Union Trust Company — a new and much stronger institution better able to serve the needs of the area's burgeoning business growth.

To house this new organization, a building was erected on Euclid Avenue at East Ninth Street featuring a magnificent Greek revival lobby which remains today the largest banking room in the United States, if not the world, and a structure of major architectural significance. More than 136,000 people toured the facility when it was dedicated in May, 1924, just one month before President Calvin Coolidge was renominated at the Republican National Convention in Cleveland.

During the calamitous Depression years, Union Trust and hundreds of other banks throughout the country were forced to close their doors. But an entirely new organization called The Union Bank of Commerce emerged out of the financial wreckage of that period, opening its doors at the same location in 1938, and through its "Cleveland Plan" immediately began helping an anemic, depression-weary

View looking north in one wing of the Union Commerce Bank (Cleveland, Ohio) lobby — the largest banking room in the United States, if not the world. Restoration of the 1924 Greek revival structure has won significant local and national recognition, including the President's Award from the National Trust for Historical Preservation in 1978. When the Union Commerce Building opened in 1924, it was the second largest office building in the world.

business community regain its footing.

New corporate trust and international banking services were introduced to business customers, and in 1954 the bank entered the retail banking field with savings and time deposits. Branch banking was begun in 1955 to serve the huge population growth and suburban development that had taken place outside of the Cleveland city limits, and installment loan and personal trust departments were activated soon after.

In 1957 the bank's name was changed to the simpler "Union Commerce Bank", and while it had built a strong foundation through its work in the commercial sector, it was clearly no longer just "the businessman's bank." In the intervening years, Union Commerce has grown through the extension of its service to all segments of the community, and by continuing its pioneering ways in bringing new banking products and services to the northeast Ohio area. To name just a few examples, it was the first Cleveland bank to introduce telephone billpaying and full service branch operations in supermarkets, and to extend this idea into the non-food retail setting. It was also the first Ohio bank to offer Sunday banking, and joined a mere handful of other banks in the country in sharing its 24-hour teller machines with a major credit union — thereby giving thousands of members easy access to bank services.

The bank has maintained its historical leadership position in assisting area business organizations through its wide range of corporate banking services and innovative marketing. For example, Union Commerce is thought to be the only major Ohio bank specializing in oil and natural gas production loans to organizations doing business in or based in Ohio, thereby making new energy available and providing added employment in the state. Through its large and expertly staffed International Division, the bank has for years helped to boost midwest exports and to satisfy the complete international business needs of companies based in Ohio and neighboring states.

Union Commerce Bank remains today a vital part of the Cleveland/Northeast Ohio scene, contributing its imagination and utilizing its resources to aid in the continued growth and development of this area so important to the nation's economic life.

Van Dorn Company

When you look over a neighbor's fence the horizon can be unlimited

At the close of the Civil War, the country's mood was to beat swords into plowshares.

At least one young man, James H. Van Dorn, took that Biblical admonition quite literally. He went to work in an agricultural implement plant in Arkon, Ohio, and quickly became a plowshare forging specialist. He later married, built his own home, and bordered the property with a handsome iron fence of his own making.

History doesn't tell us what Van Dorn's neighbors thought of his house. But they certainly liked his new fence. So much so that they dropped around to ask if he could build the same for them. Cleveland and the world are the beneficiaries of this neighborly admiration. Today, more than 100 years later, the Van Dorn Company name is world known for its innovation and expertise in the forming of metals and plastics. More than once, during that intervening century, the company has taken a direct hand in the building of a great city.

In 1878, James Van Dorn moved his burgeoning wrought iron fence business into Cleveland, closer to that city's iron making industry. The relocated company was called, appropriately enough, The Cleveland Wrought Iron Fence Company. Then, during a business trip to Milwaukee, a new idea occured to Van Dorn. Milwaukee needed a new jail. Weren't jails nothing more than fences built indoors? Within a few years, Van Dorn became the world's largest builders of jail cells. The first Cleveland application of that expertise came in the construction of the old Cleveland City Workhouse, near what is now Woodland Avenue and East 79th Street.

By 1884, in addition to fences and jail cells, all sorts of functional and ornamental iron

The original Van Dorn Iron Works Company

products were being produced. The firm was retitled The Van Dorn Iron Works Company.

Van Dorn's most apparent contributions to Cleveland's development began in 1887, when the company went into the structural steel business. Next time you pass through Cleveland's Public Square, look at the Williamson Building. Van Dorn fabricated and erected its steel frame. Drive along Cleveland's Shoreway, or sail out the breakwall entrance. You'll see the familiar five-mile intake crib, whose structural steel framework was fashioned and erected by Van Dorn. And back in the shop, Van Dorn fabricators were busy framing telescope observatory domes for the Warner Swasey Company.

In both World Wars, Van Dorn shifted its emphasis from the tools of peace to the weapons of war. World War I saw the company building a strange and terrifying new weapon — the Renault tank. Over 500 of them were delivered. Again in World War II, Van Dorn created armor plate for tanks, armored cars and aircraft. And in the years between, the company built railroad components, developed and manufactured container systems, produced truck and heavy road building equipment components, and equipped the Library of Congress with Van Dorn metal furniture.

At the close of World War II, the modern mode of Van Dorn Company began to take shape. N. T. Jones, who became president in 1938, foresaw that plastics would become one of the great industries of the late 20th century. In 1945, the company built its first, small, manually operated injection molding machine. Today, under the guidance of Lawrence C. Jones, chairman and chief executive officer, the company stands as a world leader in the manufacture of injection molding machines with clamping pressures from 75 to 1,000 tons. That work is now carried out by the company's wholly owned subsidiary, Van Dorn Plastic Machinery Company.

James H. Van Dorn, founder.

The observatory domes for Warner & Swasey under construction, right.

At about the same time the company made its first entry into the container business, with the aquisition of the Davies Can Company in 1944. Now, Van Dorn, through four container subsidiaries, is a major U.S. producer of easy-open aluminum cans, steel cans, plastic containers, as well as fibre and foil packages. These container divisions are important suppliers to the food, chemical and petroleum industries. Another division of the company is involved in heat treating of steel plate, as well as structural sections. Altogether, the company employs 2,300 people, with gross sales just under 200 million.

Which shows how far out you can move the boundaries of a well made wrought iron fence.

WEWS(TV)/Scripps-Howard Broadcasting Company

Even the test pattern drew a crowd!

The tavern with the television set was the most crowded spot in town in 1947 when WEWS(TV) went on the air giving birth to television in Ohio. No one was particularly concerned about "what was on" — Paul Hodges interviewing bums in the bus station or Gene Carroll conducting "Ring Around the Rosie" for the kids on "Uncle Jake's House." People watched because they knew for sure that this was not just some new gimmick! This was television!

Scripps-Howard Broadcasting Company had created Ohio's first television station, named after its founder, E. W. Scripps. The response was overwhelming. It is said that even the test pattern would draw a large crowd to a store window.

And from day one, WEWS has been the community's first choice for fine local programming. Lacking a network to draw upon (WEWS became a network affiliate in 1948), TV5 people had to satisfy the public demand themselves. Their commitment to excellence was evident in the maiden broadcast.

Eyewitness News coverage becomes more than face-to-face with TV5's eye-in-the sky, Chopper 5. When TV5 promises to "cover" a story, the public takes it literally.

December 17, 1947. First, the test pattern. Then, a flicker of black and white. The eager and knowledgeable but "completely lacking in television experience" staff had given notice that "We're starting this in the dark. This is brand new, but we're giving it a good shot." What they probably meant was, "Don't count on 'Roots' or 'Laverne and Shirley' — yet!"

The picture comes into focus, and a face millions had worshipped on the movie screen enters our homes — Jimmy Stewart — as master of ceremonies at the *Cleveland Press* Christmas Show, live from Public Hall! And right in our living rooms!

This began a continuing record which indexes the legends of Cleveland broadcasting including, of course, the nation's first lady of broadcasting, Dorothy Fuldheim, Cleveland's most influential news and social commentator. She has interviewed virtually every history-maker since the forties — from Hitler to Truman, Nixon to Muhammad Ali. With an armada of knowledge and experience, countless awards and honorary degrees, Dorothy Fuldheim has projected the public spirit and defended the public good, since she became America's first female news commentator in 1947.

Many "firsts" happened at TV5. The first baseball game televised here. The first remote broadcast. America's first televised college credit courses. WEWS has always been first in public service as illustrated by "In My Opinion" and "Classroom Camera" which give viewers of every age a chance to be heard. There was "Morning Exchange" — the most successful locally produced (and most widely imitated) talk show in the country. "The Gene Carroll Show," "Polka Varieties," "Academic Challenge," "Afternoon Exchange" and numerous other fine productions including the award-winning TV5 "Eyewitness News" have satisfied the dictates of Scripps-Howard's 1947 Official Operating Code Book, issued when TV5 went on the air:

> "You will deliver information, education, entertainment, news and public service as part of a balanced program which is continuously responsive to the needs, interests and desires of the population served."

The 28-page booklet also charged the newly born station's management "not to stint, to bring all the news — local, state, national and international into your studios", and offered its most memorable direction, "Give light and the people will find their own way — let this motto be your code in the presentation of all news." If they could see TV5's news helicopter, the fleet of remote "action cams", the Peabody and Emmy award-winning news and public affairs teams, they would know TV5 has fulfilled their dreams.

If you are known to the world, you're well-known by Dorothy Fuldheim. Former Clevelander Bob Hope and most notables make a point of visiting with Dorothy Fuldheim when they're in Cleveland.

Many of the pioneers are still with TV5, witnessing this fulfillment first-hand, including Donald L. Perris, now president of Scripps-Howard Broadcasting Company; Edward D. Cervenak, vice-president and general manager of WEWS; Ernest E. Sindelar, WEWS station manager; James E. Bloyd, vice president of engineering for Scripps-Howard Broadcasting and Jay S. Kerekes, executive assistant to the president. They had spirit back in 1947 when they set out to help build the most powerful medium in the history of the world. "No one knows much about this, but we're going to make it work," they promised. And WEWS continues to serve Cleveland responsibly as its "longest running show in town."

Today WEWS has more employees than they had viewers in 1947, and with today's competition the test pattern might not draw such a crowd! But TV5's programming is still *First in Cleveland*.

The Warner & Swasey Company

Marriage of tools, telescopes led to distinguished career for two entrepreneurs

Cleveland in 1881 was the 12th largest manufacturing city in America, and growing rapidly in size and population. Cleveland industries were producing iron and steel, brass, paint, fasteners, cutting tools, plumbing fixtures, sewing machines and many other products.

It was to this strong industrial base that Worcester Warner and Ambrose Swasey brought their young business in the summer of 1881. A year earlier the two New England-raised machinists had begun operations in Chicago. But they had trouble attracting skilled people and obtaining good quality materials. They had gone too far West.

The two founders decided to purchase land on East Prospect (now Carnegie Avenue) near East 55th Street, in Cleveland. A three-story structure (100'x35') was built, and the shop opened in August, 1881. This original plant has been expanded many times and is now headquarters for the Turning Machine Division.

Early production was divided between telescopes and turrets lathes, sold largely to the brass shops for producing plumbing fixtures.

Astronomy had been Warner's hobby since childhood. A 9-1/2" telescope he built and exhibited at a Chicago fair in 1880 was purchased by Beloit College for its new observatory. This was the beginning of a distinguished career for Warner & Swasey in the manufacture of telescopes.

The Warner & Swasey design resulted in more accurate and reliable drive mechanisms, and the company soon became the leading builder of equatorial and reflector telescopes. Among the company's more prominent projects were: the McDonald Observatory (Mt. Locke, Texas); Dominion Astrophysical Observatory (Victoria, B.C., Canada); the University of Chicago's Yerkes Observatory (Williams Bay, Wisconsin); United States Naval Observatory (Washington, D.C.); and Lick Observatory (Mt. Hamilton, California).

The early marriage of telescopes and machine tools was fortunate for the company. Later, the founders were to agree that Warner & Swasey had built its reputation on telescopes and its profitability on turret lathes.

Business was good in the early years, and the company prospered. Between 1900 and 1910 Warner & Swasey decided to concentrate more on machine tool production than on telescopes and other optical instruments. Telescopes were not abandoned, but were of relatively less importance and eventually were phased out. The last was built in 1970. The company turned to building larger and more universal turret lathes.

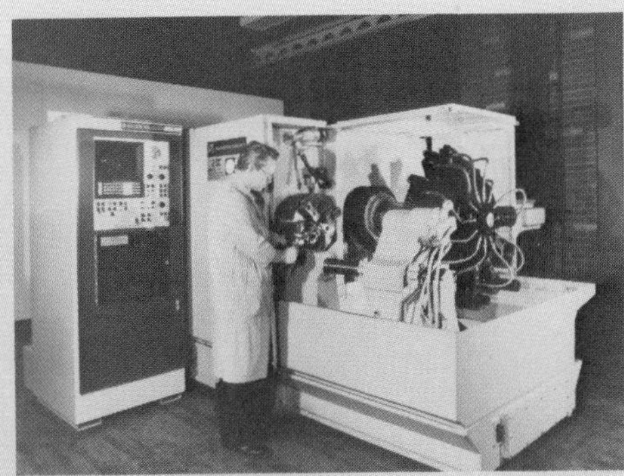

This Warner & Swasey 2-SC column-type turning machine is one in a new generation of computer numerically controlled models.

During World War I, the company became a prime military contractor for machine tools, as well as for optical instruments. As an example, Warner & Swasey produced 8,000 panoramic sights for field artillery pieces at the request of the Ordnance Department.

Warner & Swasey telescopes were known for their precision. This 36" equatorial telescope was built in 1888 for the Lick Observatory of the University of California.

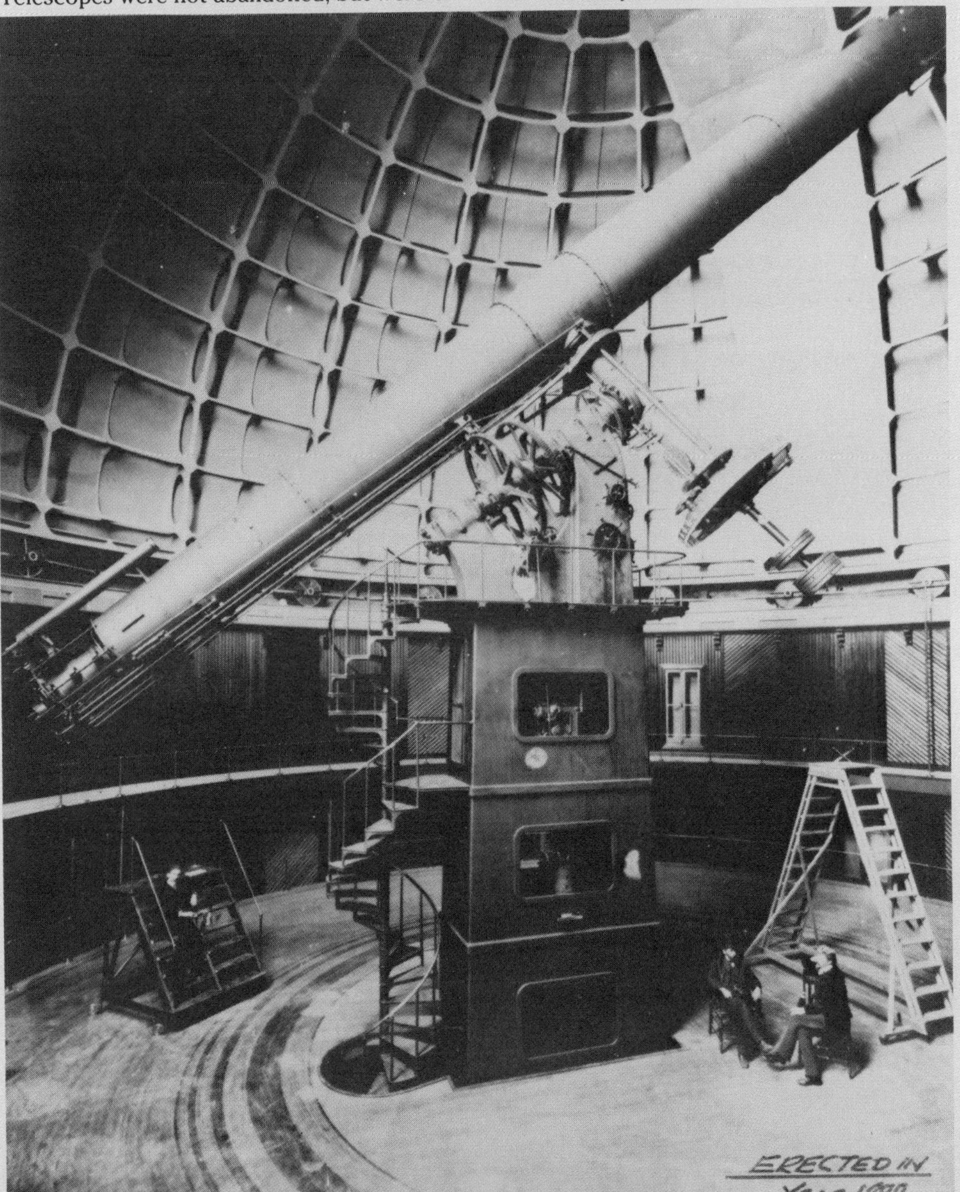

Founders Worcester Warner (left) and Ambrose Swasey are pictured with one of their smaller early model telescopes.

After World War I, however, demand for machine tools declined dramatically as surplus machines saturated the market. In those lean years following the war, company leaders began to think about ways to diversify the business. This thinking carried forward to the 1940s when, following World War II, the company expanded into textile machinery and construction equipment.

In 1936, to enhance the company's reputation and pave the way for diversification, Warner & Swasey had begun a nationwide editorial advertising campaign in *Newsweek* and *U.S. News & World Report*. The ads addressed issues of importance to the nation and its free enterprise system. It was widely acclaimed and became a door-opener for company salesmen. This program, which continues today, is the longest-running campaign of its type in American advertising history.

Today, Warner & Swasey is a leading producer of computer numerically controlled (CNC) turning machines, turret punch presses, boring mills, and grinding machines. In addition, the company manufactures hydraulic excavators, textile machinery and tools and accessories.

Warner & Swasey people are active in Cleveland. From the beginning, the founders had recognized the importance of company involvement in civic and charitable activities. Each served as president of the Cleveland Chamber of Commerce. Swasey was a founding member of the Community Chest. Both were benefactors of Cleveland universities and cultural institutions. Their gift of the Warner & Swasey Observatory to Case Western Reserve University is a monument to their impact on Cleveland.

White Consolidated Industries, Inc.

Still meeting with confidence the challenges of two worlds

The foundation of White Consolidated was this White Sewing Machine Co. plant, employing 600 "hands" in 1876 in Cleveland's industrial flats.

The lure of fame and fortune which drew Thomas H. White to Cleveland and the bustling new industrial frontiers of the midwest shortly after the Civil War are the grist which dreams are made of. But even he would have been awed by the phenomenal growth which has occurred within the firm to which he lent his name.

White Consolidated Industries, Inc., a multi-faceted, modern, diversified company with more than a century of history and tradition behind it, is an outgrowth of White Sewing Machine Company, founded by Thomas White and operated in Cleveland since 1876.

Following his instincts, Thomas White, armed with a United States patent, moved to Cleveland from his native Massachusetts in 1866. Within ten years, White's entrepreneurial spirit helped him establish White Sewing Machine Company. He and his workforce of "600 hands," working out of a five-story "manufactory" in the industrial flats on the banks of the Cuyahoga River, were turning out one of the now famous White rotary bobbin sewing machines every four minutes. Cumulative sales had reached $2,450,000 by the end of 1878.

The company's 1878 letterhead also prominently identified "improved kerosene street lamps." Other diverse products included bicycles, roller skates, phonographs, automatic lathes and screw machines and the innovative White Steam Car. Priced at $3,200 and offered as "The ideal car for shopping and for evening use," this proved to be the ideal vehicle for the formation, in 1906, of a separate company known today as the White Motor Corporation.

The hub of White Consolidated's worldwide operations is its headquarters building on Cleveland's West Side. Today, the company employs some 31,000 persons throughout the world.

In fact, White Consolidated as it is today really got its start in 1955 when a small group of men from White Motor moved into WCI. They were led by Vollmer W. Fries who came as chairman, Edward S. Reddig as president and William H. Johnson as chief financial officer. Roy H. Holdt, present WCI chairman, came to the company shortly thereafter in one of the early acquisitions.

Beginning in 1955, Reddig's team transformed White Consolidated Industries from an 80-year-old, single product, $20 million sewing machine company into the third largest U.S. manufacturer of major home appliances and a leading producer of machinery and equipment for industry with annual sales of more than $2 billion.

Today, WCI's 31,000 men and women design and manufacture a broad range of products for the home and supply massive and sophisticated tools and machinery for thriving industrial markets as basic as steel, as necessary as interstate highways, as exotic as nuclear energy, and as innovative as compact quick-copy reproduction centers for schools and offices.

The courage to get involved, the tenacity to persist, and the skill to succeed shared by Reddig and a small, closely-knit management team enabled WCI to grow into more than 80 companies with operations in 22 states, Canada, Mexico, Europe and the Far East.

That management style, applied by dedicated, cost-conscious managers has also enabled WCI to succeed in the major home appliance industry where some of its biggest rivals could not. Household names such as Westinghouse, Kelvinator, Gibson, Philco, Hamilton and Franklin have become part of WCI's network of profitable operations. Frigidaire, purchased from General Motors by Holdt and his team in 1979, is a most significant acquisition and a vital key to the future of its world of appliances.

Earlier acquisitions brought the counterbalancing effect of a strong industrial group of companies whose names read like Who's Who — Blaw-Knox, Bullard, White-Sundstrand, AFT-Davidson, and Copes-Vulcan — all leaders in their special fields of commercial, industrial and high technology products. The growth plan so wisely formulated years ago continues to work well under Roy Holdt's leadership.

The ability to thrive in its first 100 years of change and challenge puts White Consolidated in an outstanding position to face the problems and accept opportunities in the years ahead. A small, 120-person corporate staff, headed by Chairman Holdt, President Ward Smith and Senior Executive Vice President Karl E. Ware, operating out of WCI's world headquarters on Cleveland's West Side, keeps a tight rein on the company's widely diversified operations.

The same balanced approach which has enabled White to achieve success in the two widely divergent worlds it serves — the world of consumer products for the home, and the world of machinery and equipment for industry — is the basis on which WCI is planning with confidence to meet the challenges still ahead.

The Geo. Worthington Co.

Cleveland's oldest business a leader in merchandise distribution

This 1880 drawing shows the new building erected after Worthington's previous headquarters were totally destroyed by fire in 1874.

George Worthington founded the company in 1829 and served as its president for 42 years.

In 1829, riding from Utica, New York to Cleveland, 16-year-old George Worthington stopped to watch workers as they dug the new Ohio Canal. He was immediately impressed by their lack of proper tools.

Sensing a golden sales opportunity, he rode hurriedly back to Cooperstown. There, he borrowed $500 from his brother, invested it in picks, shovels and wheelbarrows, and returned via the Erie Canal to Buffalo and lake schooner to Cleveland.

He promptly "sold out" and established the "business for profit" pattern which has always characterized Worthington, Cleveland's oldest business and one of the nation's leading hardware wholesalers and industrial distributors.

In 1835, Worthington bought out its foremost competitor, McCurdy and Conklin. A yellowed clipping from the old *Cleveland Whig* indicates this was big news of that day. In 1868, increased business, incident to the Civil War, made it necessary for the firm to construct a new store and warehouse at St. Clair and West 9th St. This was almost wholly destroyed by fire in 1874, but was immediately rebuilt. Many additions later, the company is still there in a 625,000 sq. ft. working area.

George Worthington died in 1871. He was mourned by the entire community where he had gained respect as a civic leader in addition to his business success. Worthington's successor was General James Barnett, who joined the firm in 1841 after returning from service in the Civil War.

After 70 years' service to Worthington, General Barnett died in 1911. W. D. Taylor, employed by Worthington in 1867 as an office boy at a $5 per week salary, succeeded Barnett. Taylor's 63 year service was culminated upon his death in 1930.

In 1913, Worthington stock was offered for sale to its employees, who today own the company in its entirety. Seventy-six of Worthington's 450 work force have served the company for more than 25 years, tribute to the statement that Worthington is a good place to work.

Taylor's successor was A. J. Gaehr, a Worthington veteran of 39 years who successfully guided his company through the Depression years. H. E. Hulburd, who came to work for the company in 1889 as a salesman in the state of New York, took the reins in 1936.

It is a tribute to Hulburd's leadership that, during World War II, Worthington constantly improved its services to its customers. Through painstaking follow-up and supervision, the distribution of vital merchandise was expedited and hastened. Hulburd retired in 1947, turning over a sound, alert organization to A. G. Rorabeck, associated with Worthington since 1909 and previously vice president and director of sales.

Rorabeck died in 1958 and was succeeded by N. F. Luekens, who had joined Worthington in 1942 as comptroller. In 1960, Luekens negotiated the purchase of the Schaberg-Dietrich Hardware Co., a highly successful Lansing, Michigan wholesaler. In the same year, Worthington became one of the original members of Sentry Hardware Corporation, an affiliation of 14 major wholesalers throughout the country. Luekens served as president of Sentry until his death in 1975.

Dexter A. Rolla, who joined Worthington in 1959 as comptroller and treasurer, succeeded Luekens as executive vice president. Active in industry affairs, Rolla is a member of the executive committee of the National Wholesale Hardware Association, and a director and treasurer of Sentry Hardware Corporation.

In addition to its hardware wholesaling activities, Worthington is a leading industrial distributor which serves the area's major manufacturers. It has grown from the boxes and barrels of frontier trading to the computerized systems and highly automated warehousing of modern industrial supplies.

Worthington is a Cleveland landmark, which is only fitting for a concern older than the city itself. However, rather than dwelling on its highly successful past, Worthington today is totally concerned with the needs of the modern marketplace. As expressed by President Rolla on its 150th anniversary: "We pride ourselves on being an innovative company — one which leaves a trail rather than follows a path."

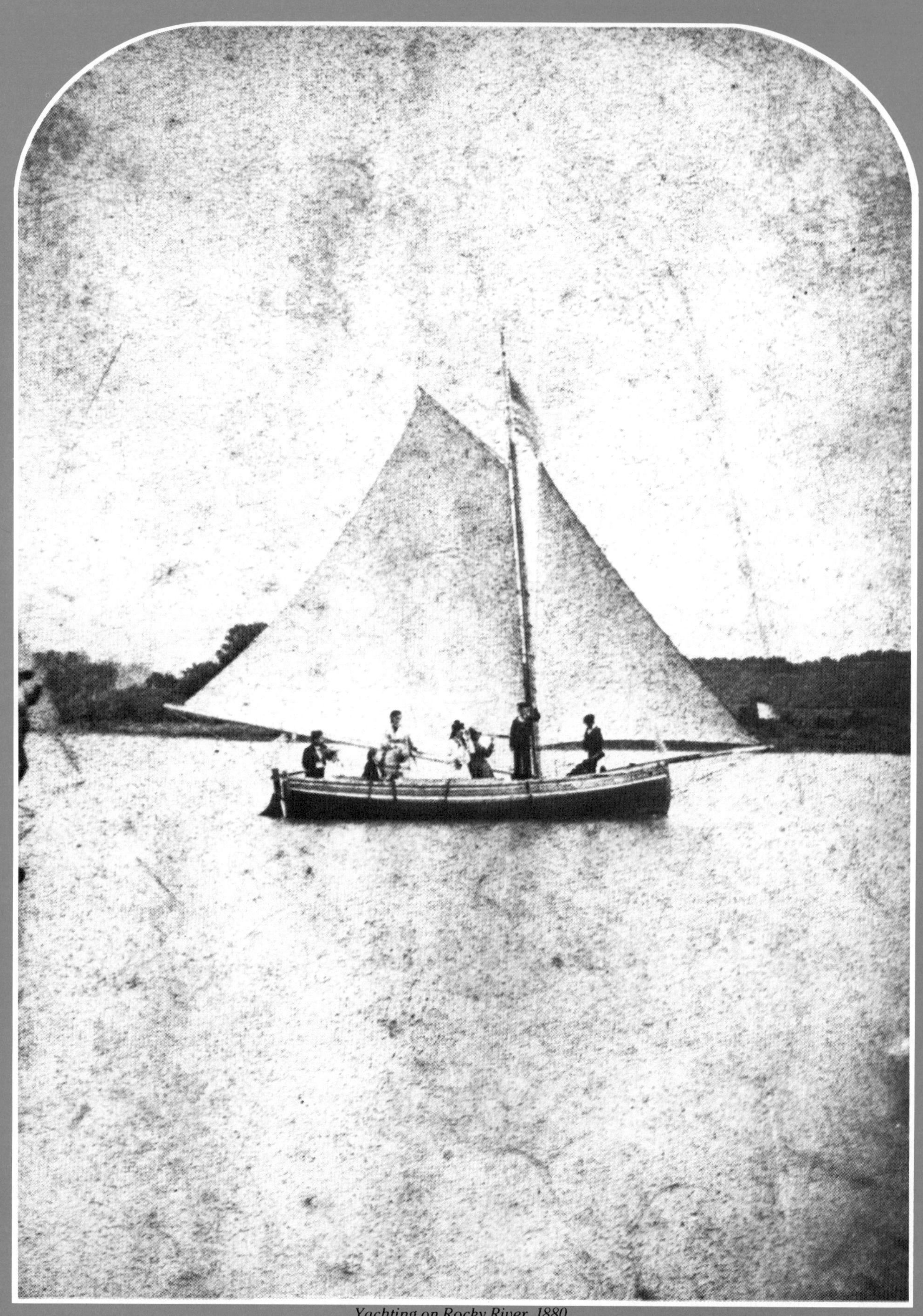
Yachting on Rocky River, 1880

Unity from diversity

The very multiformity of those who live in, work within and react to Cleveland is perhaps one of the major virtues of its many. The challenge and the adventure of the 1980s and beyond may well be to build a stronger and more cohesive, livable city utilizing the multi-faceted talents of a diverse citizenry.

Cleveland, carved from a patch of Ohio wilderness, was first home to early day Indian mound builders, later the Eries and the Senecas, and when restless colonists along the Atlantic began trickling westward, the first organized settlement in the Cleveland area was a colony of Moravians.

From that moment forward, Cleveland has been one of the world's most flavorful ethnic and philosophical melting pots — with all the accompanying crescendoes of pride and prejudice, differences of thought tempered by sometimes heroic attempts at understanding, as well as social upheaval, economic wanderlust and dedication by the many to the city's well being.

The Industrial Revolution brought economic explosion; it also brought talent and human resources from every land and of every persuasion. Cleveland churned and learned and sometimes burned. It not only survived; it cleaned off the soot and grew considerably taller, and wiser.

Cleveland has lived a dramatically fruitful life, has created major education and health centers, has endowed itself with magnificent museums, theatres, and a world of culture that is truly superior. It has built, renovated, torn down, rebuilt and rethought. Cleveland, fortunately, has never successfully resisted change.

While this city has been the object of international concern over its governmental and fiscal disparities, Cleveland, going into the last years of the twentieth century, is a place rich in human resources and ripe for unity.

Cleveland, indeed, is faced with a challenge to provide a wholesome and rich future for those whose lives and livelihoods tie it all together.

Out of diversity come the threads and the strengths of unity.

And from unity, a more economically sound and livable Cleveland, a better Cleveland, is there.

Index

Numerals in italics indicate an illustration of the subject.

Index

Credits

Sources of photographs, maps and art appearing in this book are noted here in alphabetical order and by page number (numbers in parentheses indicate multiple pictures provided by source on one page). Those photographs appearing in the chapter *Partners in Cleveland's Economy,* pages 176 through 233, were provided by the represented firms.

Abraitis, Vyto: 12-13, 152, 156, 170, 172.

Browns, The Cleveland: 143, 144, 145.

Cleveland, City of: 171.

Cleveland Orchestra: 171 (2).

Cleveland Plain Dealer: 24, 137, 146, 167 (2).

Cleveland Trust: 146.

Crawford Auto Museum, Frederick C.: 153, 154, 155, 161, 240.

Greater Cleveland Growth Association: 16, 156, 168 (3), 170, 171, 172, 174 (2).

Indians, Cleveland: 142.

Johnson, Rusty: 39, 50.

Jones & Laughlin Steel Corporation: 176.

Karabinus, Joe: Dust jacket, 1.

Kimple, Bob: 8-9, 148-149, 156, 157, 160, 163, 169, 173, 174.

Merchant, Bill: 145, 149 (2), 156, 157, 160, 164 (2), 168 (4), 170 (2), 172.

Reynolds, James: 149.

Ruffner, Howard E.: 162, 164, 166.

Western Reserve Historical Society: 2-3, 6-7, 10-11, 14-15, 17, 18 (2), 19 (2), 20, 21 (2), 22, 23, 26 (2), 27 (2), 28 (2), 29 (2), 30 (2), 31 (2), 32, 33, 34 (2), 35 (8), 36, 37, 41 (2), 42, 43, 44-45, 46 (2), 47, 48 (2), 49 (2), 51, 52, 53, 54, 55 (2), 56, 57 (2), 58-59, 58 (2), 59 (3), 60 (3), 61 (2), 62-63, 62 (2), 63 (2), 64-65, 66, 67 (3), 68 (2), 69 (3), 70, 71, 72 (4), 73, 74, 75, 76 (3), 77, 78, 79 (3), 80-81, 80, 81, 82 (3), 83 (2), 84 (2), 85, 86-87, 86 (2), 88-89, 88, 89, 90 (2), 91, 92-93, 92, 94-95, 96-97, 98, 99, 100 (2), 101 (2), 102-103, 102, 103 (2), 104 (2), 105, 106-107, 106 (2), 108 (2), 109 (2), 110, 111, 112, 113, 114-115, 114, 116 (2), 117, 118, 119 (2), 120-121, 121, 122 (2), 123, 124-125, 125 (2), 126-127, 128-129, 130-131, 132 (2), 133, 134-135, 135, 136-137, 136 (2), 137 (2), 138, 139, 140, 141, 147 (3), 148, 150-151, 150, 151, 152, 157, 158, 159, 161, 163, 165, 167 (2), 171, 234, 240.

Zampino, Frank: 4-5.

The editors and publishers of *Cleveland: Prodigy of the Western Reserve,* are indebted to a number of people and organizations who, over the many months of preparation and production, believed as we did that Cleveland citizens and visitors to Cleveland should have available an entertaining and pictorially oriented history.

Our special thanks, of course, go to author George Condon, whose perception, dedication and good humor brought to fruition an entertaining, accurate and well told story about the growth and development of Cleveland.

In addition, we thank:
The staff and volunteer leadership of the Greater Cleveland Growth Association, for their continuing support and assistance, including John A. Gelbach, Chairman; William H. Bryant, Executive Vice President; John J. Dwyer, First Vice Chairman; Robert A. Boylan, Director of Association Development, who coordinated the project for the Association; Virginia Felderman, Director of Communications, who assisted greatly in authentication and proofing of the manuscript and who researched and wrote the Association history for this book; and to staff members Linda Humphrey, Beverly Bahl, and Linda Klancher. Thanks also to Alice, Carol, Jimmy, Lynn, Shirley and Mary for their help along the way.

The professional staff of the Western Reserve Historical Society for its continued guidance, direction and photographic search assistance throughout this project, especially to Executive Director Meredith B. Colket; David C. Twining, Director of Development and Communication; John J. Grabowski, Associate Curator of Manuscripts; and Martin Hauserman, Manuscript Specialist.

For assistance and authentication of manuscript, a special thanks to Dr. David van Tassel, Professor of History and Chairman, and Dr. Carl Ubbelohde, Professor of History, Department of History, Case Western Reserve University.

Others who contributed to the success of *Cleveland: Prodigy of the Western Reserve,* include David York, Richard Sullivan, Carolotta Brandon-Hartman of The Type House, Inc., J. R. Jones of Lightshed Studios, Caroline Johnson, Kristi Martin, David Wadley, Suzan Hunter, Hobart and Sue Hammond, Ed and Mary Brett, Tim Colwell, Brian Ridgway, Pat Briggs, Kathy Wendt, Leigh Flowe, Mary Rounds and Glenda Silvey.

A class of diligent eighth-grade students at Hough School in the late 1890s.

Concept and design by Continental Heritage Press, Tulsa.
Printed and bound by Von Hoffmann Press, St. Louis.
Type set in Cheltenham by The Type House, Inc. Tulsa.
Text sheets are Warrenflo by S. D. Warren Company.
Endleaves are Antique Multicolor Oatmeal by Process Materials.
Cover is Kingston Linen by Holliston Mills.